安徽省"十三五"规划教材

外贸函电与单证实训教程
（第2版）

主　编　李奕华
副主编　姚　瑶　张龙然
编　者（以姓氏拼音为序）
　　　　陈　倩　陈新苗
　　　　李奕华　邱小玲
　　　　孙晓芳　姚　瑶
　　　　张龙然　张　鹏
　　　　张薇薇

北京师范大学出版集团
BEIJING NORMAL UNIVERSITY PUBLISHING GROUP
安徽大学出版社

图书在版编目(CIP)数据

外贸函电与单证实训教程：英文/李奕华主编.—2版.—合肥：安徽大学出版社，2020.11（2024.1重印）

ISBN 978-7-5664-2090-9

Ⅰ.①外… Ⅱ.①李… Ⅲ.①对外贸易－英语－电报信函－写作－高等学校－教材－英文②进出口贸易－原始凭证－高等学校－教材－英文 Ⅳ.①F75②F740.44

中国版本图书馆 CIP 数据核字(2020)第 160690 号

外贸函电与单证实训教程（第 2 版）
Waimao Handian Yu Danzheng Shixun Jiaocheng

李奕华 主编

出版发行	北京师范大学出版集团 安 徽 大 学 出 版 社 (安徽省合肥市肥西路 3 号 邮编 230039) www.bnupg.com www.ahupress.com.cn
印　　刷	江苏凤凰数码印务有限公司
经　　销	全国新华书店
开　　本	787mm×1092mm　1/16
印　　张	17
字　　数	393 千字
版　　次	2020 年 11 月第 2 版
印　　次	2024 年 1 月第 3 次印刷
定　　价	46.00 元

ISBN 978-7-5664-2090-9

策划编辑	马晓波　钱翠翠　李　晴	装帧设计	李伯骥　孟献辉
责任编辑	葛灵知　马晓波　钱翠翠	美术编辑	李　军
责任校对	刘婷婷	责任印制	陈　如

版权所有　侵权必究

反盗版、侵权举报电话：0551－65106311
外埠邮购电话：0551－65107716
本书如有印装质量问题，请与印制管理部联系调换。
印制管理部电话：0551－65106311

第 2 版前言

《外贸函电与单证实训教程》自出版以来受到广大使用者的好评,同时也收到读者的中肯建议。第 2 版在第 1 版的基础上进行了修订,力求做到全面改进和完善。

在内容编排上,改变传统教材中以理论知识点为体系的框架,以商务实践为主线组织编写。为了使教学目标更明确,每一章新增了学习目标(Learning Objectives);为了使理论知识与实践训练更系统,部分章节的内容有所更新,具体如下:第一章新增商务信函的写作原则,第九章新增调解信函,第十二章和第十三章分别新增提单和保单种类。全书紧紧围绕外贸业务流程,既有较为翔实的理论知识和写作指南,又配套贯穿整个业务流程的信函样本,并提供常用例句,引出英语语言运用练习和外贸函电实训练习。

在练习设计上,理论与实践相结合,各章节练习编排体例基本一致。函电部分(第一至八章)练习题型设置统一为突出商务术语和词汇使用的选择题、填空题,加强商务句型应用的英汉互译和商务信函练习的信函英译,另外还增加了根据商务背景进行信函写作的实训练习。实训练习均来自外贸公司真实的业务材料。

在模拟实训上,依托外贸模拟软件设置外贸情景,进行函电书写和单证制作及外贸各流程的实操,并新增一章涵盖外贸业务全流程信函书写和单证制作的模拟实训。

编 者

2020 年 9 月

第 1 版前言

根据教育部《关于进一步加强高校实践育人工作的若干意见》及安徽省教育厅《关于加强高等学校实践教学工作的若干意见》等文件精神,地方应用型本科院校应坚持"地方性、应用型"的办学定位,结合地方经济社会发展的需要,培养以本科层次为主的、高素质应用型创新人才。为此,应用型高等学校的课程设置、内容选取和教学过程必须强调理论、实践、知识和方法的协调发展并满足学生未来职业发展和学生综合能力培养的需要,体现应用性、发展性、实践性和创新性。

为了适应应用型高等学校商务英语专业及英语专业(商务方向)教学改革的要求,我们走访了多家外贸企业和兄弟院校,结合外贸行业对人才的实际需求,通过多年的教学实践和广泛调研与论证,遵行职业针对性、岗位实用性、实践可操作性和知识系统性的原则,编写了《外贸函电与单证实训教程》。

本教材的突出特点是"以工作流程为导向、以实践操作为指南",创造实训工作情景,构建"教、学、做"无缝对接的实训平台,实现学生"在实践中学习、在学习中实践"的学习目标,突出"以生为本、以用为先"的教学理念。

本教材由外贸函电实训、外贸单证实训和综合模拟实训三部分组成,按外贸实务发展的顺序排列。第一部分为外贸函电实训,包括信函的格式、建立贸易关系、询价、报盘、还盘、成交、支付、装运、保险、投诉、索赔等内容。第二部分为外贸单证实训,包括商业发票、汇票、信用证、提单、保单、装箱单、原产地证明和其他单证。这些内容涵盖了外贸业务流程的方方面面,内容详尽,语言简练,通俗易懂。每章包含简介、范例、实践技巧、常用例句及实训操作五个部分,让学生较全面、系统地了解外贸函电与单证的各流程。

本教材可作为应用型高等院校商务英语、国际贸易等专业的实训教材,也可供高等职业学校的相关专业学生使用,亦可供外贸从业人员参考。

本教材在编写过程中得到了池州学院外语系领导及全体教师的大力支持与帮助,尤其是商务英语专业教师的辛勤付出,本教材才得以顺利完稿。另外,本教材还引用了部分参考文献,向其作者表示感谢。

由于编者的水平有限,疏漏之处在所难免,恳请广大教师、读者及同行专家批评指正。

编 者

2015 年 4 月

Contents

Part I Business Correspondence

Chapter 1 Layout of Business Letters

1.1　Introduction ··· 4
1.2　Writing Principles of Business Letters ································ 4
1.3　The Structure of Business Letters ······································ 7
1.4　The Format of Business Letters ······································· 10

Chapter 2 Establishment of Business Relations

2.1　Introduction ··· 15
2.2　Samples ·· 15
2.3　Writing Guide ·· 18
2.4　Supplement ··· 19

Chapter 3 Enquiry, Offer and Counter-offer

3.1　Introduction ··· 26
3.2　Samples ·· 27
3.3　Writing Guide ·· 31
3.4　Supplement ··· 35

Chapter 4 Conclusion of Business

4.1　Introduction ··· 43
4.2　Samples ·· 44
4.3　Writing Guide ·· 45
4.4　Supplement ··· 48

Chapter 5 Terms of Payment

- 5.1 Introduction ······ 55
- 5.2 Samples ······ 56
- 5.3 Writing Guide ······ 58
- 5.4 Supplement ······ 60

Chapter 6 Shipment

- 6.1 Introduction ······ 68
- 6.2 Samples ······ 68
- 6.3 Writing Guide ······ 70
- 6.4 Supplement ······ 72

Chapter 7 Insurance

- 7.1 Introduction ······ 77
- 7.2 Samples ······ 78
- 7.3 Writing Guide ······ 79
- 7.4 Supplement ······ 82

Chapter 8 Complaints, Claims and Settlements

- 8.1 Introduction ······ 88
- 8.2 Samples ······ 89
- 8.3 Writing Guide ······ 92
- 8.4 Supplement ······ 94

Part II Business Documents

Chapter 9 Commercial Invoice

- 9.1 Introduction ······ 104
- 9.2 Samples ······ 104
- 9.3 Composing Details ······ 105

9.4 Supplement ·· 109

Chapter 10 Bill of Exchange

10.1 Introduction ·· 115
10.2 Samples ·· 116
10.3 Composing Details ·· 117

Chapter 11 Letter of Credit

11.1 Introduction ·· 122
11.2 Samples ·· 124
11.3 Composing Details ·· 127
11.4 Supplement ·· 130

Chapter 12 Bill of Lading

12.1 Introduction ·· 138
12.2 Samples ·· 139
12.3 Composing Details ·· 141

Chapter 13 Insurance Policy

13.1 Introduction ·· 147
13.2 Samples ·· 148
13.3 Composing Details ·· 151

Chapter 14 Packing List

14.1 Introduction ·· 157
14.2 Samples ·· 157
14.3 Composing Details ·· 159

Chapter 15 Certificate of Origin

15.1 Introduction ·· 164

15.2　Samples ……………………………………………………… 165
15.3　Composing Details ………………………………………… 167

Chapter 16　Other Bills and Documents
16.1　Inspection Certificate ……………………………………… 176
16.2　Export License ……………………………………………… 181
16.3　Customs Declaration ……………………………………… 184

Part Ⅲ　Practical Training

Chapter 17　Simulative Training
17.1　Simulative Training Ⅰ …………………………………… 194
17.2　Simulative Training Ⅱ …………………………………… 195
17.3　Simulative Training Ⅲ …………………………………… 202

Appendices
Appendix Ⅰ ……………………………………………………… 209
Appendix Ⅱ ……………………………………………………… 254
Appendix Ⅲ ……………………………………………………… 255

Bibliography ……………………………………………………… 257

Part Ⅰ Business Correspondence

Part 1 Business Correspondence

Chapter 1
Layout of Business Letters

Learning Objectives
- To know the writing principles of business letters.
- To know the format and structure of business letters.

1.1 Introduction

Business correspondence is concerned with the successful exchange of messages that support the goal of buying and selling goods or other services. It is the main carrier of business communication. So it is of great importance for students to master the skills of writing a good business letter, which can promote friendship and obtain complete understanding between the parties involved.

1.2 Writing Principles of Business Letters

Effective business letters should be easy to read and understand. So, we need to apply some specific writing principles while writing a business letter. They are courtesy, consideration, completeness, correctness, concreteness, conciseness and clarity.

1.2.1 Courtesy

Courtesy is an important language feature of business letters. It is a favorable card, helping to strengthen the present business relations and to establish new ones. Courtesy not only means politeness but also means thinking about the interests of the other party.

Compare the following pairs of sentences.

Impolite	Polite
We are sorry <u>you</u> have misunderstood us.	We are sorry <u>we</u> didn't make ourselves clear.
We <u>cannot</u> deliver the goods all at one time.	I'm afraid we <u>cannot</u> deliver the goods all at one time.
<u>You made</u> a very careless mistake during the course of shipment.	A very careless mistake <u>was made</u> during the course of shipment.

1.2.2 Consideration

Consideration emphasizes "You-attitude" rather than "We-attitude". We should

Chapter 1 Layout of Business Letters

keep the reader's requests, needs, desires as well as feelings in mind when writing a letter.

Compare the following pairs of sentences.

Less Considerate	More Considerate
We <u>allow you</u> a 2% discount for cash payment.	<u>You can earn</u> a 2% discount for cash payment.
We <u>don't believe</u> you will be dissatisfied.	We <u>feel sure</u> that you will be entirely satisfied.

1.2.3 Completeness

A business letter is successful and functions well only when it contains all the necessary information. Keep the following guidelines in mind when writing: Whom do you write to? Why do you write the letter? What are the facts? Have you answered all the questions?

Compare the following pairs of sentences.

Incomplete	Complete
We have opened through our bank an irrevocable L/C in your favor.	We have opened through our bank an irrevocable L/C in your favor which will reach you <u>on July 10 and remain valid until the end of July</u>.

1.2.4 Correctness

Correctness means not only proper expressions with correct grammar, punctuation and spelling, but also appropriate statements, accurate figures and exact terms which help to achieve the purpose.

1.2.5 Concreteness

What the letter covers should be specific and definite. The following guidelines can help us write concretely: use specific facts and figures; prefer active verbs to passive verbs; choose vivid words.

Compare the following pairs of sentences.

Vague	Concrete
Please send your proposal to us <u>as soon as possible</u>.	Please send your proposal to us <u>before May 10</u>.
We wish to confirm our telex <u>dispatched yesterday</u>.	We confirm our telex of <u>June 30</u>.

1.2.6 Clarity

The writer must try to express himself clearly so that the reader will understand it well. To achieve this goal, the writer should follow the guidelines: avoid using the words which have different or unclear meanings; put modifiers in the right place.

Compare the following pairs of sentences.

Ambiguous	Clear
We inform Mr. Smith & Brown that <u>they</u> would receive a reply in a few days.	We inform Mr. Smith & Brown that <u>the latter</u> would receive a reply in a few days.
The goods <u>not only differ</u> in quality, but also in price.	The goods <u>differ not only</u> in quality, but also in price.

1.2.7 Conciseness

Conciseness means the message is expressed with brevity without sacrificing clarity and courtesy. A good business letter should be precise and to the point. To achieve conciseness, we should keep the sentences short, avoid wordy languages or repetition and eliminate excessive details when writing.

Compare the following pairs of sentences.

Wordy	Concise
Attention should be called…	Please note…
In the early part of May…	In early May…

Chapter 1 Layout of Business Letters

1.3 The Structure of Business Letters

Every well-constructed business letter is made up of the seven parts as follows: the letterhead, the date, the inside address, the salutation, the body, the close and the signature. Some business letters may include such optional parts as attention line, subject line, enclosure notation and copy notation.

1.3.1 The Principal Parts of a Business Letter

1. The Letterhead

The letterhead includes the sender's name, postal address, telephone number, fax number, email address, etc. Usually the letterhead is printed in the up-center or at the left margin of a letter and typed in more than two lines.

2. The Date

The date should be typed in one line. It may be expressed either in cardinal numbers, e. g. ,1,2,3... or in ordinals, e. g. ,1st,2nd,3rd... The names of months are preferable spelled out in full and not abbreviated, e. g. ,December for Dec. and the -st, -nd,-rd and -th that follow the day can be omitted. It is preferably typed in the order of D/M/Y: day, month, and year; but in practice, quite a few people write the date in M/D/Y order. The date line may start from the left margin or be centered.

3. The Inside Address

The inside address of the receiver is typed at the left-hand margin below the date. It is exactly the same way as on the envelope. The ordinary courtesy titles are used to address to one person, e. g. , Mr. C. E. Eckersley.

After the name, his or her official position should follow if there is any, e. g. , Mr. C. E. Eckersley, Director/ President.

4. The Salutation

The salutation is the complimentary greeting with which the writer opens his/her letter. The usual salutation in British business letters addressed to a company is *Dear Sirs*, while the most common one in the US is *Gentlemen*.

Dear Sir or *Dear Madam* is used to address a person whose name you do not know. When you know the name of the person you are writing to, the salutation takes the form of *Dear* followed by a courtesy title and the person's surname: *Dear Mr. Eckersley.*

5. The Body

The body is the main part of the letter. It is typed two lines below the salutation, or below the subject line, if any. It expresses the writer's idea, opinion, purpose and wishes, etc. When writing, pay attention to the following:

(1) Write simply, clearly, courteously, grammatically, and to the point.

(2) Paragraph correctly, confining each paragraph to one topic.

In letters of average length, paragraphs are single-spaced and between paragraphs double spacing is used.

6. The Close

The complimentary close is simply a matter of custom or a polite way of closing a letter, two lines below the final line of the body of the letter.

The expression used for the complimentary close must match the salutation as the following table:

Dear Sirs/Mmes Dear Sir/Madam	Yours faithfully/Faithfully yours
Ladies/Gentlemen	Yours very truly/Very truly yours
Dear Mr. Smith Dear Ms. Johnson Dear Mrs. Seaver Dear Miss Malone	Yours faithfully/Yours sincerely/Best wishes/Kind regards (UK) Sincerely/Very truly yours/Best regards (the US)

7. The Signature

It is common to type the name of the writer's firm or company immediately below complimentary close. Then the person who writes or dictates the letter should sign his/her name, by hand and in ink, below it. To sign with one's given name, e. g., *David Smith* or *Diana Jenkins*, is preferable because the writer or dictator's gender is so identifiable that his/her correspondent is able to give him/her the right title when replying.

Since hand-written signature is illegible, the name of the signer is usually typed below the signature and followed by his job title or position. For example,

Yours faithfully,

The National Transport Co.

(Signature)

Wang Daming

Sales Manager

1.3.2 The Optional Parts of a Business Letter

1. The Attention Line

The attention line is used when the writer of a letter addressed to an organization wishes to direct the letter to a specific individual or section of the firm. It is generally inserted between the inside address and the salutation. For example,

Attention: Mr. Smith or *Attn: the Sales Manager* or *For the attention of the Sales Manager.*

2. The Subject Line

Subject line is actually the general idea of a letter. It is of vital importance in today's business correspondence due to the fast pace of business world. It is placed two lines below the salutation and above the body either at the left hand margin (full block form) or centrally over the body (other forms). The line may begin with or without the word *Subject* or be typed in block letters. For example,

Dear Sirs,

Subject: Request for copy of invoice

In the email, the subject is above the salutation.

3. Enclosure

If something is enclosed with the letter — such as a bill, check, proof or copy of another letter, note it below the signature in the lower left hand corner. The word can be shortened to *Enc* or *Encl* and followed by a period or colon. If necessary, you may list the enclosed documents or matters. For example,

Enc. Bill of lading (4 copies)

    Commercial invoice (3 copies)

    Insurance policy

Nowadays many business letters are sent by fax or by emails, the word *Attachment* should be used to replace *Enclosure*.

4. The Copy Notation

When you want your correspondent to know that a copy of a letter is to be sent to a third party, it is usual to indicate this by typing cc or CC followed by the name of the recipient. The usual position is at the foot of the letter two lines below the signature or immediately below the enclosure. For example,

CC Mr. William Carter, Vice-President.

1.4　The Format of Business Letters

1.4.1　Full Block Format

In the full block format, every part of a letter is typed from the left margin. It is convenient to be typed with a type writer; so it is often used in electronic correspondence. For example,

---

ABC Textile Group B. V.
Los Angeles 27524 California, the US
Tel:02-123456
Email:345678@ aol. com

Date:April 25,2018

Jiangsu Textile Import & Export Corp.
201 Jianshe Road,
Nanjing,Jiangsu,China

Dear Sirs,

Thank you for your letter of April 18, 2018. We are a company that is engaged in importing clothing items from your country.

We are interested in contacts as mentioned by you. Our Purchasing Manager, who is in Shanghai at the moment, will contact you when he returns.

Yours faithfully,

Chapter 1 Layout of Business Letters

(continued)

> ABC Textile Group B. V.
> (Signed)...
> Johnson Smith, Manager

1.4.2 Modified Block Style with Indented Paragraph

In the style, the sender's address as well as the date is typed in the up-middle part. The receiver's address starts from the left margin. The first line of each paragraph in the body is indented. The close as well as the signature is typed from the middle little toward the right. The layout of modified block form with indented style is beautiful, so some business persons use this style especially in printed letters.

> ABC Textile Group B. V.
> Los Angeles 27524 California, the US
> Tel: 02-123456
> Email: 345678@ aol. com
> Date: April 25, 2018
>
> Jiangsu Textile Import & Export Corp.
> 201 Jianshe Road, Nanjing, Jiangsu, China
>
> Dear Sirs,
>
> Thank you for your letter of April 18, 2018. We are a company that is engaged in importing clothing items from your country.
> We are interested in contacts as mentioned by you. Our Purchasing Manager, who is in Shanghai at the moment, will contact you when he returns.
>
>   Yours faithfully,
>   ABC Textile Group B. V.
>   (Signed)...
>   Johnson Smith, Manager

1.4.3 Modified Block Style

As the business letters are supposed to be simple and clear, the modified block form and simplified form come out. In the modified block format, all the parts start from the left margin, except the date, close and signature which are positioned the same as that in modified block format with indented paragraph.

ABC Textile Group B. V.
Los Angeles 27524 California, the US
Tel:02-123456
Email:345678@ aol. com

                                                     Date:April 25,2018

Jiangsu Textile Import & Export Corp.
201 Jianshe Road, Nanjing, Jiangsu, China

Dear Sirs,

Thank you for your letter of April 18, 2018. We are a company that is engaged in importing clothing items from your country.

We are interested in contacts as mentioned by you. Our Purchasing Manager, who is in Shanghai at the moment, will contact you when he returns.

                                                     Yours faithfully,
                                         ABC Textile Group B. V.
                                                 (Signed)...
                                       Johnson Smith, Manager

---

1.4.4 Simplified Format

Simplified format is somewhat like full block form; but some parts are omitted, such as salutation and complimentary close.

ABC Textile Group B. V.
Los Angeles 27524 California, the US
Tel:02-123456
Email:345678@ aol. com
Date:April 25,2018

Chapter 1 Layout of Business Letters

(continued)

> Jiangsu Textile Import & Export Corp.
> 201 Jianshe Road,
> Nanjing, Jiangsu, China
>
> Thank you for your letter of April 18, 2018. We are a company that is engaged in importing clothing items from your country.
>
> We are interested in contacts as mentioned by you. Our Purchasing Manager, who is in Shanghai at the moment, will contact you when he returns.
>
> (Signed)...

The above four styles are popularly used nowadays. Which form a sender likes to choose depends on his or her preference. The main aim of designing a letter is to make the letter not only pleasing to the eye, but also convenient to be typed. Therefore, in modern electronic correspondence, the full block style and the simplified style are preferable.

For the convenience, the letter head, inside address and sometimes the date and the signature are omitted in most of the specimen letters in this book.

Chapter 2
Establishment of Business Relations

Chapter 2 Establishment of Business Relations

Learning Objectives

- To learn to seek clients from different channels.
- To write letters to establish business relations.

2.1 Introduction

When the firms want to establish business relations with prospective dealers in other countries or regions, they will write letters to express their wishes. To establish business relations with prospective dealers is the base for starting and developing business. So, in the international trade, it is vitally important to establish good business relations with other companies or firms.

Prospective dealers abroad may be approached through different channels including official institutions and non-official organizations in the following:

(1) the chambers of commerce, the commercial counselor's office;

(2) the export commodities fairs or exhibitions;

(3) the introduction from business connections;

(4) mutual visits by trade delegations or groups;

(5) market investigations;

(6) self-introduction by customers themselves;

(7) trade directory;

(8) banks;

(9) advertisements in newspapers, magazines and other channels, such as Internet or foreign sales agents, etc.

This kind of letters should be written cordially, sincerely and courteously.

2.2 Samples

Specimen 1   An Exporter Asking to Establish Business Relations

Dear Sirs,

Through the chamber of commerce in Beijing, we have known that you are importers of

Cotton Piece Goods and interested in doing business with us. We wish to inform you that we specialize in the export of Cotton Piece Goods and shall be pleased to establish business relations with you at an early date.

Chinese Cotton Piece Goods are excellent in quality and reasonable in price. To give you a general idea of our products, we enclose a catalogue together with two pamphlets for your reference, and would be interested in receiving your enquiries.

We look forward to your early reply.

Yours faithfully,

Specimen 2　An Exporter's Self-introduction

Dear Sirs,

We write to introduce ourselves as one of the largest exporters, from China, of a wide range of machinery and equipment.

We enclose a copy of our latest catalogue covering the details of all the items available at present, and hope some of these items will be of interest to you.

It will be a great pleasure to receive your enquiries for any of the items against which we will send you our lowest quotations.

Should, by chance, your corporation not deal with the import of the goods mentioned above, we would be most grateful if this letter could be forwarded to the correct import corporation.

We are looking forward to your favorable and prompt reply.

Yours faithfully,

Chapter 2 Establishment of Business Relations

Specimen 3   An Importer Asking to Establish Business Relations

Dear Sirs,

We have obtained your name and address from the Pacific Trading Co., Ltd. in Hongkong, and are glad to establish business relations with you.

We are connected with all the major dealers here of light industrial products; moreover, there is a good demand for your electronic products. So, we feel sure we can sell large quantities of these goods.

Please let us have all necessary information regarding your products for export. If your prices are competitive, we would place a large order with you.

Yours faithfully,

Specimen 4   An Importer's Self-introduction

May 5, 2018

Dear Sirs,

We saw your Green Tea at the International Exhibition of Natural Health Products held in Beijing during April, and are keenly interested in this product.

We are writing to you and hope to receive your catalogues and price list for information.

We take this opportunity to introduce ourselves as a British importer of health products. At present, we would like to market Green Tea in our country. If you can cooperate with us on quality, price and delivery, we shall place an order with you.

We look forward to your favorable reply.

Yours faithfully,
(Signature)
Harold Piper

2.3 Writing Guide

2.3.1 Structure of a Letter for Establishing Business Relations

Opening paragraph: tell the source of the information and your intention.

Body: give a self introduction including business scope of the firm, the reference as to your firm's financial position and integrity.

Closing paragraph: express your expectation of cooperation and an early reply.

The letter may include some or all of the following main points and use the following expressions.

(1) Source of information:

- Your company has been kindly introduced/recommended to us by...
- We learn through/from... that...
- On the recommendation of...
- We owe your name and address to...
- We are writing to you at the suggestion of...

(2) Desire of establishing business relations:

- We are willing to enter into business relations with you.
- We express our desire to...
- We are now writing to you for...
- We are desirous of...
- We avail ourselves of this opportunity to approach you for the establishment of trade relations with you.

(3) Your own line of business and references of your company:

- We wish to introduce ourselves to you as one of the leading exporters of cotton goods in China.
- We are enjoying an excellent reputation through fifty-year experience in...
- Our lines are mainly...
- We specialize in...
- We take the liberty of introducing ourselves as...

Chapter 2 Establishment of Business Relations

(4) Your expectation of an early reply:

- We look forward to receiving...
- Hope to receive...
- Your early reply is appreciated.
- We are anticipating your reply...
- Your prompt reply will be greatly appreciated.

2.3.2 A Reply

A reply to the above letter includes the following points:

(1) Your appreciation of their interests:

- Thank you for your interest in...

(2) Your interests in establishing business relations with them:

- Your wish of establishing business relations coincides with ours.

(3) Your willingness to communicate further:

- We are sending you our catalogue and price list.

2.4 Supplement

Useful Sentences on Establishing Business Relations

(1) We've come to know your name and address from the Commercial Counselor's Office of the Chinese Embassy in London.

我们从中国驻伦敦大使馆的商务参赞处得知贵公司的名称和地址。

(2) By the courtesy of Mr. Black, we are given to understand the name and address of your firm.

承蒙布莱克先生的介绍,我们得知贵公司的名称和地址。

(3) We are willing to enter into business relations with your firm.

我们愿意与贵公司建立业务关系。

(4) Your firm has been introduced (recommended) to us by Maple Company.

枫叶公司向我方介绍(推荐)了贵公司。

(5) Our mutual understanding and cooperation will certainly result in important business.

我们之间的相互理解与合作必将促成重要的生意。

（6）We express our desire to establish business relations with your firm.

我们愿和贵公司建立业务关系。

（7）Your letter of August 8 addressed to our head office has been passed on to us for attention.

贵方8月8日写给我们总公司的信已转交我们处理。

（8）We now avail ourselves of this opportunity to write to you with a view to entering into business relations with you.

现在我们借此机会致函贵公司，希望和贵公司建立业务关系。

（9）We are now writing to you for the purpose of establishing business relations with you.

我们特此致函是想与贵方建立业务关系。

（10）Your desire to establish business relations coincides with ours.

贵方想同我方建立业务关系的愿望与我方是一致的。

（11）We specialize in the export of Japanese light industrial products and would like to trade with you in this line.

鉴于我方专营日本轻工业产品出口业务，我方愿与贵方在这方面开展贸易。

（12）Our lines are mainly arts and crafts.

我们经营的商品主要是工艺品。

（13）We have been in this line of business for more than twenty years.

我们经营这类商品已有二十多年的历史了。

（14）Your letter expressing the hope of establishing business connections with us has met with approval.

来函收悉，得知贵方愿与我方建立业务关系，我们表示同意。

（15）In order to acquaint you with the textiles we handle, we take pleasure in sending you by air our latest catalogue for your perusal.

为了使贵方对我方经营的纺织品有所了解，特航空邮寄我方最新目录，请过目。

（16）Our bankers are the Hong Kong & Shanghai Banking Corporation; they can provide you with the information about our business and finances.

我们的业务银行是香港上海汇丰银行，他们可以向贵方提供有关我方的业务及资金情况。

Chapter 2 Establishment of Business Relations

(17) We should be pleased if you would respond to our request at your earliest convenience.

如果贵方能尽早回复,我们将不胜感激。

(18) In order to promote business between us, we are airmailing you samples, under separate cover, for your inspection.

为了促进双方业务往来,另封航邮寄上样品,供贵方检测参考。

(19) It would be very helpful if you could send us statistics on your sales.

若能向我方提供贵方的销售统计资料,那可就太有帮助了。

(20) We would like to ask you to kindly send us the related information.

我们希望贵方能将相关资料提供给我们.

EXERCISES

◇**Language Usage**

Ⅰ. Choose the one that best completes each of the following sentences.

1. We _____ your name and address _____ the Commercial Counsellor's Office of the Chinese Embassy in Ghana.

   A. have known...in   B. have learned...by
   C. have given...by   D. have come to know...from

2. We wish to introduce _____ the largest exporter of fabrics of high quality.

   A. that we are   B. it that we are   C. ourselves as   D. ourselves to be

3. Your letter expressing the hope of entering into business connection with us _____ with thanks.

   A. have been received   B. has been received
   C. have received   D. has received

4. We take the liberty of writing to you _____ establishing business relations.

   A. hope   B. in hope   C. in the hope of   D. hoping

5. We are one of the leading exporters _____ all kinds of computers of high quality.

   A. trade in   B. trading on   C. trading in   D. trade for

6. We take the pleasure of introducing ourselves _____ an experienced importer _____ line of daily products.

A. of...on   B. as...in   C. for...by   D. be...at

7. We will forward all the necessary information of the item mentioned above _____ receipt of your reply.

A. with   B. upon   C. in   D. of

8. _____ you _____ send us samples of your new products?

A. Do...hope to   B. Do...wish to   C. Would...please   D. Will...like to

9. We _____ that with joint efforts business between us will be developed to our mutual benefit.

A. are convinced   B. are convince   C. convinced   D. convincing

10. This corporation _____ foodstuffs.

A. deals in   B. deals with   C. deals   D. deal on

II. Fill in the blanks with proper prepositions.

11. If your price is competitive, we shall be glad to place a substantial order _____ you.

12. This article is of particular interest _____ us.

13. We are gearing our production _____ your requirements and shall soon be _____ a position to offer you substantially.

14. There is nothing available for export _____ present.

15. Since you all agree to the offer and therefore enter _____ a contract.

16. We trade _____ the principle of equality and mutual benefit.

17. We take the liberty _____ writing you _____ a view to building up business relations with your firm.

18. We appreciate your sending us a special offer _____ walnut.

19. All the information you have got is up _____ date on the computer.

20. You may rest assured that _____ no case will the shipment be delayed.

III. Translate the following sentences into Chinese or English.

21. Your company has been kindly recommended to us by the Chamber of Commerce in London, Britain as one of the leading exporters of cotton textiles in your country.

22. We'd like to express our desire to establish business relations with you on the basis of equality, mutual benefit and exchange of needed goods.

Chapter 2 Establishment of Business Relations

23. Our purpose is to explore the possibilities of developing trade with you. Respecting the local customs of the buyer's country is surely one important aspect of China's foreign trade policy.

24. We now avail ourselves of this opportunity to write to you with a view to entering into business relations with you.

25. We've never have any difficulties with our Chinese partners, and we'd like to make as many new contracts as we can.

26. 我公司从事纺织品出口业务多年。我们的产品质量好、价格合理，在世界上享有极高的声誉。

27. 丝绸是我们的传统出口商品之一。丝绸女装色彩鲜艳、设计美观，在国外很受欢迎，需求量一直都很大。

28. 我已看过您上次在信中所附的目录和小册子，对贵公司的出口产品有所了解。对你们的丝绸女衫颇感兴趣。

29. 我公司是中国最大的电器产品进口商，感谢贵公司5月4日来函，我们愿意和贵公司建立贸易关系。

30. 为使贵方对我方各种款式的毛毯初步了解，今航寄我方目录、价格表和一些样品供贵方参考。

Ⅳ. **Translate the following letter into English.**

敬启者：
　　经我方驻贵国商务参赞处介绍，今特写此信。我们冒昧向贵方介绍：我方专营丝绸商品，主要向日本和欧洲出口。望与贵方建立直接的业务关系。贵方若能告知是否对上述商品生意抱有兴趣，我们将深表感谢。若有兴趣请告知所需数量。

◇**Practice**

Write a letter asking to establish business relations in the importer's name and then write a reply based on the information given below.

(1) Information about the exporter and importer.

Exporter's name and address: Tianjin ABC Cotton Goods Co., Ltd.

31 Jiuyuan Road, Baodi District, Tianjin 300801, China

Importer's name and address: Union Clothing Associate Co. Ltd.

3710 West 9th St. Los Angeles, CA 90019, the US

(2) Background information for business.

On May 8, 2018, Tianjin ABC Cotton Goods Co., Ltd. received a letter from a potential client of the US, who showed interest in its pure cotton garments, which are advertised on the Internet.

Chapter 3
Enquiry, Offer and Counter-offer

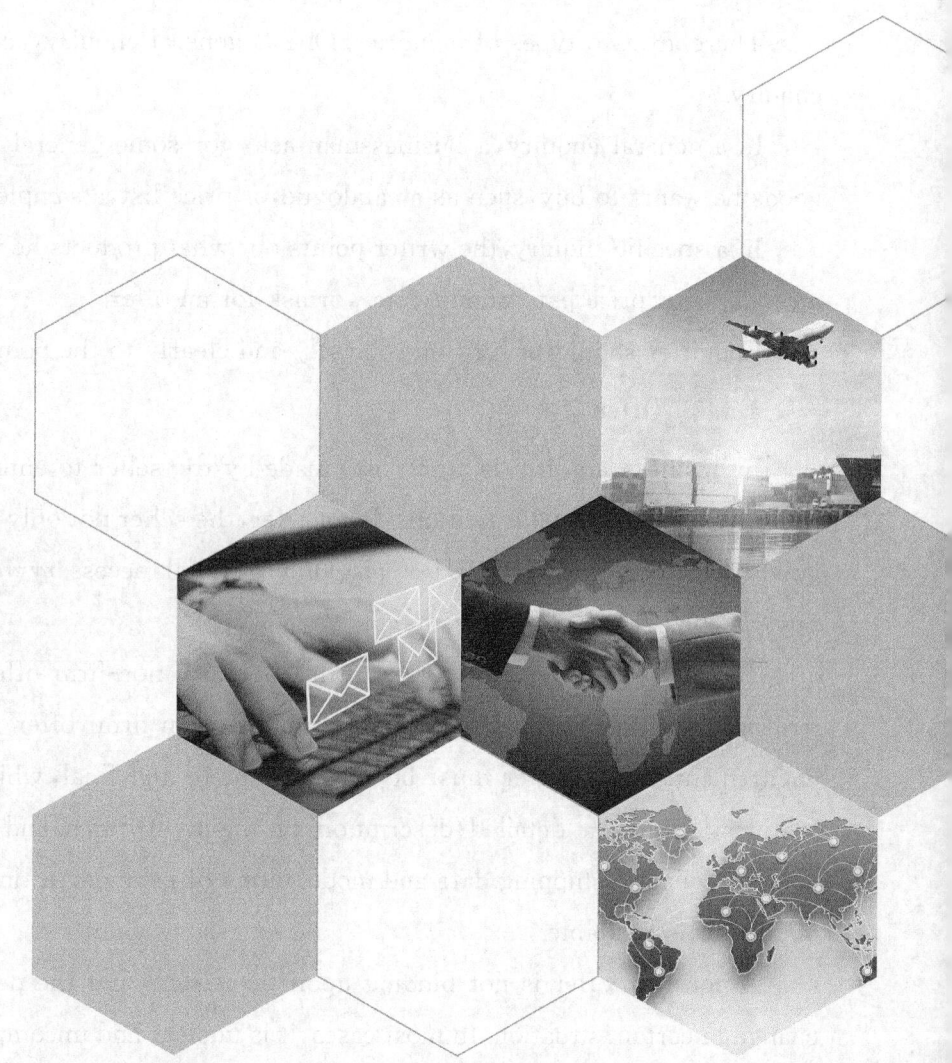

Learning Objectives

- To write letters of enquiry and reply.
- To identify firm offer or non-firm offer.
- To write letters of offer and counter-offer.

3.1 Introduction

3.1.1 Enquiry

An enquiry is a request for information about the goods to be ordered. An importer may send out an enquiry to an exporter to invite a quotation or an offer for the goods he wishes to buy or simply ask for some general information about the goods.

There are two types of enquiries. One is general enquiry, and the other is specific enquiry.

In a general enquiry, a businessman asks for some general information about the goods he wants to buy, such as a catalogue, or price list, a sample or sample book, etc.

In a specific enquiry, the writer points out what products he wants. He may ask for a catalogue, a price list, samples, etc. , or ask for an offer.

Enquiries should be written concisely and clearly to the point.

3.1.2 Offer

In business, an offer is a proposal made by the seller to enter into a contract with the buyer under special conditions. In an offer, the seller not only quotes the price of the goods he/she wishes to sell but also indicates all necessary terms of sales for the buyer's consideration and acceptance.

There are two types of offer: firm offer and non-firm offer. A firm offer is an irrevocable offer with engagement, while a non-firm offer is an offer without engagement. A firm offer must be clear, complete and final, which should contain the following points: a detailed description of the item; price and currency; packaging; quantity; quality; shipping date and mode; terms of payment; a time frame during which your offer is available.

A non-firm offer is not binding upon the sellers and the details of the offer may change in certain situation. In most cases, it is unclear and imcomplete with reservation.

Chapter 3 Enquiry, Offer and Counter-offer

The main terms and conditions are not complete.

3.1.3 Counter-offer

A counter-offer is a reply given to an initial offer and may change the terms of the deal. In fact, it is a new offer made in response to an offer received, and at the same time, the original offer lapses.

In the counter-offer, the buyer may show his disagreement to the certain term or terms and state his/her own idea instead. The counter-offer gives the original offeror three options: to accept the counter, to reject it or to make another one. This process can go on for many a round till business is finalized or called off.

If the buyer rejects the offer, he also should write a letter to express his thanks for the seller's offer and explain the reason for rejection.

3.2 Samples

Specimen 1   General Enquiry

January 20, 2018

Dear Sirs,

We have been informed by the Bank of US Commerce, New York that you are one of the leading exporters of textiles in China, and you wish to export pure silk garments to our market.

You will be pleased to note that our corporation is one of the leading importers of textile products, having over 30 years' history and high reputation.

We shall be able to give you considerable orders, if the quality of your products is fine and the prices are moderate. We would be obliged if you will send us some samples with the best terms at your earliest convenience.

Yours faithfully,

Specimen 2　A Reply to General Enquiry

January 28, 2018

Dear Sirs,

We take pleasure in acknowledging receipt of your letter of January 20, from which we learn that you are interested in bringing silk garments to the New York market.

We are enclosing our quotations sheet covering different sizes and colors of our pure silk garments that can be supplied from stock. We are also airmailing you two dozen sample garments in different sizes and colors. Delivery will be made within 30 days after your placing an order with us. Payment of the purchase is to be effected by an irrevocable L/C at sight in our favor.

This offer is subject to your immediate reply which should reach us not later than the end of next month. The price will probably be changed once this particular offer has lapsed.

Yours faithfully,

Specimen 3　An Enquiry Letter

Dear Sirs,

We learn with pleasure from your letter of April 12, 2018 that you are exporters of Chinese Blanket Cover and are willing to establish business relations with us.

At present, we are interested in the blanket cover and shall be pleased if you will send us samples and all necessary information on the blanket cover, so as to acquaint us with materials and workmanship of your supplies. Meanwhile, please quote us the lowest price CIF London, inclusive of our 3% commission, stating the earliest date of shipment.

Chapter 3 Enquiry, Offer and Counter-offer

Should your price be found competitive and delivery time acceptable, we shall place a large order with you.

Yours truly,
Johnson Smith

Specimen 4 A Reply to the Specific Enquiry—A Non-firm Offer

Dear Mr. Johnson Smith,

Thank you very much for your letter of April 28, 2018. We are pleased to send you samples and all the necessary information on the blanket cover.

As requested, we are pleased to make you an offer, subject to our final confirmation, as in the enclosure.

As you will realize from the catalogue we sent you, our blanket cover is a perfect combination of warmth, softness and easy care. We are sure that you can get benefit from our products.

We look forward to your prompt reply.

Yours truly,

Enc.
Commodity: Blanket Cover.
Size: Large (L), Medium (M), Small (S).
Price: $20 each piece CIF Hamburg inclusive of 3% commission.
Shipment: During August/September
Payment: By confirmed, irrevocable L/C payable by draft at sight.

Specimen 5 A Reply to the Specific Enquiry—A Firm Offer

Dear Mr. Johnson Smith,

Thank you very much for your letter of April 28, 2018. We are pleased to send you samples and all the necessary information on the blanket cover.

As requested, we are pleased to make you a firm offer, as in the enclosure.

As you are aware that there has been lately a large demand for the above commodities, such growing demand has doubtlessly resulted in increased prices.

This offer is firm subject to your immediate reply which should reach us not later than June 30.

Yours faithfully,

Enc.

Commodity: Peacock Blanket Cover

Size: 76 * 88 inches

Color: Red and White

Price: $20 each piece CIF Hamburg inclusive of 3% commission

Shipment: During August/September

Payment: By 100% confirmed, irrevocable L/C in our favor payable by draft at 60 days.

Specimen 6 A Counter-offer on Price of Blanket Cover

Dear Sirs,

We thank you for your offer by email of May 5 for 5,000 pieces of the captioned goods at $20 per piece CIF Hamburg.

We immediately contacted our customers and they showed great interest in the quality

Chapter 3 Enquiry, Offer and Counter-offer

and designs of your products. However they said that your price is 10% higher than the average. They told us if you can reduce your price to $18 per piece, they will increase 1,000 pieces to the quantity. So there is a good chance of concluding a bigger transaction with them if you can meet their requirement. We hope you will take advantage of this opportunity so that you will benefit from the expanding market.

We await your favorable reply with great interest.

Yours faithfully,

Specimen 7 A Counter-counter Offer

Dear Sirs,

Your counter-offer of May 19 has been received.

However, $18 per piece as you suggest is too severe for us. You mentioned you could get blanket cover of the same quality at much lower prices, but our goods are produced direct from Hangzhou, which will be offered by us at an exceedingly moderate price.

It is hard for us to accept your counter-offer of $18 per piece, but as this is our first transaction, we may concede to $19 per piece provided you give us an order for 6,000 pieces at the least.

Your earliest possible reply would be appreciated.

Yours faithfully,

3.3 Writing Guide

3.3.1 Structure of an Enquiry Letter

Opening paragraph: notify the goods you want to buy if you are well-known with you customer; if you don't know each other, this paragraph is the same as the beginning of the letter for establishing business relationship.

Body: demand the seller to send you catalogue, price list, samples, trade terms and so on; indicate the future of this trade.

Closing paragraph: restate your request and you are waiting for the reply.

The letter may include some or all of the following main points and useful expressions.

(1) To elucidate the information source:

• We read with interest your advertisement on *China Daily* and should be glad to receive particulars of your...

• We have heard from China Council for the promotion of International Trade that...

• We learn from ABC Co. Ltd, New York that you are a leading exporter in your country.

(2) To explain what you want directly:

• We are considering the purchase of...

• We are interested in importing—but we need to have further details of the costs before making a final decision.

• We are regular buyers of men's knitwear.

(3) To ask for catalogues, price list, samples, etc.:

• Will you please send us your illustrated/ latest catalogue and price list?

• It is desired that the catalogues shall be airmailed to us within one week.

• We would like to receive a copy of your latest catalogue and full details of your export prices and terms of payment, together with samples.

(4) To emphasize that the quotation should be competitive:

• If your quotation is really competitive...

• Provided prices are right...

• If your products and terms compare favorably with those of other supplies, we shall send you an order.

(5) To enquire about the discount, payment methods and delivery:

• We should like to know if you allow discounts.

Chapter 3 Enquiry, Offer and Counter-offer

• Please let us have your lowest FOB prices, together with your terms of business, and state your best delivery time.

• We require the goods delivery be effected within six weeks of order.

(6) To express the possibility of placing orders:

• Will you please let us know by April 4 so that we can place our order promptly?

• Please let us know by return of post whether you would be interested in such an order.

• We should appreciate it if you would let us know what discount you may grant us if we place an order for 20,000 pieces.

3.3.2 Structure of Replies to an Enquiry or Offer

Opening paragraph: thank for the enquiry (if this offer is replying to an enquiry); state on what terms and at what price you will supply the goods; indicate whether this offer is a firm offer or an offer subject to confirmation.

Body: reply the enquiry, and tell what you are enclosing, such as catalogue, price list and samples; present your sales terms (that is to tell the available quantity, the quality and the date of delivery); indicate the market of the enquired goods in order to interest the buyer, or indicate the benefit of this trade, such as high quality, best price and so on.

Closing paragraph: anticipate an order.

The letter may include the following main points and expressions.

(1) Your appreciation of their enquiries:

• Many thanks for your enquiry of...

• Thank you for your enquiry and for your interest in our products.

• We thank you for your enquiry of...

(2) Your willingness to send the requested items:

• We are pleased to enclose...

• We have pleasure in enclosing...

• We are sending you our latest price list and catalogue.

(3) Detailed information about the specific goods and their advantages:

• We are confident you will find our products the finest on the market and considerably better than those of our competitors who supply your market at present.

• The specimen sent will convince you of the excellent quality of our...

• We feel confident that you will find the goods are both excellent in quality and very reasonable in price.

(4) Your statement of rationality of the quoted price and validity of period for the current quotation:

• This is the most favorable offer we can make and you will agree that none of our competitors can equal these items.

• Price is valid until December 31.

• The offer is subject to goods being unsold.

(5) Your terms of payment and possible delivery time:

• Our terms of payment are cash on delivery.

• We should require payment by banker's draft on receipt of our proforma invoice.

• We can usually deliver within three weeks of receiving an order.

(6) Your hope to accept their orders and willingness to cooperate with them for long periods:

• We hope you will find our quotation satisfactory and look forward to receiving your order.

• We look forward to doing business with you.

3.3.3 Structure of a Counter-offer Letter

Opening paragraph: express thanks for the offer.

Body: state your disagreement to the certain term or terms and the reasons; point out your suggestions.

Closing paragraph: look forward to an early reply.

The letter may include the following main points and expressions.

(1) To thank the offeror for the quotation:

• Thank you for your prompt reply and detailed quotation.

• Thank you for the samples you sent in response to our enquiry of June 8.

• We thank you for your quotation of February for...

(2) To reject the offer and explain why:

• We are sorry to tell you that we cannot take you up on the offer as the price you are asking is above the market level here for the quality in question.

• I should like to point out that your choice in color and pattern is very limited and that the shades which are now fashionable are missing.

• We feel that your quotation is not proper because the price for such material is on the decline at present.

(3) To put forward your terms and conditions:

• May we suggest that you could make some allowance on your quoted prices that would help to introduce your goods on this market?

• We regret that your terms are unsatisfactory and unless you can amend those terms we shall have to place our order elsewhere.

• You should benefit from higher sale with a little concession, say a 2% reduction.

(4) To express your wishes to be accepted:

• It is hoped that you would seriously take it into consideration and let us have your reply very soon.

• We hope you will consider our counter-offer most favorable, and fax us acceptance at your earliest convenience.

• It is our hope that you would reconsider the matter and let us know your favorable decision as quickly as possible.

3.4 Supplement

Some Useful Sentences on Enquiries, Offers and Counter-offers

3.4.1 Enquiry

(1) Please let us have the information as to the price and quality of the goods.

请告知该商品的价格和质量等信息。

(2) Please quote us your lowest price for synthetic fiber goods, such as nylon, vinylon, and saran made in Japan.

请将日本生产的尼龙、维尼龙、莎纶等合成纤维制品的最低价格报给我们。

(3) Kindly favor us with the lowest cash price for the goods.

敬请告知这批货以现金支付的最低价格。

(4) Kindly let us know at what price you are able to deliver quantities of best refined sugar.

敬请告知贵公司上等砂糖的批发价格。

(5) At what lowest price can you quote for 50 bales middling Texas cotton for November?

请问50包德克萨斯州产中等棉花11月份交货的最低价格是多少？

(6) We shall be obliged by a quotation of your lowest price for the said goods free delivered at our works.

如蒙对上述产品报运至我方工厂交货的最低价格，将不胜感激。

(7) I shall be glad if you will send me your catalogue together with quotations.

请贵方惠寄商品目录并报价。

(8) If your prices are favorable, we can place the order right away.

如果你们的价格优惠，那么我们可以马上订货。

(9) We'd like to know what you can offer as well as your sales conditions.

我们想了解贵方的报盘及销售条件。

(10) How long does it usually take you to make delivery?

贵方通常要多久才能交货？

(11) Could you make prompt delivery?

贵方可以即期交货吗？

(12) Would you accept delivery spread over a period of time?

不知贵方是否接受在一段时间里分批交货？

(13) Could you tell me which kind of payment terms you'll choose?

请问贵方选择哪种付款方式？

(14) Will you please tell us the earliest possible date you can make shipment?

能告知我们最早船期吗？

(15) Do you take special orders?

贵方接受特殊订货吗？

(16) Could you please send us a catalogue of your rubber boots together with terms of payment?

请问贵方能寄来一份胶靴的目录，并告诉我们付款方式吗？

(17) He inquired about the varieties, specifications and price, and so on and so forth.

他询问了品种、花色和价格等信息。

(18) We would appreciate it if you will let us know the ruling prices of the goods.

如您能告知该商品的现行价格,我们将不胜感谢。

3.4.2　Offer

(1)We're willing to make you a firm offer at this price.

我们愿意以此价格为贵方报实盘。

(2)We can offer you a quotation based upon the international market.

我们可以按国际市场价格给您报价。

(3)We are in a position to offer tea from stock.

我们可以提供茶叶的现货价格。

(4)We offer firm for reply before 11 a.m. tomorrow.

我们报实盘,以明天上午11点答复为准。

(5)My offer was based on reasonable profit,not on wild speculations.

我的报价以合理利润为依据,不是漫天要价。

(6)We always try our best to meet your requirements in view of our long relation.

鉴于我们长期的贸易关系,我们总是尽力满足贵方的要求。

(7)Is your offer a firm one or one subject to final confirmation?

贵方报的是实盘还是以最后确认为准?

(8)This offer is based on an expanding market and is competitive.

此报盘着眼于扩大销路,而且很有竞争性。

(9)The offer is valid until June 23,2018.

报价有效期至2018年6月23日。

(10)Moreover,we've kept the price close to the costs of production.

再说,我们已经把价格压低至接近生产成本了。

(11)I think the price we offered you last week is the best one.

相信我上周的报价是最好的。

(12)All prices in the price lists are subject to our confirmation.

报价单中所有价格以我方确认为准。

(13)We'll give you the preference of our offer.

我方将优先向贵方报盘。

(14)We'll let you have the official offer next Monday.

我们下周一就给您正式报盘。

(15)You'll see that our offer compares favorably with the quotations you can get elsewhere.

您会发现我方的报价比别家更具竞争力。

3.4.3 Counter-offer

(1) I'm afraid the offer is unacceptable.

恐怕贵方的报价我不能接受。

(2) The offer is not workable.

报盘不可行。

(3) The offer is given without engagement.

报盘没有约束力。

(4) It is difficult to quote without full details.

未说明详尽细节，难以报价。

(5) Buyers do not welcome offers made at wide intervals.

买方不欢迎报盘间隔太久。

(6) We cannot make any headway with your offer.

贵方的报盘未取得任何进展。

(7) Please renew your offer for two days further.

请将报盘有效期延长两天。

(8) Please renew your offer on the same terms and conditions.

请按同样条件重新报盘。

(9) We regret we have to decline your offer.

很抱歉，我们不得不拒绝贵方报盘。

(10) The offer is withdrawn.

该报盘已被撤回。

(11) I appreciate your counter-offer but find it too low.

感谢您的还盘，但我方觉得价格太低了。

(12) Now we look forward to replying to our offer in the form of counter-offer.

现在，希望贵方能以还盘的形式对我方报盘予以答复。

(13) Your price is too high to interest buyers in counter-offer.

你的价格太高，买方没有兴趣还盘。

(14) Your counter-offer is much more modest than mine.

你们的还盘比我的要保守得多。

Chapter 3 Enquiry, Offer and Counter-offer

(15) We make a counter-offer to you of ＄150 per metric ton FOB London.

我方还价为每公吨伦敦离岸价 150 美元。

(16) I'll respond to your counter-offer by reducing our price by three dollars.

我方同意贵方的还盘,减价 3 美元。

(17) Your counter offer is too low and groundless; therefore it cannot serve as a basis for further negotiation with our manufacturers.

贵方还价太低且没有根据,因此不能作为与我方生产厂家继续磋商的依据。

(18) No other buyers have bid higher than this price.

没有别的买家出价更高。

(19) We can't accept your offer unless the price is reduced by 5%.

除非你们减价 5%,否则我们无法接受报盘。

(20) I'm afraid I don't find your price competitive at all.

恐怕你们的报价毫无竞争性。

EXERCISES

◇**Language Usage**

Ⅰ. Choose the one that best completes each of the following sentences.

1. We thank you for your letter of May 17 and the _____ catalogue.
   A. sent   B. enclosed   C. given   D. presented

2. The letter we sent last week is an enquiry _____ color TV sets.
   A. about   B. for   C. of   D. as

3. We should be pleased to send you some samples of our new typewriters on approval, _____ our own expense.
   A. at   B. on   C. for   D. in

4. If you are interested, we will send you a sample lot _____ charge.
   A. within   B. with   C. for   D. free of

5. This price is _____ of your 5% commission.
   A. includes   B. covering   C. inclusive   D. including

6. _____ your enquiry No. 123, we are sending you a catalogue and a sample book for your reference.
   A. According   B. As per   C. As   D. About

7. Your letter has _____ our careful attention.

   A. drawn   B. brought   C. received   D. invited

8. We would suggest _____ a small quantity for trial.

   A. you to buy   B. you buy   C. your buying   D. your buy

9. We anticipate _____ your early reply.

   A. to receive   B. having receive   C. receiving   D. receive

10. We confirm _____ your cable of even date.

    A. received   B. to receive   C. having received   D. receive

Ⅱ. Fill in the blanks with proper prepositions.

11. We are writing to you with a desire to open an account _____ you.

12. The lowest prices we can quote now are _____ follows.

13. This offer is firm subject _____ your reply before 10 a.m. our time.

14. We will withdraw the offer if we would not hear _____ you _____ this period.

15. The letter of credit has been opened _____ your favor.

16. In the meantime, please keep us informed _____ the developments _____ your end.

17. We take pleasure in informing you that we are _____ a position to accept new orders.

18. We have cut our price to the limit. We regret, therefore, being unable to comply _____ your request _____ further reduction.

19. On orders _____ 500 pieces or more we offer a special discount _____ 4%.

20. Can you lower the price _____ a small margin?

Ⅲ. Translate the following sentences into Chinese or English.

21. In order to start a transaction between us, we take pleasure in making you a special offer, subject to our final confirmation.

22. We can accept your offer if you can reduce your price in the price list of October 10 by 5%.

23. If you make a 10% discount, we would be glad to give you an order for 500 sets.

24. We are not in a position to entertain business at your price, since it is far below our cost price.

Chapter 3 Enquiry, Offer and Counter-offer

25. In reply to your letter of February 8, we regret that we cannot accept your price.

26. 我们对贵方生产的电脑很感兴趣,如蒙寄备有存货的电脑价格,将不胜感激。

27. 请给我们发来完整的目录及价目表,并附上大量购买的折扣。

28. 如果贵方能为我们提供一些新产品,以扩大我们的经营范围,那么我们将非常感谢。

29. 虽然贵方询问的商品眼下无货,但我们将尽最大努力尽快供货。

30. 我方的产品质量好、价格合理,因此相信贵方能大量订货。

Ⅳ. **Translate the following letter into English.**

> 敬启者:
> 　　收到贵方 5 月 10 日关于 9088 棉布的询盘,我们非常高兴。
> 　　兹报盘如下:
> 　　品名:9088 棉布
> 　　规格:36 * 36
> 　　价格:每码 1 美元 CIF 纽约
> 　　我们产品物美价廉,希望这笔交易能够成为双方之间长期业务合作关系的良好开端。近年来市场对纺织品的需求非常大,而且人民币一直在升值,请充分利用这次行市上涨的机会。
> 　　盼回复。
> 　　此致
> 敬礼!

◇**Practice**

Ⅰ. **Write a specific enquiry based on the following information.**

　　Source of information: advertisement in today's *Times*

　　The name of the commodity you want: children's shirts and skirts

　　You ask for: catalogues; price list; specification; payment terms; delivery terms; delivery date; other information

Ⅱ. **Write a reply to the above enquiry.**

Ⅲ. **Write a counter-offer according to the above reply.**

Ⅳ. **Write a counter counter-offer.**

Chapter 4
Conclusion of Business

Chapter 4 Conclusion of Business

Learning Objectives

- To get familiar with the procedures in conclusion of business.
- To learn to write letters confirming acceptance of a quotation or an order.
- To know how to translate contracts into English or into Chinese.

4.1 Introduction

In international trade, a transaction is concluded when one party accepts the terms and conditions put forward by the other party. Acceptance is a final and unconditional expression of assent to an offer, a counter-offer or an order. Generally, signing a contract is the way showing absolute assent to all the terms and conditions. There are several forms of contract in international trade, such as confirmation, agreement and memo, etc. Usually, a contract or confirmation can be drafted either by the exporter or the importer which is respectively called Sales Contract/Sales Confirmation or Purchase Contract/Purchase Confirmation. Any kind of the above is equally binding on both parties. It should be noted that the contract is more formal than the confirmation. No matter whatever form is used; a contract usually consists of three parts: preamble, body and witness clause.

(1) Preamble (heading) may include titles, number of the contract, date and place for signing the contract, names and addresses of the parties concerned and recital of whereas clause (purpose of signing the contract).

(2) Body is the most important part of the contract and reflects rights and obligations of both parties. The main clauses in this part may cover the following points: description of goods, specifications, quantity, price, packing, shipment, insurance, claims, force majeure, arbitration, etc.

(3) Witness clause (ending) usually includes language validity, copies, signature, seal and so on.

4.2 Samples

Specimen 1   Placing an Order

Dear Mr. XX,

Thank you for your letter of Dec. 15. We really appreciate your effort to pave the way for our business. So we are glad to place Order No. ME2020 as follows:

Purchase Order

PO No.: ME2020

Date: Dec. 18, 2016

Item No.	Descriptions	Quantity (M/T)	Unit Price (CIF Shanghai)	Total
CM201	24 * 16 Whole Slice	1,000	$ 210 per M/T	$ 210,000
CM202	24 * 8 Bottom Slice	1,000	$ 175 per M/T	$ 175,000
Payment: by irrevocable L/C Shipment: within 60 days upon receipt of L/C				

We expect to find a good market for the above and hope to place further and larger orders with you in the very near future.

Yours sincerely,

Specimen 2   Accepting an Order

Dear Sirs,

We have booked your order No. 789 for bed sheets and pillowcases and are sending you herewith our Sales Confirmation No. CW 0618 in duplicate.

Please sign and return one copy to us for our file. You may rest assured that we will arrange for delivery of the goods as soon as we receive the relative L/C. We have confidence that you will be completely satisfied with our products when you receive them.

Yours sincerely,

Chapter 4 Conclusion of Business

Specimen 3　Rejecting an Order

Dear Sirs,

Referring to the bed sheets under your order No. 456, we regret to tell you that we have no stock of the goods you required for the time being and do not expect further deliveries for at least another two months. Before then you may have been able to obtain the goods elsewhere, but if not we will revert to this matter as soon as our new supplies come up.

We are enclosing 2 copies of our catalogue covering all the articles available at present. If you need any of the items, please inform us. We assure you that your requirement will receive our prompt attention at all times.

Yours faithfully,

4.3　Writing Guide

Main points and requirements of letter-writing in this chapter are to be able to write a letter of placing an order and its reply as well as letters of sending a contract.

4.3.1　Placing an Order

1. Structure of an Order Letter

Opening paragraph: confirm the trade terms mentioned in the quotation or counter-offer; state the intention of placing an order.

Body: introduce in detail main contents of the order: article number, name of the commodity, specification, quantity, price terms, etc. ; point out, if any, other requirements such as packing and shipment terms.

Closing paragraph: express wish of cooperation or receiving a favorable reply.

2. Contents of an Order Letter

A satisfactory order letter should include at least the following points and some relevant useful expressions are furnished for your reference.

(1) To express your intention to place an order or pleasure in receiving the offer:

• Thank you for your quotation of... and enclose herewith our Order No. 456 for the captioned goods.

• We find both the price and quality of your products satisfactory and are pleased to give you an order for the following items.

• Your samples of... received favorable reaction from our customers, and we are pleased to enclose our order for...

(2) To confirm the deal and the full details of article number, quantity, specification, quality, unit price, total value, shipment, packing, insurance and terms of payment as agreed upon in preliminary negotiations between the buyer and the seller:

• Please supply in assorted colors: preferably 5 dozen each of red, yellow, green, blue and brown.

• We confirm the conclusion of our business. Enclosed is our order sheet No. 123.

• Please send us 350 sets so that we may tap the market. If successful, we will give you larger orders in the future.

(3) To close the letter by expressing willingness to cooperate or suggesting future business dealings:

• Your early attention to this order will be highly appreciated.

• We expect to find a good market for the goods.

• We hope to place further and larger orders with you in the near future.

4.3.2 Replying to an Order

1. Structure of a Letter for Acceptance

Opening paragraph: express appreciation for the order received.

Body: state briefly the main contents of the order received; promise that you will fill this order according to the buyer's terms.

Closing paragraph: express willingness to cooperate or suggest future business dealings.

2. Contents of a Letter for Acceptance

The following expressions can be used for your reference in reply to the buyer's order letter.

(1) To express appreciation for the order received:

• We are very pleased to receive your Order No. 123 for...

• We thank you for your Order No. 222 received this morning for...

(2) To state briefly the main contents of the order received; or promise that you'll fill this order according to the buyer's terms:

Chapter 4 CONCLUSION OF BUSINESS

• We accept the order and shall arrange delivery as soon as possible.

• As to the items A and B, we shall arrange delivery as soon as we get our L/C, and for items C and D we shall ship accordingly.

• We are enclosing a copy of our catalogue and hope that our handling of your first order will lead to further business between us.

(3) To express willingness to cooperate or suggesting future business dealings:

• Hoping the goods will turn out to your entire satisfaction and we may have further orders from you.

• We hope that our handling of your first order with us will lead to further business between us and mark the beginning of a happy working relationship.

4.3.3 Contract Cover Letter

1. Structure of a Contract Cover Letter

Opening paragraph: confirm the conclusion of business.

Body: mention the purpose of writing; remind the reader of the important points in the contract, such as the terms of payment, shipment, etc.

Closing paragraph: urge counter-signature of the contract.

2. Contents of a Contract Cover Letter

A letter of sending the covering contract consists of the following main points.

(1) To express pleasure of concluding the business:

• We are pleased to confirm our acceptance of your order.

• Referring to the lately exchange of letters, we are pleased to confirm having concluded with you a transaction of 100 tons of coal.

(2) To inform the recipient of the fact that a contract is being sent to him for counter-signature:

• As requested, we have made out and sent you our sales confirmation No. 6060 in duplicate. Please countersign and return one copy for our file.

• Attached is our sales confirmation No. 98SC in triplicate made out against your order mentioned above. Please countersign and send back one copy.

(3) To demand the buyer to establish the relevant L/C on time or expect the seller to effect shipment as soon as possible:

• Please open the relevant L/C, which must reach us one month before the date of shipment.

• We wish to point out that the stipulations in the relevant credit should strictly conform to the terms stated in our sales confirmation thus avoiding subsequent amendments.

(4) To express your promise or hope:

• We are looking forward to your early reply.

• Upon receipt of your credit, we shall effect the shipment in time.

4.4 Supplement

Some Useful Sentences on the Conclusion of a Business

4.4.1 Placing an Order

(1) We have received your offer dated Sept. 4 and are prepared to order a large quantity of the above commodity.

收到贵方9月4日报盘,我方欲大量订购上述货物。

(2) The quality and price of your products are satisfactory and we are willing to place an initial order with you for 2,000 sets.

贵方产品的质量和价格均令人满意,我方想先订2,000台。

(3) Enclosed please find our Order Sheet No. 012.

随信附上我方012号订货单。

(4) It is understood that the transaction is concluded on FOB basis. The buyer should effect insurance for 110% of the invoice value.

当然,交易是以FOB成交的,买方应按发票价值的110%投保。

(5) If this first order is satisfactorily executed, we shall place further orders with you.

倘若首次订单的履行令人满意,我们会继续下单。

(6) We are looking forward to receiving your confirmation and hope it is a good beginning for our cooperation.

盼确认并希望这是我们双方合作的良好开端。

4.4.2 Replying to an Order

(1) We are glad to receive your order No. 103 for stationery and confirm our

acceptance of it.

很高兴收到贵方关于文具的 103 号订单,我方确认接受。

(2)With reference to your letter of July 7, we have pleasure in informing you that we have booked your order for 10,000 pieces of towels.

关于贵方 7 月 7 日来函,我方很高兴接订贵方 10,000 条毛巾的订单。

(3)You may rest assured that all the items ordered will be shipped upon receipt of your letter of credit. We assure you of our careful attention to the packing of those items.

请放心,收到贵方信用证后,我们会立即发货,并保证仔细包装。

(4)Enclosed is one copy of our latest catalogue and if you are interested in any of the items, please feel free to contact us.

随信附上我方最新产品目录一本,若有兴趣可随时联系。

(5)We hope that you will be satisfied with our products.

希望贵方对我方的货物满意。

(6)We appreciate your cooperation and anticipate your further orders.

感谢配合,希望贵方能继续订货。

4.4.3 Contract Cover Letter

(1)We are pleased to confirm our acceptance of your order.

很高兴确认贵方订单。

(2)Referring to the lately exchange of letters, we are pleased to confirm having concluded with you a transaction of 100 tons of coal.

根据双方近期往来函件,特确认达成销售 100 吨煤的协议。

(3)As requested, we have made out and sent you our sales confirmation No. 6060 in duplicate. Please countersign and return one copy for our file.

遵照贵方要求,我们已缮制并寄去第 6060 号售货确认书一式两份。请会签后将其中一份回寄我方,以便我方存档。

(4)Attached is our sales confirmation No. 98SC in triplicate made out against your order mentioned above. Please countersign and send back one copy.

对于贵方上述订货,现随信附上我方销售确认书第 98SC 号一式三份,会签后即寄回一份。

(5)Please open the relevant L/C, which must reach us one month before the date of shipment.

请开立相关信用证并于装运前一个月送达我处。

(6) We wish to point out that the stipulations in the relevant credit should strictly conform to the terms stated in our sales confirmation thus avoiding subsequent amendments.

需要指出的是，信用证条款应与售货确认书严格一致，以避免日后修改。

(7) We are looking forward to your early reply.

盼早日回复。

(8) Upon receipt of your credit, we shall effect the shipment in time.

收到贵方信用证后，我们会及时发货。

EXERCISES

◇ **Language Usage**

Ⅰ. Choose the one that best completes each of the following sentences.

1. We hope you can give prompt attention to our request for the _____ of the relative L/C.

  A. establishing   B. establish   C. establishment   D. established

2. Referring to the latest _____ of letters, we are pleased to confirm having concluded with you a transaction of 100 tons of coal.

  A. exchanged   B. exchanging   C. exchange   D. being exchanged

3. Thank you for your repeat order which, as usual, is receiving our immediate attention. As _____, we will effect the shipment well in time.

  A. advised   B. referred   C. requested   D. concluded

4. We have made out and sent you our Sales Confirmation No. 6060 _____ and please send back one copy duly countersigned.

  A. in duplicate   B. of duplicate   C. of two copies   D. in duplicates

5. We will _____ you of the time of delivery as soon as we make preparation.

  A. mention   B. note   C. learn   D. advise

6. In order to ensure the requested shipment, please open the covering L/C _____ should reach us 30 days prior to the date of delivery.

  A. which   B. in which   C. on which   D. of which

Chapter 4 Conclusion of Business

7. For your information, we have recently _____ with a Japanese exporter a transaction of ＄10,000 on the terms of D/P at sight.

 A. concluded   B. brought   C. realized   D. come to

8. _____ our order of June 17, we will keep you well advised of the relative development.

 A. With reference to   B. Regards to

 C. Regards on   D. With reference on

9. We return herewith one copy _____ signed to you for your files.

 A. with   B. being   C. duly   D. due

10. Since this _____ is concluded successfully, neither party is obliged to give up the idea of destroying it.

 A. purchase   B. transaction   C. order   D. contract

Ⅱ. **Fill in the blanks with proper forms of the words given.**

effect	satisfy	comply	result	dispatch
accept	refer	enclose	purchase	regard

11. At present, supply can be _____ only in small quantities.

12. The quality of your new products _____ us in every respect.

13. As a _____ of our endeavor, we have obtained supplies for you.

14. In international business, sales confirmation is a document _____ as a contract.

15. _____ to our enquiry of Oct. 25, we invite your attention to it.

16. We are _____ these goods for our own account.

17. We would like to claim beforehand that if the quality of the goods _____ by you is not in accordance with the contract, we have a right to refuse the goods.

18. We are not sure that our quotation is _____ to you.

19. _____ with the terms stated, we send you our invoice in duplicate.

20. _____ please find S/C No. 123, one of which should be countersigned and returned for our file.

Ⅲ. **Translate the following sentences into Chinese or English.**

21. The minimum quantity of an order for the goods is 300 cases. If you order more than 500 cases, we can reduce our price by 3%.

22. The relative L/C will be established through the First National Bank, Jakarta. We thank you very much for your prompt arrangement of shipment upon receipt of it.

23. All notices of the Maritime Arbitration Commission to the parties shall be delivered by messengers, registered mail or telegraph.

24. It was a very unpleasant surprise to learn that the terms and conditions we finally agreed upon had been turned down by your company.

25. Please be informed that we have already sent the samples required.

26. 我们同意按以下条款售出下列货物。

27. 我们很高兴寄上销售合同2060号（一式两份），请贵方会签并寄回一份，以便我方存档。

28. 一收到信用证我们就按照贵方的订单，对装运作及时的安排。

29. 按照合同要求，我们将在9月10日前装运货物。

30. 质量必须与样品相符。

Ⅳ. Translate the following letter into English.

ABC公司：
　　我方对上次的印花细布供货十分满意，因此想再次订货。新订单详情如下表。

货号	数量	单价
9715	100,000码	1.5美元（每码）
9716	150,000码	1.2美元（每码）
9623	120,000码	1.4美元（每码）

　　因顾客急需这批货物，我方希望贵方接到该订货信后即刻装运。收到装船通知之后，我方将寄送相关即期信用证。

◇ **Practice**

Write a letter in response to the following purchase order, confirming your acceptance.

Dear Mr. Gilson,
Order for 2,000 Pairs of Sheep Leather Gloves
　　Please dispatch to us 2,000 pairs of sheep leather gloves as per the terms stated in your offer of May 5.

Chapter 4 Conclusion of Business

Would you please take special care of the quality and the package of this order? The leather should be of the same quality as that used in the sample. We hope that you can pack each pair in an airtight polythene bag, a dozen pairs of gloves in a box and then 20 boxes to a strong seaworthy wooden case. We will order more if the first order with you proves to be satisfactory.

We are enclosing our Purchase Confirmation No. 2018-308 in duplicate for your signature. Please sign and return one copy for our file. Upon receipt of your confirmation, an L/C will be issued.

Sincerely yours,

Chapter 5
Terms of Payment

Chapter 5 Terms of Payment

Learning Objectives

- To master the relevant terms used in international settlement.
- To be acquainted with the operation of a documentary letter of credit.
- To know how to write letters about establishment of or amendment to an L/C.

5.1 Introduction

International transactions involve longer distance and more procedures. Therefore, longer time is needed in settling an international payment. Different regulations and systems of law that are applied further complicate the payment. In international business, there are three kinds of payments commonly used: remittance, collection and letter of credit.

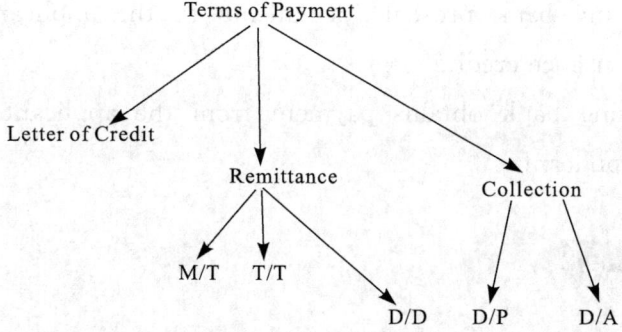

Fig. Terms of Payment

The most widely adopted method of payment in foreign trade is letter of credit. Letter of credit (L/C) is a written undertaking by a bank given to the seller at the request, and in accordance with the instructions, of the buyer to effect payment up to a stated sum of money, within a prescribed time limit and against stipulated documents. Documentary credits provide a high level of protection and security to both buyers and sellers engaged in international trade.

The seller is assured that payment will be made so long as the terms and conditions of the credit are met. The buyer is assured that payment will be released to the seller only after the bank has received the title documents called for in the credit.

The operation of a commercial L/C is as follows:

(1) The buyer and the seller conclude a sales contract stipulating to pay by L/C.

(2) The buyer instructs his bank, the issuing bank, to issue a credit in favor of the seller.

(3) After issuing the L/C instruments, the issuing bank forwards it to its chosen

advising bank.

(4) The advising bank authenticates the L/C and delivers it to the beneficiary.

(5) As soon as the seller receives the credit and is satisfied with the terms and conditions, he is in a position to load the goods and dispatch them.

(6) The seller prepares the documents called for in the L/C and presents them to the seller's negotiating bank.

(7) The negotiating bank checks the documents against the credit. If they meet the credit requirements, the bank will pay to the beneficiary according to the terms of credit.

(8) The negotiating bank generally sends a reimbursement claim together with full set of documents to the issuing bank.

(9) The issuing bank checks the documents and transfers funds to the negotiating bank against its claim.

(10) The issuing bank presents documents to the applicant for payment or acceptance if it is a usance credit.

(11) The issuing bank obtains payment from the applicant and forwards the documents to the applicant.

5.2 Samples

Specimen 1　Urging the Establishment of L/C

Dear Sirs,

We are pleased to inform you that the goods under your purchase contract No. TY213 are ready for dispatch.

According to the stipulations in the foregoing contract, shipment is to be made during May/June. The date of shipment is approaching. However, we still have not received your covering L/C to date. Therefore, we would like to ask you to rush the L/C so as to enable us to effect shipment within the stipulated time.

When establishing the L/C, please make sure that the L/C stipulations strictly conform to the terms of our contract to avoid subsequent amendments.

We look forward to your L/C soon.

Yours faithfully,

Chapter 5 Terms of Payment

Specimen 2   Replying to the Letter of Urging Establishment of L/C

Dear Sirs,

We have received your letter of April 12, urging us to establish the L/C against our contract No. TY213.

We are really very sorry for the delay in establishing the L/C, which was due to oversight of our staff. As soon as we received your letter this morning, we contacted our bank and instructed to open the L/C. We are sure that it will reach you soon.

We apologize again for the trouble we have caused you. We hope after receiving the L/C, you will ship the goods as early as possible. Thank you for your cooperation.

Yours faithfully,

Specimen 3   Asking for L/C Amendment

Dear Sirs,

We have received your L/C No. A-2234 but regret to say that we have found some discrepancies in the above mentioned L/C. Please make the following amendments in the L/C:

(1) The beneficiary should be China Machinery Imp. & Exp. Corp. and the applicant should be Smith & Co.

(2) The currency is US dollars, instead of French Francs.

(3) Delete "30 days after" in relation to the draft.

(4) Delete insurance clause.

(5) "Partial shipments prohibited" should read "Partial shipments allowed".

As the stipulated time of shipment is drawing near, please make amendments to the L/C as soon as possible so that we can effect shipment in time.

Yours faithfully,

Specimen 4   Asking for L/C Amendment

Dear Sirs,

We have duly received your L/C No. 02531, but regretfully find it contains quite a few discrepancies. You are requested, therefore, to make the following amendments:

(1) "Draft drawn on you" should read "draft drawn on them".

(2) The date of the bills of lading should be "December 31, 2019" instead of "November 30, 2019".

(3) Amend "CIF" to read "CFR".

The expiry date of this credit should be "January 15, 2019", not "December 15, 2019".

As the date of shipment is drawing near, please let us have your telex amendments without delay.

Yours truly,

5.3　Writing Guide

It is the usual practice that the letter of credit is to be opened and to reach the sellers 30 days ahead of the shipment, so as to give the seller enough time to make preparation for shipment, such as making the goods ready and booking shipping space. For prompt-shipment, it is advisable that the letter of credit be issued in good time.

No suggestion of annoyance is allowed to be shown in the letter urging establishment of L/C. It is not wise, except under special conditions, to start off too strongly by blaming the buyer for not executing the contract. The first message sent should therefore be a polite note saying that the goods ordered are ready but the relevant L/C has not yet been received. It must be written with tact. If the first message brings no reply, a second one will be sent. This one, though still restrained, will express disappointment and surprise.

Letters concerning L/C amendment and/or extension should be written with courtesy because a mere amendment to or extension of L/C will need time and money, which is always an annoying thing to the buyer.

This part focuses on the letters urging establishment of L/C and letters of L/C amendment.

5.3.1　A Letter for Urging the Establishment of L/C

1. Structure of a Letter for Urging L/C

Opening paragraph: inform the buyer that the goods are ready for dispatch or that the shipping space has already been booked.

Body: politely push the buyers to open the L/C without delay.

Closing paragraph: express expectations and asking the buyers to take immediate action.

2. Contents of a Letter for Urging L/C

The letter consists of the following contents and use the following expressions.

(1) To inform the buyer that the goods are ready for dispatch or that the shipping space has already been booked.

• Regarding the sales confirmation No. ***, we would like to draw your attention to the fact that the date of delivery is approaching, but up to now, we haven't received your relative letter of credit.

• With reference to our faxes dated... requesting you to establish the L/C covering the above mentioned order, we regret having received no news from you up till now.

(2) To politely urge the buyers to open the L/C without delay, either by referring to the stipulations of the contract or by reminding the buyers of the seriousness of not opening the L/C in time:

• We wish to remind you that it was agreed, when placing the order, that you would establish the required L/C upon receipt of our confirmation.

• If your L/C fails to reach us before Sept. 4, we cannot effect the shipment in time.

(3) To ask the buyers to take immediate action:

• We look forward to receiving your favorable response at an early date.

• As the goods have been ready for shipment for quite some time, it behooves you to take immediate action.

5.3.2 A Letter Asking for L/C Amendment

1. Structure of a Letter for Amendment to L/C

Opening paragraph: express thanks for the L/C and state that the credit has been received.

Body: state your point of amendments to L/C and telling the reasons.

Closing paragraph: express the hope for cooperation.

2. Contents of a Letter for Amendment to L/C

Such a letter consists of the following contents and useful expressions.

(1) To state that the credit has been received:

- We wish to acknowledge receipt of the L/C No. *** for the amount of... covering your order No. ***.
- Letter of Credit No. 1234 issued by the Bank of *** has duly arrived.
- We have received your captioned letter of credit.

(2) To point out the terms or conditions that do not conform to the contract (the reasons for amendment or extension):

- Among the clauses specified in your credit we find that the following two points do not conform to the relative contract.
- When we checked the L/C with the relevant contract, we found that the amount in L/C is insufficient.
- Your L/C allows us only half a month to effect delivery, but when we signed the contract we had agreed that the delivery should be made within one month.

(3) To express the hope for cooperation:

- We shall appreciate it if you will modify the L/C promptly as requested.
- As the goods are now ready for shipment, you are requested to amend your credit as soon as possible.
- In view of the above, you are kindly requested to amend the term of packing.

5.4 Supplement

Some Useful Sentences on Payment

(1) We wish to inform you that the goods under S/C No. 2567 have been ready for quite some time.

第 2567 号售货确认书项下货物已备妥多日。

(2) We wish to draw your attention to the fact that the goods have been ready for shipment for a long time but the covering credit has not been received yet.

请注意,货物已备妥待运多时,但我方还未收到相关信用证。

(3) According to the stipulations in our contract No. 473, you should send us your L/C one month preceding the date of shipment.

按照双方第 473 号合同的规定,贵方应于装运期前一个月将信用证寄往我处。

(4) We shall be unable to effect shipment within the stipulated time unless your

Chapter 5 Terms of Payment

L/C reaches us before the end of this week.

若贵方信用证不能于本周内寄到我处,我方将无法在规定时间内发货。

(5) We wish to remind you that it was agreed when placing the order that you would establish the required L/C upon receipt of our confirmation.

我们想提醒贵方,在下订单时我们双方约定:收到确认书后,贵方即开具相关信用证。

(6) Please open your L/C immediately and let us have your reply by return.

请贵方立即开立信用证并函告回复。

(7) We would be grateful if you could expedite establishment of the L/C so that we can ship the order in time.

贵方若能速开信用证以便我方及时发货,我方将不胜感激。

(8) Please amend the forgoing L/C to read "partial shipment permitted" instead of "partial shipment prohibited".

请将原信用证条款"不允许分批装运"修改为"允许分批装运"。

(9) However, on checking up its clauses, we find that the followings are not in compliance with the terms and conditions of the contract.

然而,在审核信用证后,我们发现下述条款与合同条款不相符。

(10) We refer to your L/C No. TUH4752 covering 5,000 tons of sugar.

关于5,000吨糖的第TUH4752号信用证收悉。

(11) Thank you for your L/C No. 5413.

感谢贵方的第5413号信用证。

(12) Your prompt attention to the matter will be much appreciated.

贵方若能及时处理此事,我方将不胜感激。

(13) We shall be obliged for your prompt amendments accordingly.

贵方若能对信用证条款及时作相应修改,我方将十分感激。

(14) We are confident that you will give us cooperation by extending the shipment date to June 10, and the negotiation validity to June 25 respectively.

我们相信贵方会延长信用证装船期至6月10号,有效期至6月25日。

(15) As we have checked the L/C carefully, we request you to make the following amendments.

我们在认真审核信用证之后,请求贵方作如下修改。

EXERCISES

◇**Language Usage**

Ⅰ. Choose the one that best completes each of the following sentences.

1. If the terms of trade are FOB, the responsibility for insuring the goods while in transit falls on _____ and he must make the necessary arrangements.

   A. the seller   B. the purchaser
   C. the creditor   D. the carrier

2. The exporter or his agent is normally the person named as _____ on a bill of lading or an airway bill.

   A. carrier   B. U/W   C. consignee   D. shipper

3. Payment should be made _____ sight draft.

   A. at   B. upon   C. by   D. after

4. We are faxing you this morning, asking you to amend the L/C _____ "transshipment allowed".

   A. to read   B. to reading   C. as reads   D. reads

5. _____ we would like to supply you with the product, we are unable to fill your order.

   A. As much as B. Much as   C. Very much   D. As

6. _____ , which were drawn up by the ICC, provide an internationally accepted set of standardized terms which set out where the exporter's responsibility ends as regards insurance and transport of goods.

   A. UCP   B. VAT   C. INCOTERMS   D. URC

7. The buyer suggested that the packing of this article _____ improved.

   A. be   B. was to be   C. would be   D. had to be

8. We _____ some brochures _____ to illustrate the products we manufactured.

   A. enclose, to you   B. enclose you,\   C. enclose,\   D. enclose, you

9. We have made _____ that we would accept D/P terms for your future order.

   A. clear   B. it clear   C. that clear D. it is clear

10. Financial Documents means bills of exchange, promissory note, _____ , or other similar instruments used for obtaining the payment of money.

Chapter 5 Terms of Payment

  A. invoices   B. deposit receipts   C. cheques   D. bills of lading

II. Fill in the following blanks with proper prepositions.

  11. We regret that we cannot comply _____ your request _____ payment _____ D/P at sight.

  12. _____ our disappointment, we haven't received your L/C _____ your order No. 123.

  13. We will try to meet your requirements _____ the fact that we have difficulty _____ obtaining new supplies.

  14. We are appreciative _____ your letter of March 12, _____ which you ask us _____ a better price of our raincoat.

  15. In view _____ our long-term business relations, we are prepared to wait _____ your L/C, which must reach us prior _____ November 23.

  16. _____ such circumstances, we have to cancel our sales confirmation and ask you to refund us the storage charges we have paid _____ your behalf.

  17. We apologize _____ you _____ the trouble we have caused you.

  18. Any loss arising _____ the delay _____ shipment will be _____ your account.

  19. To avoid subsequent amendments, please make sure that the L/C stipulations strictly conform _____ the terms of our contract.

  20. All the prices quoted are subject _____ change _____ notice.

III. Translate the following sentences into Chinese or English.

  21. As wages and prices of materials have risen considerably, we regret we not in a position to book the order at the prices we quoted half a year ago.

  22. Your order is receiving our immediate attention and we will keep you informed of the progress.

  23. We have received your catalogue and price list, and now we order the following goods at the prices named.

  24. We find both quality and prices of your products satisfactory and enclose our trial order for prompt supply.

  25. As the goods you ordered are now in stock, we will ship them without fail as early as possible.

  21. 很遗憾，迄今为止我们仍未收到第 2240 号订单下的相关信用证。

22. 按合同规定,贵方应该在 5 月 13 日之前开立信用证。

23. 由于贵方未能及时开立信用证,很遗憾,我方无法按规定时间交货。

24. 贵方订购的货物已备妥多时,请速开信用证,以便我方能够按时装运。

25. 核对时发现你方开立的信用证金额不足,请速修改,增加金额 200 美元。

Ⅳ. **Translate the following letter into English.**

敬启者:

关于我方 4567 号售货确认书的信用证已收到。

很遗憾,贵方此信用证已远超售货确认书确定的时间节点。由于需求越来越大,我方已不能按照合同商定的价格供货。因此,请将货物单价修改为"每件 100 美元",总价改为"10 万美元"。装运期和信用证有效期也应分别延迟一个月。

静候贵方对信用证的修改。一旦银行告知收到信用证,我方将立即装船。

此致

敬礼!

◇Practice

Go through the S/C and the L/C carefully to find the discrepancies between them and then write a letter asking for amendments to the L/C (5 discrepancies at least).

中国国际纺织品进出口公司江苏分公司
CHINA INTERNATIONAL TEXTILES I/E CORP. JIANGSU BRANCH
20 RANJIANG ROAD, NANJING, JIANGSU, CHINA

销售确认书

SALES　　　CONFIRMATION

编号 NO.: CNT0219

日期 DATE: MAY 10, 2014

买方 BUYERS: TAI HING LOONG SDN, BHD, KUALA LUMPUR

地址 ADDRESS: 7/F, SAILING BUILDING, NO. 50 AIDY STREET, KUALA LUMPUR, MALAYSIA

电话 TEL: 060-3-74236211　　　　　　　　传真 FAX: 060-3-74236212

兹经买卖双方同意成交下列商品,订立条款如下:

Chapter 5 Terms of Payment

THE UNDERSIGNED SELLERS AND BUYERS HAVE AGREED TO CLOSE THE FOLLOWING TRANSACTION ACCORDING TO THE TERMS AND CONDITIONS STIPULATED BELOW:

DESCRIPTION OF GOODS	QUANTITY	PRICE (CIF KUALA LUMPUR)	AMOUNT
100% COTTON GREY LAWN	300,000 YARDS	HK$3.00 PER YARD	HK$900,000.00
PAYMENT: IRREVOCABLE SIGHT L/C			
SHIPMENT: DURING JUNE/JULY, 2014			
INSURANCE: TO BE EFFECTED BY THE SELLER COVERING WPA AND WAR RISKS FOR 10% OVER THE INVOICE VALUE			

买方(签章) THE BUYER
TAI HING LOONG SDN, BHD, KUALA LUMPUR

卖方(签章) THE SELLER
中国国际纺织品进出口公司江苏分公司
CHINA INTERNATIONAL TEXTILES I/E CORP. JIANGSU BRANCH

信用证如下所示:

FROM BANGKOK BANK LTD., KUALA LUMPUR

DOCUMENTARY CREDIT NO.: 01/12345, DATE: JUNE 12, 2014

ADVISING BANK: BANK OF CHINA, JIANGSU BRANCH

APPLICANT: TAI HING LOONG SDN, BHD., KUALA LUMPUR

BENEFICIARY: CHINA INTERNATIONAL TEXTILES I/E CORP., BEIJING BRANCH

AMOUNT: HK$900,000.00 (HONGKONG DOLLARS NINE HUNDRED THOUSAND ONLY)

EXPIRY DATE: JULY 15, 2014 IN CHINA FOR NEGOTIATION

DEAR SIRS:

WE HEREBY ISSUE THIS DOCUMENTARY CREDIT IN YOUR FAVOR, WHICH IS AVAILABLE BY NEGOTIATION OF YOUR DRAFT(S) IN DUPLICATE AT SIGHT DRAWN ONUS BEARING THE CLAUSE. "DRAWN UNDER L/C NO. 01/12345 OF BANGKOK BANK LTD., KUALA LUMPUR

DATED JUNE 12,2014" ACCOMPAINED BY THE FOLLOWING DOCUMENTS:

—SIGNED INVOICE IN QUADRUPLICATE COUNTERSIGNED BY APPLICANT.

—FULL SET OF CLEAN ON BOARD OCEAN BILLS OF LADING MADE OUT TO ORDER, ENDORSED IN BLANK, MARKED "FREIGHT COLLECT" AND NOTIFY BENEFICIARY.

—MARINE INSURANCE POLICY OR CERTIFICATE FOR FULL INVOICE VALUE PLUS 10% WITH CLAIMS PAYABLE IN NANJING IN THE SAME CURRENCY AS THE DRAFT COVERING ALL RISKS AND WAR RISKS FROM WAREHOUSE TO WAREHOUSE UP TO KUALA LUMPUR INCLUDING SRCC CLAUSE AS PER PICC 1/1/1981.

—PACKING LIST IN QUADRUPLICATE.

—CERTIFICATE OF ORIGIN ISSUED BY BANK OF CHINA, NANJING.

—SHIP'S CLASSIFICATION ISSUED BY LLOYDS' IN LONDON.

COVERING:

ABOUT 300,000 YARDS OF 65% POLYESTER, 35% COTTON GREY LAWN. AS PER BUYER'S ORDER NO. CNT0219 DATED MAY 10, 2014 TO BE DELIVERED ON TWO EQUAL SHIPMENTS DURING MAY/ JUNE.

ALL BANKING CHARGES OUTSIDE MALAYSIA ARE FOR THE ACCOUNT OF BENEFICIARY. SHIPMENT FROM CHINA TO PORT KELANG LATEST JUNE 31, 2014. PARTIAL SHIPMENTS ARE ALLOWED. TRANSSHIPMENT PROHIBITED.

WE HEREBY ENGAGE WITH DRAWERS, ENDORSERS AND BONA FIDE HOLDERS THAT DRAFTS DRAWN AND NEGOTIATED IN CONFORMITY WITH THE TERMS OF THIS CREDIT WILL BE DULY HONORED ON PRESENTATION. SUBJECT TO UCP 600.

BANGKOK BANK LTD., KUALA LUMPUR (SIGNED)

Chapter 6
Shipment

Learning Objectives

- To identify the characteristics of the direct approach of writing letters of shipment.
- To understand the structure of letters of shipment and the ways to express the time of shipment.
- To write a letter of shipment successfully.

6.1 Introduction

Shipment means that the seller fulfills his obligation to load goods into the named carrier at the given place and the time stipulated in the contract.

The buyer and the seller should reach an agreement on time, departure, and destination, shipping advice, partial shipment and transshipment, dispatch and demurrage, etc., and specify them in the sales contract.

Clear stipulation of the shipment clause is an important condition for the smooth execution of the contract.

Before shipment, the buyers generally send their shipping requirements to the seller, informing them in writing of the packing and marking, mode of transportation, etc., and the sellers should send shipping advice to the buyers immediately after the goods are loaded on board, advising them of the shipment.

Letters concerning shipment include urging to expedite shipment, altering terms of shipment, advising shipping, delivering shipping documents, etc.

6.2 Samples

Sample 1 Urging Shipment

Dear Sirs,

Referring to the contract No. 568 covering 1,000 dozen Langli brand Men's Shirts, we wish to remind you that we have had no news from you about shipment of the goods.

As we mentioned in our last letter, we are in urgent need of the goods and may be compelled to seek an alternative source of supply if you can't provide the goods.

Your delay has caused us much inconvenience, as the goods are urgently required by our customers.

Under these circumstances, it is impossible for us to extend our Letter of Credit No. 1532 further, which expires on July 18, and we feel it is our duty to remind you of this matter again.

We look forward to receiving your shipping advice, by fax, within the next seven days.

Yours faithfully,

Sample 2   Advising Shipment

Dear Sirs,

Thank you for your letter of December 15 enquiring about the shipment of the captioned goods.

Please accept our apology for the delay that has been caused by the unavailability of shipping space from Shanghai to California. However, we are now pleased to inform you that we have shipped the mentioned goods on board S. S. "Pand" which was sailed for your port yesterday directly.

Enclosed you will find one set of shipping documents covering this consignment, which comprises:

One non-negotiable copy of the bill of lading;

Commercial invoice in duplicate;

One copy of the certificate of quality;

One copy of the certificate of quantity;

One copy of the insurance policy;

Weight memo in duplicate.

We are glad to have been able to execute your order as contracted and trust that the goods will reach you in good time and prove to be entirely satisfactory.

We avail ourselves of this opportunity to assure you that any further order from you will receive our prompt attention.

Yours faithfully,

Sample 3   Requesting Earlier Delivery

Dear Sirs,

We refer to our purchase contract No. 168 under the terms of the contract that the delivery time is scheduled of April 2020. We would now like to bring delivery forward to March 2020.

We offer our sincere apologies since we realize that the change of delivery date will probably bring inconvenience to you. We know that you will consider that we would not ask for earlier delivery if we did not have compelling reasons for doing so.

In view of our long pleasant relations, we would be very grateful if you would make a special effort to meet our request.

We look forward to hearing further from you at an early date.

Yours faithfully,

Sample 4 Apologizing for Delayed Shipment

Dear Sirs,

We are very sorry to inform you that the shipment during April covering your order No. AC-156 is impossible to execute within the stipulated date on account of manufacturers' material shortage.

The manufacturers are suffering a serious material shortage by a recent rush of orders. Although they are making every effort to deliver the goods as requested, they inform us that one month delay of shipment is unavoidable. We ask, therefore, that you approve the situation with a 3% price discount and we deeply apologize for the possible inconvenience you have been put to.

We assure you that we will take every precaution against such trouble arising in the future.

Yours faithfully,

6.3 Writing Guide

6.3.1 Letters from Importers

1. Structure of a Letter on Shipment from Importers

Opening paragraph: describe relevant goods and terms of shipment (this is used to urge to expedite shipment, explain terms of shipment and wait for shipping notice).

Body: state your reason.

Closing paragraph: put forward your suggestions and express your wishes.

2. Contents of a Letter on Shipment from Importers

Letters from importers may include some or all of the following main points and use the following expressions.

(1) To describe relevant goods and terms of shipment:

• We refer to contract No. *** signed between us on... for... which is stipulated for shipment in....

• We are very anxious to know about the shipment of our order for 5,000 cases of tin plates.

• For some special reason we request you to advance shipment of the consignment under order No. *** from October to December.

(2) To state your reasons:

• As we are in urgent need of the goods, we find it necessary to stress the importance of making punctual shipment within the validity of the L/C.

(3) To put forward your suggestions and express your wishes:

• In case you should fail to effect delivery in April, we will have to lodge a claim against you for the loss and reserve the right to cancel the contract.

• We should appreciate prompt shipment and hope to establish a regular connection for the future if this first consignment proves to conform to the samples supplied.

6.3.2 Letters from Exporters

1. Structure of a Letter on Shipment from Exporters

Opening paragraph: tell the time of shipment, port of shipment, port of destination and also the fact that you have shipped the goods.

Body: state the necessity and reasons of immediate shipment.

Closing paragraph: express your hope that the ship will port there safely and hope for further cooperation.

2. Contents of a Letter on Shipment from Exporters

Letters from exporters may use the following expressions.

(1) To tell the time of shipment, port of shipment, port of destination and also the fact that you have shipped the goods:

• We are pleased to notify you that the cargo has been shipped by... (to advise shipment)

• We feel apologetic that we really have no way to make shipment on... because of... (to explain the delay of shipment)

• The shipment will reach you within... days.

(2) To express your hope that the ship will port there safely and for further cooperation:

• We appreciate the business you have been able to give us and assure you that all your future orders will continue to receive our most careful attention.

• We should be obliged if you would kindly understand the situation and you would comply with our request.

6.4　Supplement

Some Useful Sentences on Shipment

(1) We are pleased to inform you that your order No. 100 was shipped on April 12 abroad the M/S Barkley that left Keelung for Los Angeles the next day.

谨通知贵方，贵方第 100 号订单所列货品已于 4 月 12 日装上泊克利轮，第二天从基隆港出发，驶往洛杉矶。

(2) Shipment is to be made during April to June in 3 equal monthly lots.

货物将在 4 月至 6 月分 3 批每月均装。

(3) Generally, shipments can be effected within 30 days after receipt of your L/C but a specific time is to be fixed upon receipt of your official order.

通常收到贵方信用证后 30 天内完成装运，但一收到贵方正式订单以后，即可确定具体的时间。

(4) We must insist on delivery within the time limit, and reserve the right to reject the goods, should they be delivered later.

我方要求在期限内发货，如延期发货将保留拒绝收货的权利。

(5) Your failure in delivering the goods within the stipulated time has greatly inconvenienced us.

贵方未能在规定的时间内交货已给我们带来很大的不便。

(6) We will make every effort to ship the goods as early as possible, and we feel sure that the shipment will be satisfactory to you in every respect.

我方将尽一切努力尽早装运,并确信在各方面都令贵方满意。

(7) To ensure fastest delivery, you are requested to forward the above order by air (freight).

为保证以最快的方式交货,我方要求贵方空运上述订单下的货物。

(8) In compliance with terms of contract, we forwarded you by airmail a full set of duplicate shipping documents to you immediately after the goods were shipped.

按照合同条款,在装船后我们即向贵方航寄全套装运单据副本。

(9) We have been put to considerable inconvenience by the long delay in delivery. We must insist on immediate delivery; otherwise we shall be compelled to cancel the orders in accordance with the stipulations of the contract.

交货时间延误给我方带来诸多不便。我方要求立即交货,否则我们将不得不按照合同条款取消订货。

(10) We shall be glad to know the time of transit and frequency of sailing, and whether cargo space must be reserved; if so, please send us the necessary application forms.

请告知在途中运输时间、班轮航次、货舱是否要预订。如需预订,请将订舱表寄来。

EXERCISES

◇**Language Usage**

Ⅰ. Choose the one that best completes each of the following sentences.

1. It would be appreciated if you could send us your detailed information of all the items you _____ for export.

  A. handle   B. have   C. store   D. stock

2. _____ Contract No. 123, we are agreeable to D/P payment terms.

  A. With regard for   B. With regards for

  C. With regard to   D. With regards to

3. Mr. Turner told us yesterday that our price was _____ and asked us to get ready for the supplies.

  A. managerial   B. unfortunate   C. acceptable   D. impossible

4. We hope that the amendment can reach here before March 12, _____ the shipment cannot be effected as requested.

  A. and   B. or   C. unless   D. but

5. We regret to say that we cannot make any offer as the goods are _____.

   A. out of stock   B. without stock   C. no stock   D. not in stock

6. If you can make us a firm offer at a _____ price, we will place an order with your corporation.

   A. competitive   B. comparative   C. subjective   D. objective

7. We request you to _____ your price because we think it too high.

   A. put   B. reduce   C. take   D. handle

8. We desire to establish _____ beneficial business relations.

   A. mutual   B. mutually   C. equal   D. equally

9. Please _____ by telex the shipment date of your L/C to December 3, 2019, thus enabling us to effect shipment of the goods in question.

   A. prolong   B. lengthen   C. expand   D. extend

10. We offer you our lowest price, _____ we have done a lot business with other customers.

   A. which   B. that   C. at which   D. with which

Ⅱ. Fill in the blanks with proper words.

Dear Sirs,

   (11)_____ to our previous letters and cables, we wish to call your (12)_____ to the fact that up to the present moment no news has come from you about the shipment (13)_____ the captioned contract.

   As you have been informed in one of our previous letters, the users are in urgent (14)_____ of goods contracted and are in fact pressing us for assurance of early (15)_____.

   Under the circumstances, it is obviously impossible for us to again (16)_____ L/C No. 2450, which expires on August 10, and we feel it our duty to remind you (17)_____ this matter again.

   As your (18)_____ attention to shipment is most desirable to all parties concerned, we hope you will let us have your telegraphic shipping (19)_____ without (20)_____ delay.

                                                      Yours faithfully,

Ⅲ. Translate the following sentences into Chinese or English.

21. Please rest assured that we would have the goods shipped before April 20.

22. We take this opportunity to inform you that we have loaded the above goods on board S. S. "Victoria", which is due to sail for your port tomorrow.

23. The duplicate shipping documents were airmailed to you yesterday.

24. It has to be stressed that the shipment must be made within the prescribed time limit, as a further extension will not be considered.

25. Please see to it that the packing is suitable for a long sea voyage.

26. 装运期的任何延误都会增加货物的存储费用。

27. 我们将尽快通知你们装船日期。

28. 兹确认已收到贵方对标题项下货物的发盘。

29. 我们跟生产商联系一下，看他们怎么说。

30. 由于承约过多，我方目前不能接受贵方昨日的订单。

Ⅳ. **Translate the following letter into English.**

敬启者：

　　兹确认收到贵方8月10日来信，谢谢。关于50,000吨小麦，5％溢短装由买方选择，我方装船效率是晴天工作日每昼夜5,000公吨，包括节、假日在内，倘若超过此数字，按比例计算时间。

　　由于我方还有其他的装运任务，在此提醒贵方须提交最后确认的受载日期，以便我们对受载作适当安排。我方同意卖方与承运人之间直接结算滞期费和速遣费；同时，我方坚持：贵方应在受载船只到达目的港的前15天通知我们受载船只预计到达的时间，以便我方与港务当局取得联系并确切地谈妥迅速装船的事项。

　　此致

敬礼！

◇**Practice**

Write a letter as per the following particulars.

(1) 提请贵方注意用以支付我方第6767号订单项下的500匹蓝色毛哔叽呢(Woolen Serge)，我方已于25天前寄给贵方有效期截止到5月20日的不可撤销的信用证。

(2) 由于销售季节已来临，我方客户急需所订货物。因而要求贵方立即装运以便我方能赶上销售旺季。

(3) 我方想重申：在装运方面的任何延误都无疑会使我方陷入极大的困境之中。

Chapter 7
Insurance

Chapter 7 Insurance

Learning Objectives
- To learn the phrases and expressions about insurance.
- To know about how to make insurance.
- To learn how to write a business letter about insurance.
- To fill out the insurance policy in accordance with the terms of the contract and the insurance requirements.

7.1 Introduction

In international trade, the transportation of goods from the seller to the buyer is generally over a long distance and has to go through the procedures of loading, unloading and storing. During this process, it is quite possible that the goods will encounter various kinds of perils and sometimes suffer losses. In order to protect the goods against possible risks in case of such perils, the buyer or seller, before the transportation of the goods, usually applies to an insurance company for insurance covering the goods in transit.

The insured pays insurance premium to the insurance company on the basis of insurance amount, insurance cover as well as insurance premium rate, and obtains the insurance policy. The insurer shall compensate the insured for the losses of, and damage to the goods, if any, during the transportation within the scope of insurance cover.

The three basic risks are as follows:

1. All Risks;

2. Free from Particular Average(FPA);

3. With Particular Average(WPA).

The general additional risks are as follows:

1. Theft, Pilferage & Non-delivery(TPND);

2. Fresh and/or Rain Water Damage Risk;

3. Shortage Risk;

4. Clash and Breakage Risks;

5. Leakage Risk.

The special additional risks are as follows:

1. War Risks(WR);
2. Strike, Riots, Civil Commotion Risks(SRCC).

The insurance coverage should be in strict compliance with the letters of credit. If there isn't any specific coverage in the L/C, or there's only "Marine Risk" "Usual Risk" or "Transport Risk" in it, you should cover insurance against All Risks, WPA, or FPA, and one or several additional risks can be added.

The insurance should not cover the additional risks only. Premiums and insurance rates usually should not be marked specific figures but "As arranged" premiums are also written "to be paid" or "prepaid".

In addition to the name of the risks, the date and version of the insurance should be marked.

7.2 Samples

Specimen 1 Covering Insurance for the Buyer

Dear Sirs,

In reply to your letter of November 3 enquiring about the insurance on our CIF offer for Double Offset Ring Spanners made to you on October 20, we wish to give you the following information.

For transactions concluded on CIF basis, we usually effect insurance with The People's Insurance Company of China against All Risks, as per Ocean Marine Cargo Clauses of The People's Insurance Company of China, dated January 1, 2020. Should you require the insurance to be covered as per Institute Cargo Clauses, we should be glad to comply; but if there is any difference in premium between the two, it will be charged to your account.

We are also in a position to insure the shipment against any additional risks if you so desire, and the extra premium is to be borne by you. In this case, we shall send you the premium receipt issued by the relative underwriter.

Usually, the amount insured is 110% of the total invoice value. However, if a higher percentage is required, we may do accordingly but you have to bear the extra premium as well.

We hope our above information will provide you with all the information you wish to know and we are now looking forward to receiving your order.

Yours faithfully,

Specimen 2　　Informing Customer of Insurance Rate

Dear Sirs,

　　I am replying to your enquiry of yesterday. We are prepared to insure the consignments in question. Considering that you will be our regular customer, our rate for $100,000 A. R. policy on 1,000 sets of TCL Color Television from Shanghai to New York is 1‰ of declared value.

　　This is an exceptionally low rate and we trust you will be satisfied with it and give us the opportunity to handle your insurance business. We are ready to assist you at any time on all future insurance contracts.

Yours faithfully,

Specimen 3　　Asking for Charge

Dear Sirs,

　　Thank you for doing business with us. On your instructions, we have insured your shipment of 1,000 sets of TCL Color TV shipped at Shanghai on board S. S. "Princess", sailing for New York on July 15, as per the policy enclosed. Please remit $1,100 to our account for this policy.

　　We trust this business will be the first of a series of deals between us.

Yours faithfully,

7.3　Writing Guide

7.3.1　Insurance Instruction

1. Structure of a Letter on Insurance Instruction

Opening paragraph: make out the insurance and coverage and the insurance value of goods.

Body: state payment methods of premiums.

Closing paragraph: express your further request of insurance arrangements.

2. Contents of a Letter on Insurance Instruction

The letter may include some or all of the following main points and useful expressions.

(1) To make out the insurance and coverage and the insurance value of goods:

• Please see to it that the insurance is covered for...% of the invoice value against...

• As we now desire to have the consignment if you will kindly arrange to insure the goods on our behalf against... for the invoice value plus...%, amounting to...

(2) Payment methods of premiums:

• If you like, you may draw on us at sight for the amount required.

• As we understand that as per your customary practice, you only insure the shipment for 10% above the invoice value, the extra premium for additional coverage shall be for our account.

(3) Further request of insurance arrangements:

• We sincerely hope that our request will meet with your approval.

• Please arrange insurance according to our request.

7.3.2 A Reply to Insurance

1. Structure of a Reply Letter to Insurance Instruction

Opening paragraph: acknowledge the receipt of the letter.

Body: inform the particulars of the insurance.

Closing paragraph: ask for compensation for the premium.

2. Contents of a Reply Letter to Insurance Instruction

The letter may include some or all of the following main points and useful expressions.

(1) To acknowledge receipt of the letter:

• This is to acknowledge receipt of... requesting us to effect insurance on the shipment for your account.

• We have received your letter of... asking us to insure the goods for an amount of... above the invoice value.

(2) To inform the particulars of the insurance:

• We are pleased to inform you that we have covered the shipment with... against... for the amount of...

• Though it is our usual practice to take our insurance for the invoice values plus 10%, we are prepared to comply with your request for getting cover for 130% of the invoice value.

(3) To ask to be compensated for the premium:

• The policy is being prepared accordingly and will be forwarded to you by next Tuesday together with our debit note for the premium.

• The extra premium will be for your account.

7.3.3　A Letter to Insurance Company

1. Structure of a Letter to Insurance Company

Opening paragraph: state the purpose of writing.

Body: list the requirement of insurance.

Closing paragraph: look forward to an early and favorable reply.

2. Contents of a Letter to Insurance Company

The letter may include some or all of the following main points and useful expressions.

(1) To state the purpose of writing:

• We have known that your company is the largest insurance company in China.

• We write this letter to you in the hope of getting some information about the special rate of insurance.

(2) To put forward the requirement of insurance:

• We wish to insure with your company a shipment of... valued at... against...

• Would you please tell us whether you can cover All Risks for the consignments?

• We wish to know whether you can issue a special rate for this consignment.

(3) Looking forward to an early and favorable reply:

• We shall appreciate it if the goods could be incurred at favorable rate.

• We are awaiting your early reply.

7.3.4　A Reply by Insurance Company

1. Structure of a Reply by Insurance Company

Opening paragraph: acknowledge the receipt of the letter.

Body: inform the particulars of insurance.

Closing paragraph: wish for an early confirmation.

2. Contents of a Reply by Insurance company

The letter may include some or all of the following main points and use the following expressions.

(1) To acknowledge receipt of the letter:

• We have acknowledged receipt of your letter of... and are pleased to note your readiness to insure with us a shipment of...

• We are pleased to receive your letter of... in regard to insurance.

• In reply, we would like to inform you of...

(2) To inform the particulars of insurance:

• The prevailing rate for the shipment against... is... subject to Ocean Marine Cargo Clauses.

• Generally we cover insurance... in the absence of definite instructions from our clients.

• If you desire to cover... we can provide such coverage at slightly higher premium.

(3) To express wish to be confirmed early:

• If you find our rate acceptable, please let us know.

• We trust the information will serve your purpose and await your further news.

7.4 Supplement

Some Useful Sentences on Insurance

(1) We have covered insurance on 1,000 cases of beer for 110% of the invoice value against All Risks.

我们已将1,000箱啤酒按发票金额的110%投保一切险。

(2) If you desire us to insure against a special risk, an extra premium will have to be charged.

你方若想投保特殊险别,需收取额外保费。

(3) This risk is coverable at a premium of 0.25%.

该险种的保险费率是0.25%。

(4) The insurance company insures this risk with 5% franchise.

保险公司对这个险种有5%的免赔额。

(5) We can serve you with a broad range of coverage against all kinds of risks for sea transport, such as Free of Particular Average (FPA), With Particular Average (WPA), All Risks and Extraneous Risks.

我们可以承保海洋运输的所有险别,如:平安险、水渍险、一切险和附加险。

(6) WPA plus Risk of Breakage suits your consignment.

贵方货物适合投保水渍险及破碎险。

(7) The premium is calculated according to the premium rate or rates for risks to be covered.

保险费是根据投保险别的保险费率计算的。

(8) They will undertake to compensate you for the losses according to the risks insured.

他们将根据所投保险的险别对损失予以理赔。

(9) We are able to cover all kinds of risks for transportation by sea, land and air.

我们可以办理海运、陆运和空运的所有险别。

(10) We won't have such a risk included, as it is not stipulated in the Ocean Marine Cargo Clauses.

我们不能投保此项险别,因为海洋运输条款中没有包括这一险别。

(11) Do you cover risk other than WPA and War Risk?

除了水渍险和战争险外,你们还投保其他险吗?

(12) As a rule, the extra premium involved will be for buyer's account.

按常规,额外保险费应由买方承担。

(13) Please note that our insurance coverage is for 110% of the invoice value only.

请注意我们的保额只是发票金额的110%。

(14) If you wish to secure protection against TPND, it can be easily done upon the payment of an additional premium.

如果贵方想要我方投保偷窃、提货不着险,非常容易办到,只要支付附加保险费即可。

EXERCISES

◇**Language Usage**

Ⅰ. Choose the one that best completes each of the following sentences.

1. The goods are _____ against FPA only.

   A. cover   B. covering   C. to cover   D. to be covered

2. _____, the extra premium involved will be for buyer's account.

   A. As usually   B. At usual   C. As a rule   D. At a rule

3. We can _____ insurance on 1,000 sewing machines against All Risks.

   A. get   B. effect   C. take   D. make out

4. Please extend the _____ to include TPND.

   A. coverage   B. rate   C. premium   D. policy

5. We often insure shipment for the invoice value _____ 10%.

   A. plusing   B. add   C. plus   D. adding

6. After loading the goods on board the ship, you must ask the insurance company to have them _____.

   A. insure   B. to be insured   C. to insure   D. insured

7. The extra premium _____ by us.

   A. is born   B. will be taken
   C. will be borne   D. will be born

8. Please insure us on the _____ goods.

   A. follow   B. following   C. follows   D. as follows

9. If cargoes cannot be found within a few days, we will file our claim for the full _____ of them.

   A. settlement   B. solution   C. solve   D. answer

10. Insurance _____ or certificate is an evidence of insurance issued by the insurer or underwriter to the insured.

    A. rate   B. policy   C. premium   D. coverage

Ⅱ. Fill in the following blanks with the given words in their proper forms.

account	extra premium	comply with	insurance policy	shipment
effect	according to	insurance	compensate	arrange

11. Please send us the _____ together with your receipt for the premiums paid as soon as you can.

12. WA coverage is narrow for a _____ of this nature.

13. We shall provide such _____ at your cost.

14. Please _____ provisional insurance, FPA on the goods for ＄500,000.

15. We quote CIF prices on the basis of WA, with additional clauses for the buyers' _____ .

16. _____ your fax instructions, we have today arranged insurance as usual with an approved underwriter.

17. We regret our inability to _____ the buyer's request for covering insurance for 150％ of the invoice value.

18. And any _____ for additional insurance, if required, shall be borne by the buyer.

19. If we insure against Free Particular Average, can you _____ us for all losses if the ship sinks or burns, or gets stuck?

20. You should _____ for the insurance.

Ⅲ. Translate the following sentences into Chinese or English.

21. How long is the period from the commencement to termination of the insurance?

22. We adopt the warehouse-to-warehouse clause that is commonly used in international insurance.

23. According to international practice, we do not insure against such risks unless the buyers call for them.

24. Breakage is a special risk, for which an extra premium will have to be charged.

25. Because they aren't delicate goods and not likely to be damaged on the voyage.

26. 请为这批货投保水渍险。

27. 我们可以应你方要求,按发票价的130％投保,但必须请你方注意:额外的保险费用应由你方负担。

28. 一旦货物发生损失,你方可以在货物到达60天内,向保险公司提出索赔。

29. 除水渍险与战争险之外,你们保险公司还保其他险吗?

30. 并不是所有的破碎险都属于单独海损,只有因自然灾害和意外事故所造成的破碎,才属于单独海损。

Ⅳ. Translate the following letter into English.

> 兹收到贵公司8月7日来函,信中要求我方为货物投保,费用由贵方负担。欣告我方向中国人民保险公司按发票金额的110%投保了一切险。保险单正在开立之中,并将于下周二寄出。
>
> 　　盼早复。

◇**Practice**

Write a letter as per the following particulars.

(1)销售合同单号是 S/C NO. 386。

(2)要求增加一切险和战争险,增加保额至合同金额的130%。

(3)保费由己方承担。

(4)请对方寄送索款通知。

Chapter 8
Complaints, Claims and Settlements

Learning Objectives

- To familiarize with the causes of complaints and claims.
- To be able to write letters of complaint, claim and settlement.

8.1 Introduction

Today, businesses are expanding overseas to a greater extent. Hence, unintentional mistakes are bound to happen and so you must know the right way to deal with it. As a buyer, if you are suffering from the bad quality of services or any kind of financial loss, then you have the right to complaint. A complaint letter is written in such a scenario to the serve the purpose of complaint. It is important for you to make use of the polite tone while writing a complaint letter.

Though the purpose of complaints is to claim a refund/free repair or exchange goods, it is only in a preparatory stage. If the clients are compensated, they won't lodge claims. Therefore, the complaints should be valued as equally as claims.

Here are the few causes of drafting a complaint letter:

(1) Goods are not delivered properly.

There can be many problems related to delivering wrong products in terms of color, pattern, brand, etc., or the delivered goods are defective, underweight, damaged, unfinished, etc. Buyer can claim to the seller, only when the delivered goods are not up to the mark or the wrong package has been delivered to you.

(2) The quality may not be satisfactory.

(3) Defective packaging that leads to damage of goods.

(4) The prices charged may be excessive, or not as agreed.

When one side's breach of the rules causes loss to the other side, the loss party has the right to request compensation or take remedial action. The action taken by the loss party is called claim. Generally speaking, when the clients lodge claim, they must enclose the certificates made by the inspection organization. The responsible party has to settle the claim according to the request of the loss party. Claim and settlement are the two sides of one thing. Settlement of claim is the action taken by the breach party to settle the claim. The first step is to find the problem, confirm the responsibility and estimate the sum of the damage or loss. Then calculate and make compensation plan

Chapter 8 Complaints, Claims and Settlements

which could be acceptable by two parties. The breach party usually replaces goods, gives discount or compensates cash to settle the claims.

Claim should be filed during the period of claim. The loss party should definitely come up with methods and sum of claim in detail. If necessary, relevant photos and inspection certificates are enclosed to support the argument and requirement made in the claim letters.

If two sides can't reach an agreement, they will go to arbitration. They sign a written agreement and submit the dispute to a third party to arbitrate. The arbitration has legal force on two parties.

8.2　Samples

Specimen 1

A. Complaint of Wrong Goods Delivered

Dear Sirs,

<u>Our Order No. 1487</u>

We duly received the documents and took delivery of the goods in arrival of S. S. "Chunlin" at Hamburg.

We are much obliged to you for the prompt execution of this order. Everything appears to be correct and in good condition except in Case No. 71.

Unfortunately when we opened this case we found it contained completely different articles, and we can only presume a mistake was made and the contents of this case were for another order.

As we need the articles we ordered to complete deliveries to our new customers, we must ask you to arrange for the dispatch of replacements at once. We attach a list of the contents of Case No. 71, and shall be glad if you will check this with our order and the copy of your invoice.

In the meantime we are holding the above-mentioned case at your disposal.

Please let us know what you wish us to do with it.

Yours faithfully,

Encl.

B. Complaint Accepted

Dear Sirs,

Your Order No. 1487 per S. S. "Chunlin"

Thank you for your letter dated April 24. We were glad to know that the consignment was delivered promptly, but it was with much regret that we heard Case No. 71 did not contain the goods your ordered.

On going into the matter we find that a mistake was indeed made in the packing through a confusion of numbers, and we have arranged for the right goods to be dispatched to you at once. Relative documents will be mailed as soon as they are ready.

We have already emailed to inform you of this, and we enclose a copy of the email.

Please keep Case No. 71 and its contents until called for by our Commercial Counselor's Office, whom we have informed of the matter accordingly.

Your faithfully,

Encl.

Specimen 2

A. Claim for Short Weight

Dear Sirs,

Claim for Shorthanded Fertilizers under S/C No. 6543

Further to our cable dated August 26 reading:

CHEMICAL FERTILIZER EXDACHING 36 BAGS BROKEN MATERIAL IRRETRIEVABLY LOST SHORTW/T ESTIMATED 1,540 LBS AWAITING SURVEY REPORT.

We have just received the Survey Report from the Dalian Commodity Inspection Bureau evidencing the broken bags being due to improper packing, for which the suppliers are definitely responsible.

On the strength of the DCIB's Survey Report, we hereby register our claim with you as follows:

Our claim on short-delivered quantity £3,570.00

Plus survey charges £250.00

Total amount of claim £3,820.00

Survey Report No. TE (80)305 is enclosed and we look forward to your settlement

Chapter 8 Complaints, Claims and Settlements

at an early date.

Yours faithfully,

Encl.

B. Settlement of Claim

Dear Sirs,

<u>Your Claim on 1,000 M/T Chemical Fertilizers</u>

With reference to your letter of September 6, in which a claim was lodged for a short delivery of 1,540 LBS Chemical Fertilizers, we wish to express our deepest regret over the unfortunate incident. You must have had much difficulty in meeting the orders of your clients.

After check-up by our staff at the warehouse in Glasgow, it was found that some 10 bags had not been packed in strong paper bags as stipulated in the contract, thus resulting in the breakage during transmission. This was due entirely to negligence on the part of the warehouse managers, for which we, the exporters, tender our apologies.

In view of our long-standing relations, we trust that there is a good prospect of further development, and we will make payment by cheque for £3,820.00, the amount of claim, into your account within the Bank of China, upon receipt of your agreement.

We hope this matter will not affect our good relation in future dealings.

Yours faithfully,

Specimen 3

A. Claim for Damaged Carpets

Dear Frank,

<u>Our Order No. ST-PS 1200C per S. S. "Smooth"</u>

We duly received the documents and took delivery of the goods on arrival of S. S. "Smooth" at Melbourne on July 20, 2017.

To our regret, we have found 10 cartons of the consignment are badly damaged, and the 100 boxes of carpets are seriously damped and dirty, which are quite unsalable. Therefore, we would like to lodge a claim for 100 boxes of damaged carpets.

You will find a list of the damaged cartons and articles with photos attached. We anticipate your early reply and settlement.

Best regards,
Billy

B. Settlement of Claim

Dear Bear,

Cartons of Damaged Carpets under Your Order No. ST-PS 1200C

We regret to learn from your letter of September 17 that your Order No. ST-PS 1200C of 10 cartons carpets arrived in poor condition.

After a clear investigation, we would like to inform you that the goods were carefully packed by experienced workmen and the clean B/L proves fully the goods in question to have been loaded in perfect condition. Therefore, we assume that the cartons were damaged through rough handling in transit.

As the shipment is covered against All Risks, we would rather advise you to file the claim with the insurance company as soon as possible. We would, of course, do anything in our power to help you in your insurance claim.

Attached herein is our survey report and we hope everything will be fine.

Best wishes,

Frank

8.3 Writing Guide

8.3.1 A Complaint or Claim Letter

1. Structure of a Letter for Complaints or Claims

Opening paragraph: state the reason—the incidents of complaints or claims.

Body: complain and give the details, such as the evidence; suggest the settlement, such as claim, replacement or cancellation the orders.

Closing paragraph: express an expectation of early reply such as hope to meet your demands and express your wish of cooperation.

2. Contents of a Letter for Complaints or Claims

The letter may include some or all of the following main points and useful expressions.

(1) To lodge a claim and expressing your regret:

- Much to our regret about...

- We regret to say that...

Chapter 8 Complaints, Claims and Settlements

(2) To state your reasons for claims:

• We have just received the Survey Report from... evidencing that...

(3) To explain the inconvenience caused and requesting the other party to settle:

• The inferior quality of... causes us considerable difficulty and it is hard for us to dispose of it.

(4) To put forward your thought about the issue:

• We must ask you to arrange for the dispatch of replacements at once.

• On the basis of the survey report, we hereby register a claim with you for... in all.

(5) To express your anticipation of an early and favorable reply:

• We would like you to inform us of what you decide to go regarding our losses.

8.3.2 A Response Letter to Complaint or Claim

1. Structure of a Response Letter to Complaint or Claim

Opening paragraph: express your regret to receive the complaint or the claim.

Body: explain the incident and giving the result.

Closing paragraph: suggest the settlement, such as discount, replacement or cancellation of the order; apologize for inconvenience and wish for further cooperation; give advice if you are not responsible.

2. Contents of a Response Letter to Complaint or Claim

A reply complaint letter is written in a professional setting when some issues or misunderstandings crop up. It may be different to a reasonable claim and an unreasonable claim. The reply letter may include some or all of the following main points and useful expressions.

* **Responding to a Reasonable Claim**

(1) To express our regret for such a matter:

• Thank you for your letter of... but it was with great that we heard...

(2) To inform that you are investigating the matter:

• On going into the matter we find that...

• After a check-up by our staff, it was found that... thus resulting in... for which we tender our apologies.

(3) To introduce the measures to be taken:

• We have arranged. . . at once.

• In view of our long-standing business relations, we'll make payment for. . . into your account.

(4) To show your apology:

• We regret the inconvenience you have sustained.

• Please accept our apologies for the trouble caused to you.

(5) To express your hope of settling the matter in a satisfactory way:

• We trust that the arrangement that we have made will satisfy you.

* **Responding to an Unreasonable Claim**

(1) To express your regret or surprise:

• We feel deeply sorry that. . . in your letter of. . .

• We are sorry to learn from your letter of. . .

(2) To state the causes for the loss after investigation:

• After going into the matter carefully, we estimate that. . . might be due to. . .

• We can assure you that the goods in question were in perfect condition when they left have. May be the damage complained of must have occurred in transportation.

• The loss should be borne by others.

• The responsibility should rest with either of the parties concerned.

• This being the case, we would like to advise you to claim on the shipping company who should be held responsible.

(3) To show your regret for the losses and refusal to the claim:

• Consequently we find no ground to compensate you for the loss.

• We think we are apparently not liable for the damage.

• At any rate, we deeply regret about the unfortunate incident.

8.4 Supplement

Some Useful Sentences on Claims, Complaints and Settlements

8.4.1 Concerning Delay in Shipment

(1) The goods under our Order No. 123 should have reached us a week ago.

第123号订单下的货物本应在一周前到达我处。

Chapter 8 Complaints, Claims and Settlements

(2) You have confirmed our order, but to our surprise, we have not yet received the goods or any advice from you when we may expect delivery.

贵方已确认我方订单,但令人诧异的是我方至今尚未收到货,也未收到何时可以交货的通知。

(3) The articles have just been received after a delay of two weeks, for which no explanation has yet been given to us.

货物延误两周后才到货,贵方至今尚未对延误作出任何解释。

8.4.2 Concerning Poor Packing

(1) On unwrapping/opening the cases, we find the goods partly soaked by rain.

开箱后,我们发现部分货物因淋雨受潮。

(2) We have examined them one by one, and found that each of them was leaking more or less.

我们已逐件检查,每一件都或多或少有渗漏的情况。

(3) The seams of the gunny bags do not appear to have been strong enough, with the result that they have given away, thus allowing the contents to run out.

麻袋的缝口似乎不够牢固,导致麻袋开裂,袋内物品外漏。

8.4.3 Concerning Poor Quality

(1) On comparing the goods received with the sample, we were surprised to find that the color is not the same.

将收到的货物与样品比较,我们惊讶地发现颜色不一致。

(2) The goods delivered are not up to the standard of samples. The pattern is uneven in places and the color varies.

所交货物未达到样品质量标准,多处花样不匀,存在色差。

8.4.4 Concerning Shortage

(1) We regret to point out that a shortage in weight of 20 kg was noticed when the goods arrived.

我们遗憾地发现,收到的货物短重20千克。

(2) Carton 17 was found to be 5 packages short. As the carton was in good shape and does not appear to have been tampered with, we surmise that they must have been short-shipped.

第 17 号箱少 5 包,由于箱子完好,似未撬动,推测是短重。

8.4.5 Concerning Wrong Goods Delivered

(1)Evidently some mistake was made and the goods have been wrongly delivered.

显然发生了差错,以致发错了货。

(2)The wrong pieces may be returned per next available steamer for our account, but it is preferable if you can sell them out at our price in your market.

错发的货物请由下一班货轮运回,费用由我方承担,但如能在你方市场按我方价格出售则最好。

8.4.6 Accepting Claims

With mutual efforts, this case has been settled amicably and we shall remit to you an amount of... in compensation for the loss rising therefrom.

在双方的共同努力下,这件事已经得到妥善解决。我方将汇付你方……以补偿这件事造成的损失。

8.4.7 Making Adjustments

(1)Such case does exist but it counts for little. It is our hope that you will waive the claim and we shall then see if we can do something for your orders to follow.

类似事件确实存在,但是无关紧要,我方希望你方能放弃索赔,并在以下的订单中给予你方一些优惠。

(2)We are prepared to make you a responsible compensation, but not for the amount you claimed, because we cannot see the reason why the loss should be 50% more than the actual value of the goods. Please reconsider the matter.

我方准备给予合理的补偿,但不是你方要求的数字。因为我方不理解为何损失会比实际价值高 50%,请重新考虑。

(3)It would not be fair if the loss be totally imposed on us as the liability rests with both parties. We are ready to meet you half way, i.e. to pay 50% of the loss only.

由于双方都有责任,若损失都由我方承担有失公平。我方愿折中赔偿 50%的损失。

(4)We believe that this is the most advantageous solution to you, since you can get the complete goods at a specially reduced price.

我方相信这是对你方最有利的解决方式,因为你方可以以非常低的价格购买这些货物。

Chapter 8 Complaints, Claims and Settlements

(5) We may compromise but the compensation should, in no case, exceed... otherwise this case will have to be submitted to arbitration.

我方可以作出让步,但补偿决不能超过……否则这件事就要交由仲裁机构来解决。

8.4.8 Rejecting Claims

(1) As it is a matter concerning insurance, we hope you will refer it to the insurance company or their agents at your end.

由于涉及保险,我方希望你方能把这件事移交给保险公司或保险公司在贵地的代理人处理。

(2) We can hardly be expected to accept your claim after a lapse of over one month.

时隔一个月,我方很难接受你方提出的索赔要求。

(3) We regret we cannot entertain your claim.

很遗憾,我方不能接受你方的索赔要求。

(4) We are sorry we cannot agree to the view put forward by your client, and must repudiate our liability for the claim on account of lack of evidence.

很抱歉我方不能同意你方诉讼委托人提出的观点,由于缺乏证据,我方必须拒绝承担赔偿责任。

EXERCISES

◇**Language Usage**

Ⅰ. Choose the one that best completes each of the following sentences.

1. Even though the two sides are very cautious, these situations still _____.
   A. rise   B. arise   C. raise   D. rose

2. Complaints and claims occur in the international trades, such as one party does not comply _____ the contract.
   A. with   B. to   C. in   D. at

3. The goods you delivered are below the standard we expected _____ the sample.
   A. to   B. on   C. in   D. from

4. The analysis of the first shipment is not satisfactory _____ certified by the China Commodity Inspection Bureau.
   A. after   B. has been   C. as is   D. which is

5. Case No. 10 was found to be 2 packages _____.

A. too short   B. short   C. shortage   D. shortened

6. We lodge a claim _____ you _____ the short-weight.

A. with...with   B. for...for   C. with...for   D. for...with

7. We have _____ the drums one by one and found that most of them are leaking.

A. tested   B. rolled   C. traced   D. examined

8. After inspection of the shipment, we found 5 cases _____.

A. missing   B. losing   C. missed   D. lost

9. We hope this unfortunate incident will not affect the friendly relations _____ us.

A. for   B. with   C. to   D. between

10. We trust you will do your best to have this matter _____ right away.

A. settle   B. settled   C. settling   D. to settle

II. Fill in the blanks with proper words given.

| received | receipt | damage | damaged | bear |
| divided | convinced | to | under | attributed to |

Dear Sirs,

　　We have ___11___ your letter of October 15, informing us that the washing machines we shipped to you arrived in a(an) ___12___ condition ___13___ improper packing.

　　Upon ___14___ of your letter, we have given this matter our immediate attention. We have studied your surveyor's report very carefully.

　　We are ___15___ that the present ___16___ was due to extraordinary circumstances ___17___ which they were transported to you. We are therefore not responsible for the damage; but as we do not think that it would be fair to have you ___18___ the loss alone, we suggest that the loss be ___19___ between both of us, ___20___ which we hope you will agree.

　　　　　　　　　　　　　　　　　　　　　　　　　　　　Yours sincerely,

III. Translate the following sentences into Chinese or English.

21. Unfortunately, there have been similar delays on several previous occasions and their increasing frequency in recent months compels us to say that business between us cannot be continued under conditions such as these.

Chapter 8 Complaints, Claims and Settlements

22. This does not appear to us to be reasonable, as we sent you an advance sample prior to shipment, and not hearing from you to the contrary, presumed it to be acceptable to you.

23. However, considering our long-standing business relations and since the goods were examined by a Public Surveyor upon arrival, we will meet you halfway by offering a discount of 5%.

24. We have just received the Survey Report from the Dalian Commodity Inspection Bureau evidencing the broken bags being due to improper packing, for which the suppliers are definitely responsible.

25. It would not be fair if the loss be totally imposed on us as the liability rests with both parties. We are ready to meet you half way, i. e. , to pay 50% of the loss only.

26. 我方认为有必要将我方的想法讲清楚,倘若供应商无法按时交货,我方就无法向客户交代。

27. 如果你方继续坚持取消订单,那么我方将保留要求你方赔偿我方的损失的权利,因为以其他方式处理这批货物我们将蒙受损失。

28. 在你方许诺确定向我们公司下订单以后,声称进口我们公司的纺织品没有任何利益可言是不讲道理的。

29. 由于装箱单完好无损,毫无疑问在发货之前货号就缺失了。

30. 我方希望你方尽快考虑解决这次赔偿问题。

Ⅳ. Translate the following letter into English.

敬启者:
　　很遗憾,我方不得不申诉关于10月1日所订服装迟交一事。虽然你方曾承诺在12月中旬交货,但直到本周我方才收到货,我方是在你方保证如期交货的基础上才订货的。
　　很遗憾,在此之前也出现了数次类似的迟交事件。这迫使我方向你方说明,如总是迟交,业务就无法继续下去了。
　　我方觉得有必要将我方的想法表达清楚,倘若供应商无法按时交货的话,我方就无法向客户交代。
　　我方希望你方能理解我方的处境并从现在开始保证按期交货。

◇**Practice**

Write a letter as per the following particulars.

- 第 150 号订单 65 箱瓷器已收到。
- 其中 7 只箱子破损,内装瓷器损坏。
- 检验报告证明损坏是不良包装所致,要求赔偿损失费及检验费计 8,000 美元。

Part Ⅱ Business Documents

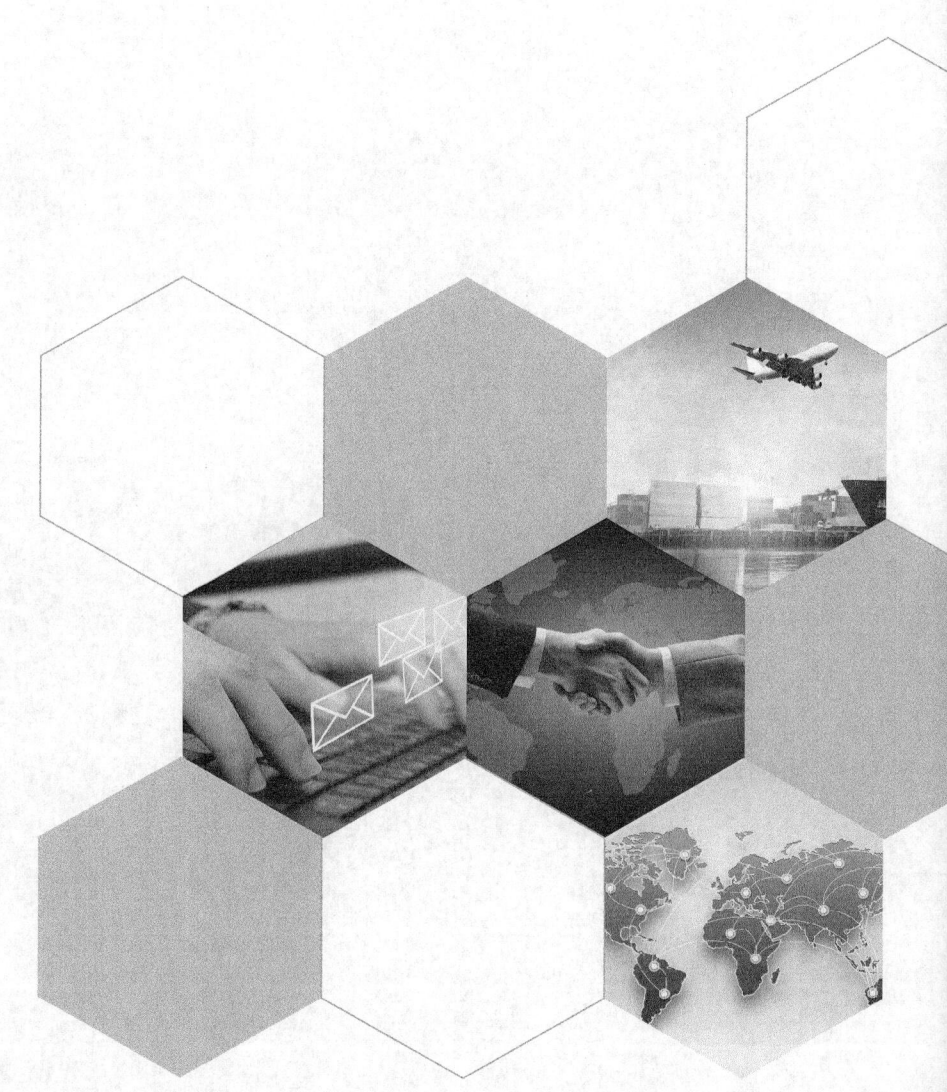

Part II Business Documents

Chapter 9
Commercial Invoice

Learning Objectives

- To know the contents and functions of commercial invoice.
- To learn how to make out a commercial invoice according to the relevant stipulations of L/C.

9.1 Introduction

A commercial invoice is a shipping document used in foreign trade. It is used as a customs declaration provided by the person or corporation that is exporting an item across international borders. The commercial invoice is the primary document used for importation control, valuation, and duty determination. This document identifies the products being shipped.

A commercial invoice containing the correct information ensures that the goods can be legally transported between countries.

9.2 Samples

Specimen 1

上海机械进出口公司 SHANGHAI MACHINERY IMPORTANT & EXPORT CORP. 383, JIANGNING ROAD, SHANGHAI CHINA				
TO: RIFA INDUSTRIAL CO., LTD. 9-4, 5-KA, DANGSAN-DONG, YOUNGDEUNGPO-KU, SEOUL, KOREA			INVOCIE NO.: NE99C573063 DATE: AUG. 23, 2011 S/C NO.: 99SNEI-CO65MZ L/C NO.: M42U4908ES08171	
FROM:				TO:
Marks & Numbers	Description of Goods	Quantity	Unit Price	Amount
BUSAN DRUM NO	ACID N/BULE BC CONC. (C. I. ACID BULE 113)	5,000 KGS	CIF BUSAN PORT, KOREA $ 35.00	$ 175,000.00
TOTAL: $ 175,000.00				

Chapter 9 Commercial Invoice

(continued)

SAY US DOLLARS ONE HUNDRED SEVENTY FIVE THOUSAND ONLY. TOTAL PACKED IN 200 IRON DRUMS. TOTAL G. W. 5,350 KGS.

Specimen 2

<table>
<tr><td colspan="4" align="center">商业发票
COMMERCIAL INVOICE</td></tr>
<tr><td colspan="2">发货人
Shipper's information:
Shenzhen Seaman Printing Plant Co. , Ltd.
4th Dongfang Industrial Zone, Songgang Town, Bo'an District, Shenzhen City</td><td colspan="2">收货人
Consignee's information:
Restaurant Suntory USA. INC2233 Kalakaua Ave. , Suit 307 Honolulu, the US</td></tr>
<tr><td colspan="2">发货人电话
Telephone NO. : 0755-2708150</td><td colspan="2">收货人电话
Telephone NO. : 8089225690</td></tr>
<tr><td colspan="2">承运人
Shipped via: United Parcel Service</td><td colspan="2">运单号
Awb No. : 1Z31T28T0499800883</td></tr>
<tr><td>件数 Number of Units</td><td>内容 Description</td><td>单价 Unit Value</td><td>总价 Total Value</td></tr>
<tr><td>1,000</td><td>Printed Matter for Menu</td><td>$1.2</td><td>$1,200</td></tr>
<tr><td></td><td>发票登记总价值 Total Value</td><td></td><td>$1,200</td></tr>
<tr><td colspan="2">发货人签名及盖章
Shipper's Signature:</td><td colspan="2">日期
Date:</td></tr>
<tr><td colspan="4">I/We hereby certify that information on this invoice is true and correct and that the contents of this shipment are stated above. I/We do hereby authorize United Parcel Service to execute any additional necessary for the export of merchandise described herein on my/our behalf.</td></tr>
</table>

9.3 Composing Details

Commercial invoices are usually used to provide information to customs and should include all necessary details related to the goods. It adequately describes the goods being transported, the location, quantity, cost, location of the transport and the name of the company involved in the payment. Although there is no standard formats, the content of which corresponds with the demands of L/C or contract. A commercial invoice containing the correct information ensures that the goods can be legally transported between countries.

The form should include:

9.3.1 Invoice No.

Invoice No. is numbered by companies respectively. It is the core document with which other documents correspond, such as draft, exporting declaration and subsidiary documents.

9.3.2 Place and Date

The date and place of issue are written in the upper right corner of invoice.

(1) The place of issue should be the beneficiary's place provided by the L/C.

(2) In the whole set of documents, invoice should be sighed and issued earliest, no earlier than the signing date of contract and no later than that of the bill of lading.

9.3.3 S/C No.

Contract number should correspond with that in L/C. If there are several contracts in a deal, it should be reflected in the invoice.

9.3.4 L/C No.

If the payment is made by L/C, L/C No. should be filled out. If there is no requirement in the L/C, it may not be filled out. Or other terms of payment is adopted, it also needn't filling.

9.3.5 Consignee

In this column, you can see "To" "Sold to Messrs" "For Account and Risk of Messrs" and so on.

Consignee is the buyer's name, which must be correspond with the provision in the L/C. If there is no special provision in L/C, the name and address of the applicant of L/C or consignee could be filled out. Or if there is no applicant's name, payer of the draft is filled out. In general, it is composed according to L/C. For example, the applicant of L/C is ABC Co., Ltd., New York, but it provides that invoice to be made out in the name of XYZ Co., Ltd., New York, the latter will be printed out.

9.3.6 From... to... / Port of Shipment and Destination

Port of shipment and destination should be filled in this column. If there is transshipment, it should be marked, which should correspond with the related part in L/C, and transshipment place also needs to be marked out. For instance, From Qingdao to New York. USA. W/T Shanghai.

9.3.7 Marks and Numbers

It is made up of three parts:

1. The abbreviation of the customer's name (Customer's name can be replaced by invoice number, contract number or order number.).

2. Port of destination.

3. Number of units.

Notes:

(1) If there is no mark, N/M can be printed out.

(2) The mark in invoice should correspond with that in bill of lading.

(3) It can be made out according to the requirement of the customer.

9.3.8 Quantity and Description

The description of goods in the invoice should conform to that in the L/C. It can be filled out according to the specific situation if the payment is made by collection.

Description includes four main clauses of the contract: quantity, quality, packing, details in contract. For example, 2,500 Dozen Gloves, Article No. FS23, Packed in 12 Bags, as per contract No. 331.

9.3.9 Unit Price

Unit price includes currency, charge unit, unit price and trade terms. If they are provided in the L/C, the content in invoice should conform to it. The amount in invoice should be the same as that in draft and cannot exceed that in the L/C.

At the bottom of the invoice, E&O. E. "Errors and Omissions Excepted". It means once the composer makes mistakes, it can be corrected. For instance, $60 PER SET FOB DALIAN.

Notes:

(1) The unit price in invoice should correspond with that in the L/C.

(2) Name of currency and unit of measure must be specified.

(3) Trade terms should be composed correctly for it is concerning risk division

between the two parties, expense burden as well as the basis of customs tax.

9.3.10　Amount

The amount cannot exceed the amount of the credit if the L/C does not provide.

1. When composing the invoice, the commission must be deducted if it is requested. So does the discount. For example, "From Each Invoice 8 Percent Commission Must Be Deducted", the amount is "$20,000.00 FOBC 8 OSLO", the sum should be calculated as follows,

FOBC 8 OSLO $20,000.00.

—C 8 1600.00.

FOB OSLO $1,8400.00.

In addition, on CFR and CIF terms, commission should be calculated on FOB terms after deducting freight and insurance.

2. Sometimes the opposite party requires freight and insurance to be listed on CIF terms, and FOB price to be showed. In this case, the invoice can be composed in the following format. For instance,

TOTAL FOB VALUE $20,000.00

FREIGHT $1,200.00

INSURANCE $900.00

TOTAL CIF VALUE $22,100.00

If they have too many demanding requirements, we can request them to revise the clauses.

9.3.11　Certificate/Statements

If L/C demands that in certificate, the name of shipment, origin and number of import license should be listed, they must be listed one by one when composing.

9.3.12　Signature or Stamp

Commercial invoice can only be issued by the beneficiary in the L/C.

If there is no other stipulation, the invoice made out by photocopy, computer processing or copy ought to be marked ORIGINAL and signed by the issuer.

"UCP600[1]" stipulates it is not necessary to sign on the invoice. If the customers request that the invoice be handwritten, it cannot be stamped. If the exporting countries are Mexico or Argentina, it must be signed by hand despite no stipulations.

9.4 Supplement

9.4.1 Some Useful Expressions in the L/C

(1) Description of goods.

(2) Covering shipment of.

(3) Description of merchandise.

(4) Covering the following goods by.

(5) Covering value of.

(6) Shipment of goods.

9.4.2 Some Useful Certifying Expressions

(1) We certify that the goods named have been supplied in conformity with order No. 123.

兹证明本发票所列货物与第 123 号合同相符。

(2) We hereby certify that the above mentioned goods are of Korean Origin.

Or: This is to certify that the goods named herein are of Korean Origin.

兹证明所列货物系韩国原产。

(3) We certify that the goods mentioned in this invoice have not been shipped on board of any vessel flying Japanese flag or due to call at any Japanese port.

兹证明本发票所列货物不装载悬挂日本国旗或驶靠任何日本港口的船只。

(4) We certify that this invoice is in all respects true and correct both as regards to the price and description of the goods referred herein.

兹证明本发票所列货物在价格和品质规格各方面均真实无误。

---

① 跟单信用证统一惯例(Uniform Customs and Practice for Documentary Credits,简称 UCP),是国际银行界、律师界、学术界自觉遵守的"法律",是全世界公认的、到目前为止最为成功的一套非官方规定。《跟单信用证统一惯例》于 1951 年、1962 年、1974 年、1978 年、1983 年和 1993 年进行了多次修订,被各国银行和贸易界广泛采用,成为信用证业务的国际惯例;2006 年 10 月 25 日,国际商会又对 1993 版《UCP500》进行了修订,成为 2007 年版本《UCP600》。

(5) This is to certify that two copies of invoice and packing list(装箱单) have been airmailed direct to applicant immediate after shipment.

兹证明发票、装箱单各两份,已于装运后立即直接航邮开证人。

9.4.3 Some Useful Expressions on Invoice

in duplicate	in triplicate	in quadruplicate
一式两份	一式三份	一式四份
in quintuplicate	in sextuplicate	in septuplicate
一式五份	一式六份	一式七份
in octuplicate	in nonuplicate	in decuplicate
一式八份	一式九份	一式十份
signed commercial invoice	已签署的商业发票	

EXERCISES

◇**Practice**

Ⅰ. **Make out an invoice according to the given L/C.**

WESTDEUTSCHE LANDESBANK

Date: October 29, 2010

IRREVOCABLE DOCUMENTARY CREDET	CREDIT NUMBER 3—10509
Advising bank Bank of China Shanghai Branch E. 1 Zhongshan Road Shanghai China	Applicant Messers. H. Rieke & Co. Lederwarenfabrik D—4905 Spenge/Westf.
Beneficiary Shanghai Morning Star Corp. 375 Dongdaming Road Shanghai China	Amount $76,500.00 (US DOLLAS SEVENTY SIX THOUSAND AND FIVE HUNDRED ONLY)
Expiry Date: January 29, 2010. At the country of: Advising bank	

We hereby issue in your favour this irrevocable documentary credit which is available by negotiation of beneficiary's draft(s) at 30 days' sight drawn on us together with the following documents in triplicate (unless otherwise specified):

—Commercial invoice duly signed in 4 copies

—Full set clean on board ocean bills of lading, issued to order and endorsed in blank, marked "freight prepaid" notify applicant

—Packing list

Chapter 9 Commercial Invoice

Covering 18,000 pcs. Goat and box calf leather wallets in black color, Art No. P75506/P75507 as per S/C No. 91AP3210 dated October 20,2010.

Terms: CFR 5% Hamburg

Dispatch/Shipment from Chinese port To Hamburg, latest: Jan. 15, 2011	Partial shipment Not Permitted	Transshipment Not Permitted

Special conditions:

Documents must be presented within 14 days after the date of issuance of the bills of lading or other shipping documents.

All drafts must indicate this credit number and name of the issuing bank.

We hereby engage that payment will be duly made against documents presented in conformity with the terms of this credit.

Subjects to Uniform Customs and Practice for Documentary Credits (1994 Revision), International Chamber of Commerce.

COMMERCIAL INVOICE

(1) SELLER	(3) INVOICE NO.	(4) INVOICE DATE
	(5) L/C NO.	(6) L/C DATE
	(7) L/C ISSUED BY	
(2) BUYER	(8) CONTRACT NO.	(9) DATE
	(10) FROM	(11) TO
	(12) SHIPPED BY	
(13) MARKS	(14) DESCRIPTION OF GOODS	(15) QUANTITY/WEIGHT
(16) PRICE TERM	(17) UNIT PRICE	(18) AMOUNT
(19) ISSUED BY (20) SIGNATURE		

Ⅱ. Make out an invoice according to the materials given.

ISSUING BANK: TOKYO BANK LTD., TOKYO

L/C NO.: 9929

DATE OF ISSUE: June 15, 2019

APPLICANT: SAKA INTERNATIONAL FOOD CO.

26 TORIMI-CHO NISHI-PU, NAGOYA 546, JAPAN

BENEFICIARY: SHANGHAI NATIVE PRODUCTS CO. NO. 115 DONGFENG ROAD, SHANGHAI, CHINA

LOADING IN CHARGE: SHANGHAI, CHINA

FOR TRANSPORTATION TO: NAGOYA, JAPAN

DESCRIPTION OF GOODS: 25M/T FRESH BAMBOO SHOOTS AT CIF NAGOYA $1,050.00 PER M/T AND 20 M/T FRESH ASPARAGUS AT CIF NAGOYA $1,500.00 PER M/T AS PER CONTRACT NO. NP94051

DOCUMENTS REQUIRED:

+COMMERCIAL INVOICE IN TRIPLICATE AND CERTIFY THAT THE GOODS ARE OF CHINESE ORIGIN.

...

SHIPPING MARKS: NO MARKS

DATE OF INVOICING: JUNE 19, 2019

COMMERCIAL INVOICE	
TO:	Date: Invoice No.: Contract No.:
FROM:	TO:
Letter of credit No.: Issued by:	

Marks & Numbers	Quantities and Descriptions	Unit Price	Amount

Ⅲ. Make out an invoice according to the following information.

Beijing Yulin Trading Co., Ltd. (Red Villa Zhongshan Road, Xuanwu Dvlp Zone, Beijing, China) 与韩国 Daiwan Art and Crafts Co., Ltd. (No. 5001 Seocho-Dong Seocho-gu, Seoul, Korea) 于 2019 年 6 月 6 日签订一份出口瓷器(china)的合同,合同号: RD303/010. 开证行 INDUSTRIAL BANK OF KOREA(HEAD OFFICE SEOUL)

Chapter 9 Commercial Invoice

SEOUL(50,ULCHIRO 2-GA,CHUNG-GU SEOUL,KOREA)于2019年6月13日开来信用证,号码是:TF010M057678。信用证的最晚装运日期是2019年7月30日,有效期至2019年8月13日与发票有关的信用证条款如下:

32B:AMOUNT: $3,980.00

44A:LOADING ON BOARD/DISPATCH/TAKING IN CHARGE AT/FROM...:ANY PORT IN CHINA

44B:FOR TRANSPORTATION TO:BUSAN PORT,KOREA

45:DESCRIPTION OF GOODS/SERVICES:

GLASSWARE AS PER SALES CONFIRMATION NO. RS303/008 DATED 7-25-2019,CIF-BUSAN PORT,KOREA

46:DOCUMENTS REQUIRED

DOCUMENTS IN TRIPLICATE (UNLESS OTHERWISE SPECIFIED)

+SIGNED COMMERCIAL INVOICE

卖方于7月28日装船完毕,取得提单。

货物品名为瓷器,明细如下:

货号	单价 (USD)	数量 (PSC)	箱号 (NO.)	尺码 (CM)	毛重 (KGS)	净重 (KGS)
09—21/22	6.5	100	1—49	70×45×25	635	540
09—11/20	5.6	100	50—98	70×45×25	635	540
09—49/20	5.5	100	99—147	70×45×25	635	540
09—27/30	7.4	100	148—196	70×45×33	885	780
09—37/30	7.4	100	197—245	70×45×33	885	780
09—24/30	7.4	100	246—294	70×45×33	885	780

唛头:无

船名:NORTHWIND

航次:F.011 B

装运港:天津

Chapter 10
Bill of Exchange

Chapter 10 Bill of Exchange

Learning Objectives

- To learn how to fill in bill of exchange under different modes of payment.
- To master how to make bill of exchange according to the relevant stipulations of L/C.

10.1 Introduction

Instruments used in international trade include bill of exchange, promissory note and check. They are all used for the payment or transfer of money. The most often used is bill of exchange.

10.1.1 Definition

A bill of exchange or "draft" is an unconditional order in writing, addressed by one person to another, signed by the person giving it, requiring the person to whom it is addressed to pay on demand or at a fixed or determinable future time a sum certain of money to or to the order of a specified person, or to bearer.

10.1.2 Types

According to different criteria, a bill of exchange can be grouped into different types.

1. Bank (Banker's) Bill vs. Commercial (Trader or Trader's) Bill

In terms of different drawers, bills may be classified into bank bill and commercial bill. Bank bill is issued or accepted by a bank. Commercial bill is issued by the corporation, company, firm or individual and paid by other firm, individual or bank.

2. Sight Bill vs. Usance (Term or Time) Bill

In terms of different payment time, bills may be classified into sight bill and usance bill. Sight bill is payable when it is presented, rather than at a given length of time after presentation or after a date indicated on the bill. Usance bill is payable at a specified/fixed future date.

3. Clean Bill vs. Documentary Bill

In terms of the documents affiliated, bills may be classified into clean bill and documentary draft. Clean bill is presented for payment without the required documents such as insurance, certificated of origin. Documentary bill is presented for payment with the required documents.

10.2 Samples

Specimen 1

No. G 103/86   Suzhou, China

April 26, 2016

EXCHANGE FOR $1,850.00

At XXX Sight of this (FIRST of) exchange (the SECOND of the same tenor and date being unpaid)

Pay to the order of Bank of China, Suzhou the sum of US Dollars One Thousand Eight Hundred and Fifty Only.

Drawn under Bank A, London

L/C NO16358

TO: Bank A, London

                                                                           Suzhou Crafts Corp.

Specimen 2

NO. 679/47   Beijing, China

Exchange for £485   March 8, 2017

At 120 days sight of this FIRST of exchange (the SECOND of the same tenor and date being unpaid)

Pay to the order of Beijing Carpet Export Corporation the sum of Pound Sterling Four Hundred and Eighty-five Only.

To West Coast Import, Ltd.

44 Dock Street,

    Liverpool, England   Beijing Carpet Export Corporation

                                                                   Manager(signed)

                                                                  (Inv. NO. 679/47)

Specimen 3

凭

Drawn under DEUTSCHE BANK (ASIA) HONGKONG

信用证　第　　　号

Chapter 10 Bill of Exchange

L/C No. <u>756/05/1495988</u>

日期

Dated <u>NOV. 20,2019</u>

按息付款

Payable with interest @.................% per annum

号码　　　　　　汇票金额　　　　　　中国广州　　年　　月　　日

No：<u>ITBE001121</u> Exchange for $ <u>19,745.00</u> Guangzhou,China <u>DEC. 20,2019</u>

见票　　　　　　日后（本汇票之副本未付）

At <u>*****</u> Sight of this FIRST of Exchange (Second of exchange being unpaid) pay to the order of <u>BANK OF CHINA,TIANJIN BRANCH</u> 或其指定人付金额

The sum of <u>SAY US DOLLARS NINETEEN THOUSAND SEVEN HUNDRED AND FORTY FIVE ONLY.</u>

To <u>DEUTSCHE BANK (ASIA) HONG KONG</u>

　　　　　　　　　　　　　　　　　　　　STAMP AND SIGNATURE

10.3　Composing Details

10.3.1　Bill Number

It is usually in accordance with the invoice number in order to check each other easily.

10.3.2　The Amount of Exchange

The amount is written both in words and in figures. The amount in figures is after "exchange for". The amount in words is after "the sum of". The draft amount in figures consists of two parts：the name of the currency abbreviation；the amount of the number of Arabic numerals. The currency name should be stated in the credit and invoice currency. First fill in the name of the currency abbreviation, and then fill in the amount of the number of Arabic numerals. The draft amount requires two decimal places. The sum is followed by the amount in words, and ONLY should be written after the amount in words.

For example,$ 8,900.20. The sum of *SAY US DOLLARS EIGHT THOUSAND NINE HUNDRED AND TWENTY CENTS ONLY.*

10.3.3 Date and Place of Issue

The date is often filled in by the negotiation bank, which is the issuing date of the draft, after the date of all the other documents and before the date of the L/C expiry. The place is the negotiating place, often printed on the draft. The date of issue must be entirely and certainly specified. The absence hereof could lead to the nullity of the bill of exchange.

10.3.4 Tenor

Tenor refers to the period of time after which a bill becomes payable. Thus, where a bill is payable after 90 days from the date of drawing or acceptance, the tenor of the bill is 90 days. If this is a sight bill, the drawer just uses symbols such as "XXX""…" "***" to fill out between "at" and "sight" or fill out "AT SIGHT". If this is an insane bill, the drawer just fills out a fixed period. The time stated in the bill runs from the day of acceptance of the bill or the protest. If the bill is not accepted, or the date of acceptance is not stated, the bill must be protested.

10.3.5 Payee

The party in whose favor the bill is drawn or is payable is called the payee. The payee will be indicated next to "pay to" wording of bill of change and usually a purchasing bank is to be indicated with L/C transaction.

The payee can be written in three types:

1. A Restrictive Payee (restrictive order)

Such as "pay A Co. only" "pay B Co. not transferable".

2. To Order (demonstrative order/indicative order)

Such as "pay to A Co." "pay to A Co. or order" "pay to the order of B Co." "pay to order".

3. To Bearer (bearer order)

Such as "pay to bearer" "pay to A Co. or bearer".

10.3.6 Drawee

Put after "TO" at the left bottom. The drawee refers to the party upon whom the bill is drawn. He gives the order to pay to the third party. He is the person to whom the bill is addressed and who is ordered to pay. He becomes an acceptor when he indicates

Chapter 10 Bill of Exchange

his willingness to pay the bill.

10.3.7 Drawer

Full name of the drawer, the exporter and the legal representative are stamped at the bottom—the right corner of the draft, when stipulated in the L/C. The signature by hand can be added. Without the signature, the bill is not valid.

EXERCISES

◇**Practice**

Ⅰ. **Check the bill of exchange according to the L/C and correct the mistakes.**

L/C

FROM: HUADI BANK, HONG KONG
TO: BANK OF CHINA, SHANGHAI BRANCH JAN. 2, 2019
IRREVOCABLE DOCUMENTARY CREDIT NO. : 234-10788
ADVISING BANK: BANK OF CHINA, SHANGHAI BRANCH
BENEFICIARY: SHANGHAI BEIFULAI AUTO PARTS CO. , LTD.
             TUNXI ROAD, SHANGHAI, CHINA
APPLICANT: HONG KONG SANRUI CO. 5/F RONGLI BUILDING TAIKOKTSUI KOWLOON, HONG KONG
AMOUNT: $ 23,100.00
EXPIRY DATE: MAR. 16, 2019
DEAR SIRS,
  WE HEREBY ISSUE AN IRREVOCABLE DOCUMENT CREDIT IN YOUR FAVOUR WHICH IS AVAILABELE BY NECOTIATION OF YOUR DRAFTS AT SIGHT DRAWN ON US, FOR 100% INVOICE VALUE MARKED AS DRAWN UNDER THIS CREDIT ACCOMPANIED BY THE FOLLOWING DOCUMENTS:
  SEPECIAL CONDITIONS: ALL DOCUMENTS MENTIONING THIS CREDIT NUMBER. DOCUMENTS TO BE PRESENTED WITHIN 15 DAYS AFTER DATE OF ISSUANCE OF TRANSPORT DOCUMENTS BUT WITHIN VALIDITY OF CREDIT.

BILL OF EXCHANGE

NO. 234—10788   DATE <u>MAR. 11, 2019</u>
EXCHANGE FOR <u>$ 23,100.00</u>
AT <u>15</u> DAYS AFTER SIGHT OF THIS FIRST OF EXCHANGE (THE SECOND OF EXCHANGE BEING UNPAID)
PAY TO THE ORDER OF <u>HUADI BANK, HONG KONG</u>
THE SUM OF <u>SAY US DOLLARS TWENTY THREE THOUSAND ONE HUNDRED.</u>

(continued)

DRAWN UNDER THIS CREDIT TO BANK OF CHINA, SHANGHAI BRANCH

HONG KONG SANRUI CO.

II. Make out a draft according to the following information.

Issuing Bank: Societe General Paris, France
L/C NO: 6081 dated April 1, 2019
L/C Amount: $82,800.00
Applicant: A NAVY&CO. Hamburg
Advising Bank: Bank of China, Suzhou Branch
Beneficiary: Jiangsu Huayu Trading Co.
Expiry Date: May 31, 2019
B/L Dated: May 5, 2019
Beneficiary's draft at sight drawn on the issuing bank and pay to the order of Bank of China, Suzhou Branch
Invoice No: 04HY34—95

BILL OF EXCHANGE

Drawn under _____

    L/C No. _____

    Dated _____

    Payable with interest @.................... % per annum

    No: 08HY34—95   Exchange   for   _____   Suzhou China _____

    At _____ Sight of this FIRST of Exchange (The SECOND of exchange being unpaid)

    pay to the order of _____

    the sum of _____

    To _____

Jiangsu Huayu Trading Co.

Chapter 11
Letter of Credit

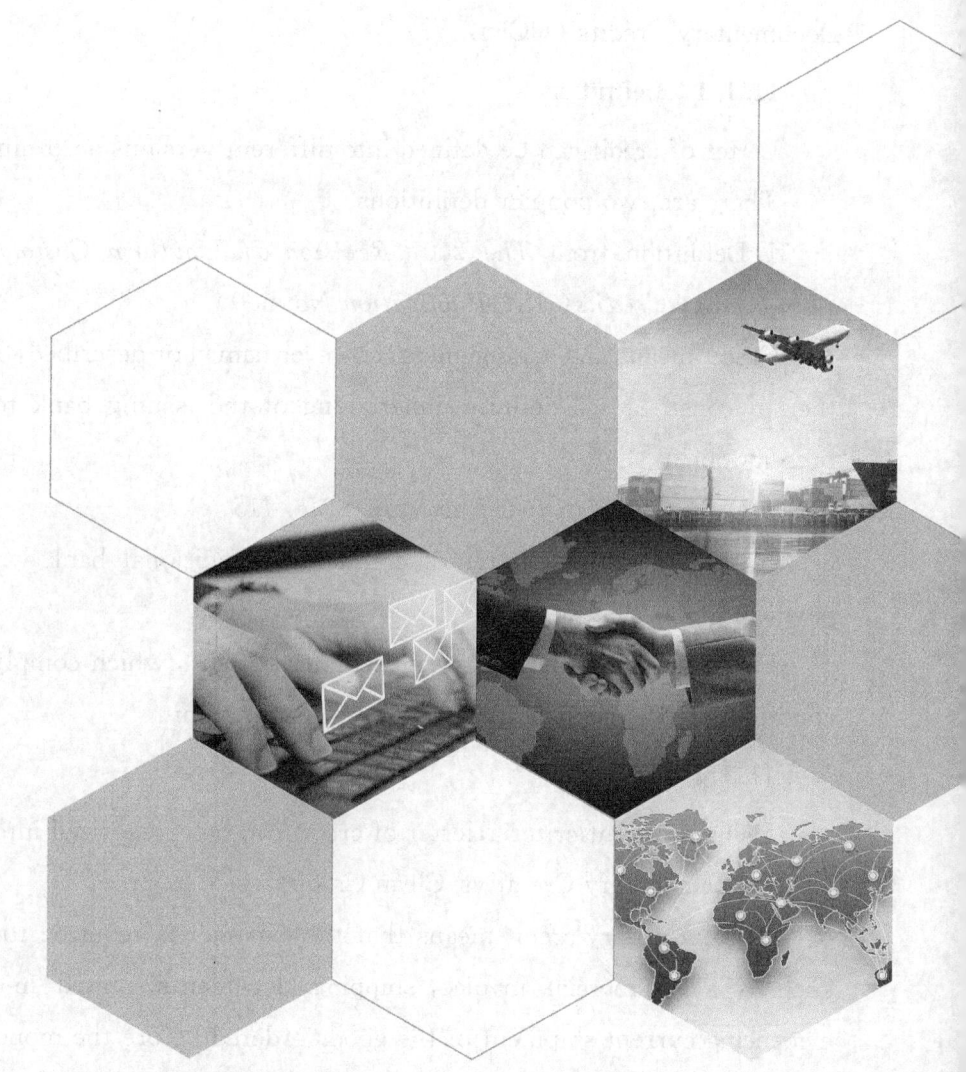

Learning Objectives

- To know the procedures of L/C establishment.
- To understand how to urge the L/C establishment and how to request L/C extension.
- To learn how to request the L/C amendments.

11.1 Introduction

Letter of credit is the most important and common type of payment. The term "letter of credit" is often abbreviated as "LC" or "L/C". An international code of rules pertaining to Letter of credit is known as The Uniform Customs and Practices for Documentary Credits (UCP).

11.1.1 Definition

Letter of credit can be defined into different versions according to different laws. There are two popular definitions:

1. Definition from *The 2007 Revision of Uniform Customs and Practice for Documentary Credits* (ICC Publication No. 600)

Credit means any arrangement, however named or described, that is irrevocable and thereby constitutes a definite undertaking of the issuing bank to honor a complying presentation.

2. Definition from *ICC Publication No. 415*

In simple terms, a letter of credit is a conditional bank written undertaking of payment.

Conditional: the beneficiary presents documents which comply with the terms and conditions of the credit within a prescribed time limit.

11.1.2 Types

Using different criteria, letter of credit can be categorized into different types.

1. Documentary Credit vs. Clean Credit

A documentary credit means that the exporter is required to produce documents, such as a commercial invoice, shipping documents, stated in the letter of credit evidencing current shipment of the goods ordered before the money is released. Letters of credit used by traders are often documentary credits. By contrast, a clean credit does not require any document other than a written demand for payment by its beneficiary, usually, a draft.

2. Revocable Credit vs. Irrevocable Credit

A revocable L/C can be amended or canceled by the buyer (the account party) at any moment without the approval of the seller (the beneficiary). Since it does not give the beneficiary great assurance of payment, it is rarely used. An irrevocable L/C cannot be amended or canceled without the consent of all parties to the credit transaction.

3. Usance Credit vs. Sight Credit

A usance credit is payable at a determined future date after presentation of conforming documents. An L/C can specify any credit period that you have negotiated with the importer. A sight credit is a kind of credit in which the announcer checks all the documents immediately and pays the required money to bank after observing the carriage documents.

4. Transferable Credit vs. Untransferable Credit

A transferable credit means a credit that specifically states it is "transferable". A transferable credit may be made available in whole or in part to another beneficiary ("second beneficiary") at the request of the beneficiary ("first beneficiary"). An untransferable is a kind of credit that the seller cannot give a part or completely right of assigned credit to somebody or to the persons he wants. In international commerce, it is required that the credit be untransferable.

5. Confirmed Credit vs. Unconfirmed Credit

A confirmed credit isused when a second guarantee is added to the document by another bank. The advising bank, the branch or the correspondent which the issuing bank routes the letter of credit to, adds its undertaking and commitment to pay according to the letter of credit. An unconfirmed letter of credit is used when the document bears the guarantee of the issuing bank alone. The advising bank merely informs the exporter of the terms and conditions of the letter of credit, without adding its obligation to pay.

11.1.3 The Operation Flow of L/C

(1) The buyer applies to a bank for a letter of credit.

(2) The buyer's bank approves the letter of credit and forwards this information to the seller's bank.

(3) The seller's bank confirms the letter of credit and then notifies the seller.

(4) The seller transfers the goods to the buyer.

(5) The seller notifies the buyer's bank that the goods have been transferred to the buyer.

(6) The seller is paid by his or her bank.

(7) The seller's bank apprises the buyer's bank of the transaction.

(8) The seller's bank is reimbursed by the buyer's bank.

(9) The buyer's bank notifies the buyer of the transaction.

(10) The buyer reimburses his or her bank.

11.2 Samples

Specimen 1 SWIFT Letter of Credit

27   SEQUENCE OF TOTAL:1/1

40A FORM OF DOC. CREDIT:IRREVOCABLE

20   DOC. CREDIT NUMBER:132CD6372730

31C DATE OF ISSUE:190702

40E APPLICABLE RULES:UCP LATEST VERSION

31D DATE AND PLACE OF EXPIRY:DATE 190915 PLACE IN CHINA

51D APPLICANT BANK:ING BELGIUM NV/SV(FORMERLY BANK BRUSSELS LAMBERT SA),GENT

50   APPLICANT:NU BONNETERIE DE GROOTE AUTOSTRADEWEG 69090 MELLE BELGIUM

59   BENEFICIARY:SHANGHAI WILL TRADING CO.,LTD
         NO. 25 JIANGNING ROAD,SHANGHAI,CHINA

32B AMOUNT:CURRENCY USD 91,500.00

41A AVAILABLE WITH... BY ANY BANK IN CHINA BY NEGOTIATION

42C DRAFTS AT... AT SIGHT

42A DRAWEE: ING BELGIUMNA/SV (FORMERLY BANK BRUSSELS

LAMBERT SA),GENT

43P PARTIAL SHIPMENTS:ALLOWED

43T TRANSSHIPMENT:ALLOWED

44E PORT OF LOADING:SHANGHAI

44F PORT OF DISCHARGE:ANTWERP,BELGIUM

44C LATEST DATE OF SHIPMENT:190831

45A DESCRIPTION OF GOODS

3,000 PCS WORK SHORT TROUSERS— 100PCT COTTON TWILL AT USD10.50/PC AS PER ORDER D1900326 AND SALES CONTRACT NUMBER WILL09068.

5,000 PCS WORK SHORT TROUSERS — 100PCT COTTON TWILL AT USD12.00/PC AS PER ORDER D1900327 AND SALES CONTRACT NUMBER WILL19069.

SALES CONDITIONS:CIF TERMS

PACKING:50PCS/CTN

46A DOCUMENTS REQUIRED

1. SIGNED COMMERCIAL INVOICES IN 4 ORGINAL AND 4 COPIES
2. FULL SET OF CLEAN ON BOARD OCEAN BILLS OF LADING, MADE OUT TOORDER, BLANK ENDORSED, MARKED FREIGHT PREPAID NOTIFY THE APPLICANT.
3. CERTIFICATE OF ORIGIN.
4. PACKING LIST IN QUADRUPLICATE STATING CONTENTS OF EACH PACKAGE SEPARARTELY.
5. INSURANCE POLICY/CERTIFICATE ISSUED IN DUPLICATE IN NEGOTIABLE FORM, COVERING ALL RISKS AND WAR RISK, FROM WAREHOUSE TO WAREHOUSE FOR 110 PCT OF INVOICE VALUE. INSURANCE POLICY/CERTIFICATE MUST CLEARLY STATE IN THE BODY CLAIMS, IF ANY, ARE PAYABLE IN BELGIUM IRRESPECTIVE OF PERCENTAGE

47A ADDITIONAL CODITIONS

1. ALL DOCUMENTS PRESENTED UNDER THIS L/C MUST BE ISSUED IN ENGLISH.

2. IN CASE THE DOCUMENTS CONTAIN DISCREPANCIES, WE RESERVE THE RIGHT TO CHARGE DISCREPANCY FEES AMOUNTING TO EUR 75 OR EQUIVALENT.

71B CHARGES: ALL BANKING CHARGES OUTSIDE THE OPENING BANK ARE FOR BENEFICIARY'S ACCOUNT.

48 PERIOD FOR PRESENTATION: WITHIN 15 DAYS AFTER THE DATE OF SHIPMENT, BUT WITHIN THE VALIDITY OF THIS CREDIT.

49 CONFIRMATION INSTRUCTION: WITHOUT

Specimen 2 A Letter of Credit Opened by Airmail

THE BANK OF CALIFORNIA
DOCUMENTARY CREDIT IRREVOCABLE

Documentary credit number: 99/50,000
Date of issue: 19/06/20
Validity date and place: 19/08/15 at Shanghai
Applicant: The Angeles Importing Co., Inc.
　　　　　3710 West 9th St. Los Angeles, CA 90019, US
Beneficiary: Wantong Trading Co., Ltd
　　　　　P. O. Box 1257 Shanghai, China
Currency code and amount: $ 950,000.00 only
Draft at... drawn on...: Draft at 60 days after sight
Partial shipment: Not allowed
Tran-shipment: Not allowed
Shipment from... to...: From Shanghai to Los Angeles by 19/07/31
Shipment of goods: 500 refrigerators Model DRF-F600
Documents required:
Commercial invoice in quintuplicate
Full set of clean on board bill of lading made out to shipper's order marked freight prepaid
Charges: All banking charges outside USA are for the beneficiary's account.

　　　　　　　　　　　　　　　　　　　John F. William
　　　　　　　　　　　　　　　　　　Authorized Signature
　　　　　　　　　　　　　　　　THE BANK OF CALIFORNIA

11.3 Composing Details

11.3.1 Applicant (Opener)

The applicant means the party on whose request the credit is issued. The applicant requests the issuing bank to open an L/C. The applicant usually is the importer. A letter of credit contains the name and address of the applicant.

11.3.2 Issuing Bank

The issuing bank accepts the requirement and opens an L/C. The issuing bank is usually a local bank of the importer. It issues an L/C, sending it to the advising bank by airmail or electronic means such as telex or SWIFT.

11.3.3 Advising (Beneficiary's) Bank

The advising bank is the correspondent bank in the exporter's country. It receives the L/C from the issuing bank for authenticating and informing the exporter of the issuance, but it doesn't undertake other responsibilities.

11.3.4 Beneficiary

The beneficiary is the party in whose favor the L/C is issued. The beneficiary is usually the exporter. A letter of credit contains the name and address of the beneficiary.

11.3.5 Negotiating Bank

The negotiating bank is the beneficiary's bank which agrees to pay the beneficiary by purchasing a negotiable instrument.

11.3.6 Paying Bank

The paying bank is responsible for the payment specified by the L/C. Usually it is the issuing bank or appointed by the issuing bank.

11.3.7 Confirming Bank

The confirming bank is the bank which guarantees the L/C established by the importer will be honored once the conditions therein are fully complied with.

11.3.8 Form and Number of Credit, Date and Place of Issue

A letter of credit should bear the form and number of credit, date and place of issue. For example,

40A:FORM OF DOCUMENTARY CREDIT

IRREVOCABLE

20:DOCUMENTARY. CREDIT NUMBER

764351

31C:DATE OF ISSUE

AUG. 12, 2019.

11.3.9　Terms of Payment

All terms of sale should be clearly specified, since payment is made according to the document's contents. For example, "net 30 days" should be specified as "net 30 days from acceptance" or "net 30 days from date of bill of lading" to avoid confusion and delay of payment. Likewise, the currency of payment should be specified as "USDxxx" if payment is to be made in US Dollars. International bankers can offer other helpful suggestions.

11.3.10　Terms of Shipment

In general, time of shipment should be prescribed in the L/C. The beneficiary should ship the goods during the prescribed period, and get the Bill of Lading. Sometimes the L/C prescribes transshipment and partial shipment. Clauses of shipment include:

(1) Port of loading or shipment; (2) Port of discharge or destination; (3) Time of shipment; (4) Partial shipment and transshipment are allowed or prohibited; (5) Mode of shipment. For example,

43P:PARTIAL SHIPMENTS

ALLOWED

43T:TRANSSHIPMENT

ALLOWED

44A:ON BOARD/DISP/TAKZNG CHARGE

London, Britain

44B:FOR TRANSPORTATION TO

DALIAN PORT, P.R.CHINA

44C:LATEST DATE OF SHIPMENT

SEP. 18, 2019.

11.3.11 Expiry Date and Place

All credits must be of limited duration. The seller should submit the documents to the bank, and present the documents to the bank for settlement during the limited duration.

The expiry place refers to the place where the seller must present documents before the L/C expires.

11.3.12 Description of the Goods

The description of the goods should be precise and complete. The description of the goods in the invoice should be the same as that in the letter of credit. In general, the description of the goods contains the name, amount, unit price, quantity, size and specification, etc.

11.3.13 Documents Required

In a credit, the documents required should be specified as follow:

1. Documents About the Goods

They include invoice, packing list, certificate of origin, inspection certificate, etc. According to UCP600, a commercial invoice must be issued by the beneficiary, with the name of the applicant as letterhead, and in the same currency as the credit, and the goods, service or the performance of the contract must be described in the same way as the credit.

2. Shipping Documents

The most important document is the ocean bill of lading, which is the warrant of cargo ownership. Usually, a bill of lading is described in a credit as: "Full set clean on board ocean bill of lading, made out to order, blank endorsed, marked freight prepaid, notify applicant."

3. Insurance Documents

An insurance document, such as an insurance policy, an insurance certificate or a declaration under an open cover, must appear to be issued and signed by an insurance company, an underwriter or their agents or their proxies. When the insurance document indicates that it has been issued in more than one original, all originals must be presented.

11.3.14 Special (Additional) Conditions

Each business has different provisions according to business needs and changes in the political, economic and trade situation of the importing country. An L/C sometimes includes special conditions concerning the negotiation, payment route, or confirmation or not.

11.3.15 Bank's Promise of Payment

For example, we hereby agree with the drawers, endorsers and bona fide holders of drafts drawn under and in compliance with the terms of this credit that such drafts will be duly honored on due presentation to the drawee if negotiated on or before expiry date and paid on maturity.

11.3.16 A Declaration to Subject to UCP600

For example, this credit is subject to the Uniform Customs and Practice of Documentary Credit 2007 Revision by ICC (International Chamber of Commerce) and Publication No. 600.

11.4 Supplement

(1) Issue of a Documentary Credit 开立信用证(开证行一般为出口商的往来银行，须视开证行的信用程度决定是否需要其他银行保兑)。

(2) Open by Airmail 信开本。

(3) Type of Documentary Credit 跟单信用证类型。

(4) Irrevocable 信用证性质为不可撤销。

(5) Letter of Credit Number 信用证号(如：LC97E0081/39. 信用证号码，一般做单时都要求标注此号码)。

(6) Date and Place of Expiry 信用证到期时间、地点，即通常最后装船期的时间加上单据提示的时间就是信用证到期时间。

(7) Available with... by... 指定的有关银行和信用证兑付方式。ANY BANK BY NEGOTIATION, 意为任何银行议付; ANY BANK BY PAYMENT, 为银行付款后无追索权。

(8) Drafts at 45 Days After Sight 汇票付款期限，见证 45 天内付款。

(9) Drawee 汇票付款人受票人，亦称受票行（drawee bank），通常也是付款行（paying bank），付款人不能为信用证申请人。

(10) Partial Shipment：NOT ALLOWED 分装条款，此为分装不允许。

(11) Transshipment：NOT ALLOWED 转运条款，此为转船不允许。

(12) Shipping on Board/Dispatch/Packing in Charge at/from 装船、发送和货物接收监管的地点。

(13) Latest Date of Shipment 最迟装运期。

(14) FULL SET OF CLEAN ON BOARD OCEAN BILLS OF LADING MADE OUT TO ORDER AND BLANK ENDORSED, MARKED "FREIGHT PREPAID" NOTIFYING QINGDAO QOF GROUP CO., LTD. 一整套已装船提单，抬头为 TO ORDER 的空白背书，且注明运费已付，通知人为青远渔（集团）公司。

(15) PACKING LIST/WEIGHT MEMO IN 4 COPIES INDICATING QUANTITY/GROSS AND NET WEIGHTS OF EACH PACKAGE AND PACKING CONDITIONS AS CALLED FOR BY THE L/C 装箱单/重量单 4 份，显示每个包装产品的数量/毛净重和信用证要求的包装情况。

(16) BENEFICIARY'S CERTIFIED COPY OF FAX DISPATCHED TO THE ACCOUNTEE WITH 3 DAYS AFTER SHIPMENT ADVISING NAME OF VESSEL, DATE, QUANTITY, WEIGHT, VALUE OF SHIPMENT, L/C NUMBER AND CONTRACT NUMBER 提交受益人证明的传真复印件。该复印件在船开后 3 天内将船名航次、日期、货物的数量、重量、价值、信用证号和合同号通知付款人。

(17) CERTIFICATE OF ORIGIN IN 3 COPIES ISSUED BY AUTHORIZED INSTITUTION 当局签发的原产地证明一式三份。

(18) CERTIFICATE OF HEALTH IN 3 COPIES ISSUED BY AUTHORIZED INSTITUTION 当局签发的健康/检疫证明一式三份。

(19) CHARTER PARTY B/L AND THIRD PARTY DOCUMENTS ARE ACCEPTABLE 可以接受租船提单和第三方单据。

EXERCISES

◇ **Practice**

Ⅰ. Fill in the blanks based on the L/C.

ABC Bank

Address: 26 North Square, London WS5R 5KL, UK

Tel: 020 7342 2369 Fax: 020 7342 2901

Irrevocable Letter of Credit

Credit Number: 45845

Date: May 20, 2019

Applicant: WIR Company, London

Beneficiary: Dongmei Corporation, Qingdao, China

Gentlemen:

We hereby open our irrevocable credit in your favor for the sum or sums not to exceed a total of Fifty Eight Thousand US Dollars ($58,000), to be made available by your request for payment at sight upon the presentation of your draft accompanied by the following documents:

1. Signed commercial invoice in three copies indicating the buyer's Purchase Order No. ED/WF-3I3.
2. Insurance Policy for invoice amount plus 10%.
3. Evidencing shipment of 300 Cartons of 34' Color Television Receivers (CIF London).
4. Clean shipped Bills of Lading in complete set marked Freight Prepaid.

Shipment from Qingdao, China to London, England

Partial Shipments: Prohibited   Transshipment: Permitted

We hereby engage that payment will be duly made against documents presented in conformity with the terms of this credit.

Yours faithfully,

Tom Brown

Manager, ABC Bank, London, International Division

Opener	
Beneficiary	
Opening bank	
Advising bank	
Kind of L/C	
Amount covered	
Type of draft agreed	
Accompanying documents	
Goods covered	
Port of departure	
Port of destination	

II. Check the L/C according to the sales contract and correct the mistakes.

Sales Contract:

The Seller: MAITY INTERNATIONAL CO., LTD..　　Contract No. MT13008

Address: NO. 29 JIANGNING ROAD, SHANGHAI, CHINA　　Date: Dec. 6, 2019

Signed at: Shanghai, China

The Buyer: DESEN EUROPE GMBH

Address: GIRARDETSTRASSE 2-38, EINGANG. 4 D-45131 ESSEN, GERMANY

This Sales Contract is made by and between the Seller and the Buyer, whereby the Seller agrees to sell and the Buyer agrees to buy the under-mentioned goods according to the terms and conditions stipulated below:

Description of Goods	Quantity	Unit Price	Amount
"RAIKOU" Homewear RH1140 Blue RH1150 Pink DRRW005 Gray DRRW008 Purple AS PER ORDER NO. MY1301	400PCS 400PCS 400PCS 400PCS	CIF Hamburg £5.88 £6.08 £5.38 £5.18	£2,352.00 £2,432.00 £2,152.00 £2,072.00
TOTAL	1,600PCS		£9,008.00
Total Amount: Say Euro Nine Thousand and Eight Only			

Packing: 40pcs are packed in one export standard carton.

Shipping Mark: RAIKOU
  MT13008
  HAMBURG
  C/No. 1-40

Time of Shipment: NOT LATER THAN FEB. 15, 2020

Loading Port and Destination: From Shanghai, China to Hamburg, Germany

Partial Shipment: Not Allowed

Transshipment: Allowed

Insurance: To be effected by the seller for 110% invoice value covering All Risks and War Risk as per CIC of PICC dated 01/01/1981

Terms of Payment: By L/C at sight, reaching the seller before Dec. 31, 2019, and remaining valid for negotiation in China for further 15 days after the effected shipment. L/C must mention this contract number. L/C advised by BANK OF CHINA. All banking Charges outside China (the mainland of China) are for account of the Drawee.

Documents:

+ Signed commercial invoice in triplicate
+ Full set (3/3) of clean on board ocean Bill of Lading marked "Freight Prepaid" made out to order blank endorsed notifying the applicant
+ Insurance Policy in duplicate endorsed in blank for 110% of invoice value covering All Risks and War Risk as per CIC dated 01/01/1981
+ Packing List in triplicate
+ Certificate of Origin issued by China Chamber of Commerce

Signed by:

THE SELLER:	THE BUYER:
MAITY INTERNATIONAL CO. ,LTD.	DESEN EUROPE GMBH
GU TAO	LUTY

The Letter of Credit:

27: Sequence of total: 1/1

40A: Form of Documentary Credit: Irrevocable

20:Documentary Credit Number:00190010018208A1

31C:Date of Issue:200101

40E:Applicable Rules:UCP LATEST VERSION

31D:Date and Place of Expiry:200220 GERMANY

50:Applicant:DESEN EUROPE GMBH
　　GIRARDETSTRASSE 2-38,INGANG. 4 D-45131ESSEN,GERMANY

59:Beneficiary:MATY INTERNATIONAL CO. ,LTD.
　　NO. 29 JIANGNING ROAD,SHANGHAI,CHINA

32B:Currency Code,Amount:＄9,008.00

41A:Available With...By...:BANK OF CHINA BY NEGOTIATION

42C:Drafts at...:30 DAYS AFTER SIGHT

42A:Drawee:DESEN EUROPE GMBH

43P:Partial Shipments:Not Allowed

43T:Transshipment:Not Allowed

44E:Port of Loading/Airport of Departure:ANY CHINESE PORT

44F:Port of Discharge/Airport of Destination:HAMBURG BY SEA

44C:Latest Date of Shipment:200210

45A:Description of Goods and/or Services:
　　1,600 pcs Babywear as per Order No. MY1301 and s/c no. MT19008 CFR HAMBURG packed in carton of 20 pcs each

46A:Documents Required

+ SIGNED COMMERCIAL INVOICES IN TRIPLICATE INDICATING L/C NO. AND CONTRACT No.

+ FULL SET(3/3) OF CLEAN ON BOARD OCEAN BILLS OF LADING MADE OUT TO ORDER AND BLANK ENDORSEDMARKED " FREIGHT TO COLLECT" NOTIFYINGTHE APPLICANT.

+ SIGNED PACKING LIST IN TRIPLICATE SHOWING THE FOLLOWING DETAILS:TOTAL NUMBER OF PACKAGES SHIPPED; CONTENT(S) OF PACKAGE(S);GROSS WEIGHT,NET WEIGHT AND MEASUREMENT.

+ CERTIFICATE OF ORIGIN ISSUED AND SIGNED OR AUTHENTICATED BY A LOCAL CHAMBER OF COMMERCE LOCATED IN THE EXPORTING

COUNTRY.
+ INSURANCE POLICY/CERTIFICATE IN DUPLICATE ENDORSED IN BLANK FOR 120% INVOICE VALUE, COVERING ALL RISKS OF CIC OF PICC(1/1/1981).
71B: CHARGES: ALL CHARGES AND COMMISSIONS ARE FOR ACCOUNT OF BENEFICIARY INCLUDING REIMBURSING CHARGES.

Chapter 12
Bill of Lading

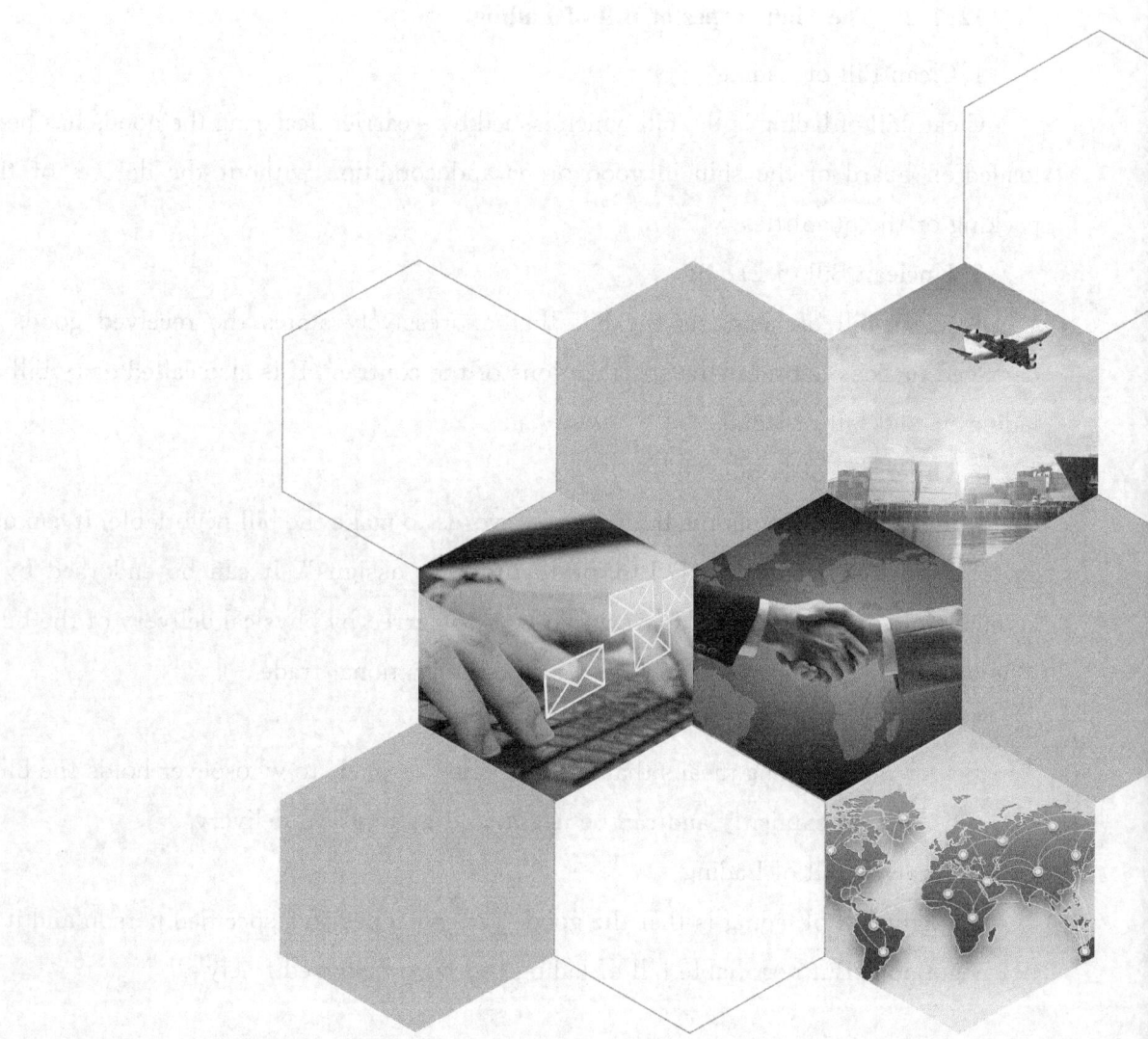

Learning Objectives

• To master different types of bill of lading.

• To know how to make out a bill of lading.

12.1 Introduction

12.1.1 Definition

A bill of lading (B/L) is a document issued by a carrier to a shipper, acknowledging that specified goods have been received on board as cargo for conveyance to a named place for delivery to the consignee who is usually identified.

12.1.2 The Main Types of Bill of Lading

1. Clean Bill of Lading

Clean bill of lading is the bill which issued by a carrier declaring the goods has been loaded on board of the ship in good order and condition without the defects of the packing or the quantities.

2. Unclean Bill of Lading

Unclean bill of lading is the bill that expressively states the received goods is damaged or does not meet the specifications of the contract. It is also called dirty bill of lading or foul bill of lading.

3. Order Bill of Lading

Order bill of lading is the bill that uses words to make the bill negotiable. It can use words such as "delivery to B Ltd. or to order or assigns". It can be endorsed by a company or the right to take delivery can be transferred by physical delivery of the bill. The order bill of lading is widely used in the international trade.

4. Bearer Bill of Lading

Bearer bill of lading means that delivery shall be made to whosoever holds the bill. It can be created explicitly and can be negotiated by physical delivery.

5. Straight Bill of Lading

Straight bill of lading is that the goods are consigned to a specified person and it is not negotiable. But negotiable bill of lading can be transferred freely.

6. Shipped on Board Bill of Lading

This bill of lading is issued when cargo is loaded on board which is in apparent good condition. It is also named on board bill of lading.

7. Received for Shipment Bill of Lading

This bill is sent from agent/charterer to shipper and indicates that goods have been received by the carrier, and have not been loaded on the ship.

12.1.3 The Main Functions of a B/L

(1) It is a cargo receipt made out by the ship owner.

(2) It is the evidence of a contract of carriage between the consignor and the shipping company.

(3) B/L is a document of title to the goods.

12.2 Samples

Specimen 1

1. SHIPPER		B/L NO. SHOSCO SHANGHAI OCEAN SHIPPING CO. ORIGINAL Combined Transport Bill of Lading			
2. CONSIGNEE					
3. NOTIFY PARTY					
4. PR-CARRIAGE BY	5. PLACE OF RECEIPT				
6. OCEAN VESSEL VOY. NO.	7. PORT OF LOADING				
8. PORT OF DISCHARGE	9. PLACE OF DELIVERY	10. FINAL DESTINATION FOR THE MERCHANT'S REFERENCE			
11. MARKS	12. NOS. & KINDS OF PKGS	13. DESCRIPTION OF GOODS	14. G. W. (KG)		15. MEAS(M^3)
16. TOTAL NUMBER OF CONTAINERS OR PACKAGES(IN WORDS)					
17. FREIGHT & CHARGES	REVENUE TONS	RATE	PER	PREPAID	COLLECT
PREPAID AT	PAYABLE AT	18. PLACE AND DATE OF ISSUE			

(continued)

TOTAL PREPAID	19. NUMBER OF ORIGINAL B(S)L	22. SIGNED FOR THE CARRIER
20. DATE	21. LOADING ON BOARD THE VESSEL BY	上海远洋运输总公司 SHANGHAI OCEAN SHIPPING CO. ×××

Specimen 2

Shipper 托运人	B/L NO. 提单号码_____ **PACIFIC INTERNATION LINES(PTE)LTD** (Incorporated in Singapore) **COMBINED TRANSPORT BILL OF LADING** 　　Received in apparent good order and condition except as otherwise noted the total number of container or other packages or units enumerated below for transportation from the place of receipt to the place of delivery subject to the terms hereof. One of the signed bills of loading must be surrendered dulyen dorsed in exchange for the goods or delivery order. On presentation of this document (duly endorsed) to the Carrier by or on behalf of the Holder, the right and liabilities arising in accordance with the terms hereof shall (without prejudice to any rule of common law or statute rendering them binding on the Merchant) become binding in all respects between the Carrier and the Holder as though the contract evidenced hereby had been made between them. **SEE TERMS ON ORIGINAL B/L**	
Consignee 收货人		
Notify Party 被通知人		
Vessel and Voyage Number 船名及航次	Port Loading 装运港	Port of Discharge 卸货港
Place of Receipt 转运	Place of Delivery 交货地	Number of Original B/L 提单份数
PARTICULARS AS DECLARED BY SHIPPER—CARRIER NOT RESPONSIBLE		

Chapter 12 Bill of Lading

(continued)

Container Nos/Seal Nos Marks and/ Numbers 运输标志(唛头)	No. of Container/Packages/ Description of Good 商品名称、包装描述	Gross Weight (Kilos)重量	Measurement(Cu. meters)尺寸
FREIGHT & CHARGE 运费支付	Number of Containers/Packages(in words)商品数量大写		
	Shipped on Board Date：上船日期		
	Place and Date of Issue：签发提单的地点与日期		
	In Witness Where of this number of Original Bills of Lading stated. Above all of the tenor and date one of which being accomplished the others to stand void. For PACIFIC INTERNATIONAL LINES(PTE)LTD as Carrier		

12.3 Composing Details

12.3.1 Parties of a Bill of Lading

The main parties on a bill of lading are shipper, consignee, notify party and carrier. The shipper is the person, usually the exporter, who sends the goods. Consignee refers to the person entitled to take delivery of the goods. Carrier is the person or company who has concluded a contract with the shipper for carriage of goods. Notify party is the party that the carrier must notify when the goods arrive at the port of destination. The carrier issues an arrival notice informing the notify party about the cargo discharge point, number of packages and other information.

12.3.2 Date of a Bill of Lading

It is important to date bills of lading correctly, and as per date on which the cargo is actually loaded. Cargo quantity and condition should also be adequately and correctly described in the bills of lading.

12.3.3　Signing of a Bill of Lading

All bills should be signed by either shipping company or by a duly authorized agent. If time does not permit the ship's master to sign the bills, a letter is usually drawn up giving the port agent appropriate authority to sign bills of lading. The bill of lading must show how many signed originals were issued.

12.3.4　Original of a Bill of Lading

The originals are marked as "original" on their face and all have equal value, that is, all have the same validity. The purpose of issuing more than one original is to ensure that the port of destination will receive the original when dispatched separately. The originals of Bs/L are proof of ownership of goods, one of which must be surrendered to the carrier at destination, duly endorsed by the title holder in the goods in exchange for the goods or the delivery order. When one of the originals is surrendered to the carrier, the others became invalid.

12.3.5　A Full Set of Original Bills of Lading

In some cases, a shipper may request a "full set" of original bills of lading, rather than just one original document. A set contains at least two originals. In practice, a set of three originals is the most common. The number of original bills of lading may be expressed as 3/3 or 2/2. If the L/C did not contain the expression "Full set 3/3", then the number of original bills of lading required would depend on the number as so issued by the carrier. It can be a sole original B/L, that is, one original only.

EXERCISES

◇**Practice**

Ⅰ. **Make out a bill of lading according to the given information.**

我国上海 LHZ 公司向美国 HPH 公司出口烟台苹果 240 吨,每吨 220 美元 CIF 纽约,单层新麻袋装,每袋净重 60 千克。唛头为:

S. M.

NEWYORK

Nos:1_4000

货物于 2019 年 3 月 16 日在上海港装"瑛宝"号轮运往美国纽约。

BILL OF LADING

Shipper (1)_____

Consignee (2)_____

Notify Party (3)_____

Ocean Vessel (4)_____ Voy. 368   S/O No. 898   B/L No. 567

Port of Loading (5)_____   Port of Discharge (6)_____

Freight prepaid at (7)_____

Particulars furnished by the Shipper

Marks and Numbers	No. of Packages	Description of Goods	Gross Weight	Measurement
(8)_____	(9)_____	(10)_____	(11)_____	

◆Total Packages (In words)

◆Freight and Charges (12)_____ Date (13)_____ at (14)_____

Ⅱ. Make out a bill of lading according to the given information.

ISSUING BANK: DE BANK LTD, FINLAND

Term of Doc. Credit: IRREVOCABLE

Credit Number: KHL02-22656

Date of Issue: 190505

Expiry Date: 190716

Place: CHINA

Applicant: CG CORP. SAN AUTO P. O. BOX12, FINLAND

Beneficiary: GUANGDONG HEPING TRADE CO. LTD.

59, GUOTAI ROAD, GUANGZHOU, CHINA

Amount: Currency $38,400.00

Pos. / Neg. Tol. (%): 5/5

Available with/by: ANY BANK IN ADVISING COUNTRY BY NEGOTIATION

Partial Shipments: Not Allowed

Transshipment: Allowed

Loading in Charge: HUANGPU

For Transport to: HANKO

Shipment Period：AT THE LATEST JULY 16,2019

Description of Goods：9600PCS OF WOMEN'S SWEATERS

UNIT PRICE：$4.00/PC,CFR HANKO

PACKING：12 PCS/CTN

Documents required：FULL SET OF CLEAN ON BOARD MARINE BILLS OF LADING, MADE OUT TO ORDER OF DE BANK LTD, FINLAND, MARKED "FREIGHT PREPAID" AND NOTIFY APPLICANT.

提单号码：KTT0243165

货物总毛重：6,500KGS 货物总尺码：25CBMS

船名：GRACE V.07 唛头：HPH/ HANKO/ NO. 1-800

集装箱号码：SIHU365487-2(20') SEAL NO. 9080 CY/CY

提单签发日期：2019 年 7 月 10 日 提单签发地点：黄埔

承运人：HPH SHIPPING CO. 提单签发人：王飞

货物由托运人负责装箱及计数

Shipper (1)_____		B/L No. (4)_____
Consignee (2)_____		BILL OF LADING
Notify party (3)_____		For Delivery of Goods Please Apply to：
Pre-carriage by	Place of Receipt	
Ocean Vessel Voy. No (5)_____	Port of Loading (6)_____	
Port of Discharge (7)_____	Place of Delivery	Final Destination for the Merchant's Reference Only
Container, Seal No. & Marks & Nos. (8)_____	No. of Packages & Description of Goods (9)_____	Gross Weight KGS (10)_____	Measurement m³ (11)_____

(continued)

FREIGHT & CHARGES	Revenue Tons.	Rate Per	Prepaid	Collect
Ex. Rate:	Prepaid at	Payable at	Place and Date of Issue (13)_____	
	Total Prepaid	No. of Original B(s)/L (12)_____	Stamp & Signature (14)_____	

Chapter 13
Insurance Policy

Chapter 13　Insurance Policy

Learning Objectives

- To master the basic concepts of insurance documents.
- To know how to make out the insurance policy.

13.1　Introduction

13.1.1　Definition

Insurance policy is the most commonly used document that contains all the details concerning the goods, premium and the insured value.

13.1.2　Different Types of Insurance Documents

1. Insurance Policy

Insurance policy, issued by the insurer, is a legal document setting out the exact terms and conditions of an insurance transaction. It also serves a written contract of insurance between the insurer and the person taking out insurance.

2. Insurance Certificate

Insurance certificate is a kind of simplified insurance policy and only indicates the name of the insured, name of the insured cargo, quantity, mark, conveyance, place of destination, insurance coverage, and insurance amount. But the rights and obligations of two parties are omitted. The insurance certificate has the same legal validity as the insurance policy.

3. Open Policy

Open policy is a convenient method for insuring the goods where a number of consignments of similar export goods are intended to be covered. An open policy covers these shipments, as soon as they are made, under the precious arrangement between the insured and the insurance company.

4. Combined Certificate

Combined certificate is the combination of the invoice and insurance policy, much simpler than the insurance certificate.

13.1.3　The Functions of Insurance Policy

(1) The insurance policy is the insurance contract.

(2) The insurance policy is the certificate that claims for reasonable compensation.

13.2 Samples

Specimen 1

中国人民保险公司

发票号码	保险单号次
Invoice No.	Policy No.

海 洋 货 物 运 输 保 险 单

被保险人：
INSURED： SHANGHAI TRADE COMPANY

　　中国人民保险公司(发下简称本公司)根据被保险人的要求，以及所交付约定的保险费，按照保险单承担险别和背面所载条款与下列货物运输保险，特签发本保险单。

　　("The Company") at the request (hereinafter called the "Insured") and in consideration of the agreed premium paying to the Company by the Insured, Undertakes to insure the under mentioned Goods in transportation subject to the conditions of this Policy as per Clauses printed overleaf and other special clauses attached hereon.

标　记 Marks & Nos	包装及数量 Quantity	保险货物项目 Description of Goods	保险金额 Amount Insured
	1,000 CASES	SHOES	$550,000

总保险金额：
Total Amount Insured：SAY UNITED STATES DOLLARS FIFTY-FIVE HUNDRED THOUSAND ONLY

保费	费率		装载运输工具
Premium：as arranged	Rate：as arranged	Per conveyance	S. S：KOTA TIANG V. O47

开航日期　　　　　　　　　自　　　　　　　　至
Sig on or abt September 2, 2019　From SHANGHAI　To SINGAPORE

承保险别
Conditions　　ALL RISKS

所保货物，如遇出险，本公司凭本保险单及其他有关证件给付赔款。

Chapter 13 Insurance Policy

Claims, if any, payable on surrender of this Policy together with other relevant documents.

所保货物,如发生本保险单项下负责赔偿的损失事或事故,应立即通知本公司下述代理人查勘。

In the event of accident whereby loss or damage may result in a claim under this Policy, immediate notice applying for survey must be given to the company's Agent as mentioned hereunder.

赔款偿付地点

Claim payable at   DESTINATION

日期   中国人民保险公司

DATE   September 27,2019   THE PEOPLE'S INSURANCE CO. OF CHINA

Specimen 2

中国人民保险公司

THE PEOPLE'S INSURANCE COMPANY OF CHINA

总公司设于北京   一九四九年创立

Head Office:BEIJING   Established in 1949

发票号码   保险单   保险单号次

INSURANCE POLICY

中国人民保险公司(发下简称本公司)

This Police of Insurance witnesses that The People's Insurance

Company of China (hereinafter called "The Company")

根据

at the request of   **China First Automobile Group Corporation**

(以下简称被保险人)的要求,由被保险人

(hereinafter called the "Insured")and in consideration of the agreed premium

向本公司缴付约定的保险费,按照本保险单

paying to the Company by the Insured, Undertakes to insure the undermentioned

承保险别和背面所载条款与下列特款承保

Goods in transportation subject to the conditions of this Policy as per Clauses

下述货物运输保险,特立本保险单。

printed overleaf and other special clauses attached hereon.

149

标 记 Marks & Nos	包装及数量 Quantity	保险货物项目 Description of Goods	保险金额 Amount Insured
	10 sets	Car(1.8L)	$300,000.00

总保险金额：

Total Amount Insured: SAY UNITED STATES DOLLARS THREE HUNDRED THOUSAND ONLY

保费　　　　　费率　　　　　　装载运输工具

Premium as arranged Rate as arranged Per conveyance S.S Vessels

开航日期　　　　　　　　　　　至

Sig on or abt 2019.11　From　NAGOYA　To　DALIAN.CHINA

承保险别　投保一切险，按照中国人民保险公司1981年1月1日生效的有关海洋货物运输条款为准。

　　Conditions　ALL RISKS AS PER AND SUBJECT TO THE RELEVANT DCEAN MARINE CARGO CLOUSES OF THE PEOPLE'S INSURANCE COMPANY OF CHINA DATED 1/1,1981.

所保货物，如遇出险，本公司凭本保险单及其他有关证件给付赔款。

Claims, if any, Payable On, surrender of this Policy together with other relevant documents.

所保货物，如发生本保险单项下负责赔偿的损失事或事故，应立即通知本公司下述代理人查勘。

In the event of accident whereby loss or damage may result in a claim under this policy immediate notice applying for survey must be given to the company's Agent as mentioned hereunder.

赔款偿付地点

Claim payable at　CHANGCHUN,CHINA

日期　　　　　　　　　　　中国人民保险公司长春分公司

DATE　　20/11　2019　　THE PEOPLE'S INSURANCE CO. OF CHINA CHANGCHUN BRANCH

13.3 Composing Details

13.3.1 Number of Originals

It should be made according to L/C stipulations. When there is no stipulation in the L/C, exporters usually submit a full set of insurance policy, which covers one original and one duplicate.

13.3.2 Policy Number

It should be given number by insurance company.

13.3.3 Invoice Number

It should keep the same as that in the invoice.

13.3.4 Insured

Unless otherwise stated in the L/C, under terms of CIF and CIP, insurance should be covered by exporters, so the insured should be the beneficiary in the L/C.

13.3.5 Descriptions of Goods

It can use the general name of goods and keep the same as that both in the L/C and other documents.

13.3.6 Packing, Unit and Quantity

It is the number of the biggest packages (or "In Bulk"), quantity (gross or net weight), and unit.

13.3.7 Amount Insured

The amount usually will be 110% of the invoice value.

13.3.8 Conditions

Usually the insurance company should stamp the insurance clauses at the requirements of the insured.

13.3.9 Marks of Goods

It should be the same as that in the L/C and the relevant invoice.

13.3.10 Total Amount Insured

It should be the total amount in words.

13.3.11 Premium

Usually the insurance company will print "as arranged" on the insurance policy. If L/C asks for details, premium shall be specified.

13.3.12 Per Conveyance SS

The name of the vessel and the second ship (in case of transshipment) will be specified. "As per B/L" can be also filled in.

13.3.13 Sailing on or About

It can be the issuing date of B/L, or any date within 5 days before or after the issuing date or "As per B/L date".

13.3.14 From… to

It should be the port of shipment and port of destination. If any transshipment occurs, port of transshipment should be filled in, such as "FROM XXX（装运港）TO XXX（目的港）W/T AT XXX（转运港）(WITH TRANSSHIPMENT AT XXX)".

13.3.15 Insurer

It should be the stamp of the insurer, and the signature of the person in charge.

13.3.16 Claim

It should comply with the L/C. If there is no stipulation in the L/C, it will be the port of destination for the purpose of claim. The currency should also be indicated.

13.3.17 Date

It is the issuing date of insurance policy, no later than the date of B/L.

13.3.18 At

It should be the place of beneficiary.

13.3.19 Address

It is the address of insurance company.

13.3.20 Agent of the Insurance

The name and address of an agent of the insurance company at port (place) of destination should be mentioned here for the sake of insured.

13.3.21 Endorsement (on the overleaf of the policy)

The consignor should make an endorsement on the overleaf of the policy so as to

Chapter 13 Insurance Policy

transfer all rights of it to the consignee. The endorsement is always to be made in blank except otherwise required by the consignee.

EXERCISES

◇**Practice**

Ⅰ. **Make out an insurance policy according to the given information.**

DOC. CREDIT NUMBER	20: TT45664565
DATE OF ISSUE	31C: MAR. 5,2019
EXPIRY	31D: DATE:JULY 15,2012 PLACE:CHINA
APPLICANT	50: DIADORA S. P. A.

VIA MAZZINI,20

310310 CAERANO SAN MARCO (TV),ITALY

BENEFICIARY   59: CHINA NATIONAL NATIVE PRODUCT AND ANIMAL BY-PRODUCT IMP. AND EXP. CO. GUANGDONG ANIMAL BRANCH-JIANMIN ROAD, GUANGZHOU-GUANGDONG-CHINA

......

PARTIAL SHIPMENTS	43P: NOT ALLOWED
TRANSSHIPMENT	43T: ALLOWED
LOADING IN CHARGE	44A: ANY PORT IN CHINA
FOR TRANSPORTATION TO	44B: NAPLES,ITALY
LATEST DATE OF SHIPMENT	44C: JUNE 30,2019
DESCRIPIT OF GOODS	45A:

1110PCS DOWN FILLED JACKET MODEL:115 AT USD 28. 50/PC

1110PCS DOWN FILLED JACKET MODEL:116 AT USD 30. 00/PC

CIFNAPLES,ITALY LESS 3% DISCOUNT

PACKED IN CARTONS AS PER S/C NO. 00GABP07

SHIPPING MARK: DIADORA/MOD: 115/116/NAPLES/CTN. NO. /MADE IN CHINA

DOCUMENTS REQUIRED   46A:

INSURANCE POLICY COVERING W. P. A. AND RISK OF SHORTAGE AND SRCC AS PER C. I. C. FOR 110 PCT OF INVOICE VALUE, CLAIMS, IF ANY,

PAYABLE AT THE PORT OF DESTINATION IN THE CURRENCY OF DRAFT.

ADDITIONAL COND. 47A:

L/C NO. SHOULD BE INDICATED IN ALL DOCUMENTS PRESENTED FOR NEGOTIATION

Other Information:

Down filled jacket packed in cartons of 222 cartons total.

G. W.:35KG/CTN   N. W.:33KG/CTN

M.:40X38X20CM/CTN

Port of Loading:SHENZHEN,CHINA

Port of Transshipment:SINGAPORE

Name of Vessel:GRACE V598/CONCORD

Date of B/L:JUNE 27,2019

Invoice No.:685

中保财产保险有限公司
The People's Insurance (Property) Company of China, Ltd
No. of Original, one

发票号码
Invoice No. 685

保险单号次
Policy No.

海 洋 货 物 运 输 保 险 单
MARINE CARGO TRANSPORTATION INSURANCE POLICY

Insured:(1)_____

中保财产保险有限公司(以下简称本公司)根据被保险人的要求,及其所缴付约定的保险费,按照本保险单承保险别和背面所载条款与下列条款承保下述货物运输保险,特签发本保险单。

This POLICY Of Insurance witnesses that The People's Insurance (Property) Company of China, Ltd. (hereinafter called "The Company"), at the request of the Insured and in consideration of the agreed premium paid by the Insured, undertakes to insure the undermentioned goods in transportation subject to the conditions of this Policy as per the Clauses printed overleaf and other special clauses attached hereon.

保险货物项目 Deserptions of Goods (2)_____	包装单位数量 Packing Unit Quantity (3)_____	保险金额 Amount Insured (4)_____

承保险别   货物标记
Conditions: Marks of Goods:

COVERING FOR 110% OF INVOICE VALUE AGAINST (5)_____

W. P. A. AND RISK OF SHORTAGE AND SRCC AS

PER AND SUBJECT TO THE OCEAN MARINE CARGO

Chapter 13 Insurance Policy

(continued)

CLAUSES OF THE PEOPLE'S INSURANCE COMPANY
OF CHINA DATED 1/1,1981.
总保险金额
Total Amount Insured: ____(6)_____

保　费　　　　　　　　运输工具　　　　　　　　　开航日期
Premium:__(7)____　　Per conveyance S. S. __(8)__　　Slg. On or abt. __(9)__
起运港　　　　　　　　目的港
From __(10)_____　　To　__(11)_____

所保货物,如发生本保险单项下可能引起索赔的损失或损坏,应立即通知本公司下述代理人查勘。如有索赔,应向本公司提交保险单正本(本保险单共有　份正本)及有关文件。如一份正本已用于索赔,其余正本则自动失效。
In the event of loss or damage which may result in a claim under this Policy, immediate notice must be given to the Company's Agent as mentioned hereunder. Claims, if any, one of the Original Policy which has been issued in Original(s) together with the relevant documents shall be surrendered to the Company. If one of the Original Policy has been accomplished, the others to be void.

中保财产保险有限公司
THE PEOPLE'S INSRURANCE(PROPERTY) COMPANY OF CHINA LTD.

赔付地点
Claim payable at　__(12)_____
日期　　　　　　　　　　　　在
Date __(13)_____　　at　__(14)_____
地址
Address

Ⅱ. **Make out an insurance policy according to the given information.**

常州食品国际贸易有限公司出口一批货物,从上海装船直达新加坡。价格术语为 CIF,货物名称为中国丝绸(Chinese Silk),毛重 35 吨,净重 34 吨,无唛头;保险金额为 9,000 美元,参照中国人民保险公司保险条款,投保一切险和战争险。装载货物的船名为 Sunflower,航次为 V.33,要求 2019 年 3 月 7 日前装运。(备注:合同号是 FS 1035,发票号是 FS2015)

人民大道 18 号　　　中国人民保险公司江苏省分公司
电话:05321267

Chapter 14
Packing List

Chapter 14 Packing List

Learning Objectives

- To master the general concepts and functions of packing documents.
- To learn how to make out a packing list according to the relevant documents.

14.1 Introduction

14.1.1 Definition

Packing documents refer to all documents which record or describe the packing conditions of the commodity. They are the supplements to the commercial invoice. According to the requirements of the importer, different kinds of packing documents are used, such as packing list, weight list, measurement list, packing declaration, etc. Packing list is the most frequently used one.

Packing list is an itemized list usually requested by the importer to confirm the name of commodity, specification, quantity, marks, number of packages, weight of the contents, the packing conditions, etc. There is no unified format or fixed contents for a packing list. Thus it is usually made according to the specific request of the importer and the kind of goods. In addition, packing list should not show the unit price or the total amount of goods.

14.1.2 Functions

(1) To make up the deficiency of an invoice.
(2) To enable the consignee to declare the goods at the Customs.
(3) To distinguish and check the goods when they arrive at the port of destination.
(4) To facilitate settling insurance claims in case of loss or damage.

14.2 Samples

Specimen 1

Issuer 出单方	PACKING LIST 装箱单	
To 收单方	Invoice No. 发票号码	Date 出单日期

(continued)

Marks 唛头	Number and kind of package Description of goods 包装种类和件数 货物描述	Qua. 数量	G. W. 毛重	N. W. 净重	Meas. 尺码

Total 小计
SAY TOTAL PACKAGES IN WORDS 包装件数大写

Specimen 2

A COMPANY
NO. 123 CHANGJIANG STREET, SHANGHAI, CHINA
TEL: 021-88888888
PACKING LIST

To: B COMPANY NO. 123-4 JALAN STREET, LONDON ENGLAND	INVOICE NO: XYZ0001 DATE: JUNE 12, 2010 S/C NO: SH12345 L/C NO: 00/1212-BC

SHIPPING MARKS
SH12345
B COMPANY
LONDON
C/NO. 1-230
FROM   SHANGHAI   TO   LONDON   BY   SEA

PACKAGES	DESCRIPTION	QUANTITY	G. W.	N. W.	MEASUREMENT
100 CTNS	GREAT CITY COLOR TELEVISION	@1SETS	@20KGS	@18KGS	@0.8*0.5*0.6M
TOTAL: 100CTNS		100SETS	2,000KGS	1,800KGS	24M³

SAY TOTAL PACKAGES IN WORDS:

A COMPANY
(SIGNATURE)

Chapter 14 Packing List

14.3 Composing Details

14.3.1 Name of the Packing Document/Packing List

The name of the packing document should be in strict accordance with that in the credit.

14.3.2 Name of the Issuer

The issuer is the exporter. The name and address of the exporter should be given in detail here. And it should be the same as that in the invoice.

14.3.3 To/Buyer's Name and Address

The name and address of the importer should be filled in here. And it should be the same as that in the invoice.

14.3.4 Invoice No.

The number of the invoice.

14.3.5 Issuing Date

The date of a packing list can be the same as the issuing date of invoice. The above four are the heading of a packing list.

14.3.6 Marks and No.

Marks refer to the shipping mark. It should be the same as that in the invoice and B/L.

14.3.7 Number and Kind of Packages, and Description of Goods

It includes the name, specification and kind of goods, the condition of packing, such as "30PCS/CTN", and the total number of packing as "100CTNS". And this part should be filled in according to the invoice. If goods are not packed, state "In bulk" here.

14.3.8 Quantity

When there is more than one kind of specifications of package, different specifications should be listed respectively and then the total quantity should be given.

14.3.9 G.W.

Gross weight of each package such as "@20kg/CTN".

14.3.10 N.W.

Net weight of each package.

14.3.11 Meas.

Measurement of each package.

14.3.12 Total

When there is more than one kind of commodity, the total gross weight, net weight, quantity, measurement and packages in figures should be given here.

14.3.13 Say Total

The total gross weight, net weight, quantity, measurement and packages in capitalized words should be given here. It should be in accordance with that in figures.

14.3.14 Signature of Issuer

This is the signature of the exporter. When a packing list is more than one page, each page should carry the same signature.

EXERCISES

◇Practice

Ⅰ. **Make out a Packing List according to the given information.**

L/C Information:

BANK OF CHINA, SINGAPORE

DATE: SEP. 20. 2019

FORM OF DOCUMENTARY CREDIT: INRREVOCABLE

CREDIT NO.: YN8812

ADVISING BANK: BANK OF CHINA, NANJING BRANCH

APPLICANT: A COMPANY, NO. 18 HONGKONG STREET, SINGAPORE

BENEFICIARY: B COMPANY, NO. 78 CHANGJIANG ROAD, NANJING, CHINA

AMOUNT: $98,500.00 (SAY US DOLLARS NINETY EIGHT THOUSAND FIVE HUNDRED ONLY)

EXPIRY DATE: DEC 15, 2019 IN THE COUNTRY OF BENEFICIARY.

DEAR SIR(S),

WE HEREBY ISSUE AN IRREVOCABLE DOCUMENT CREDIT IN YOUR

Chapter 14 Packing List

FAVOUR WHICH IS AVAILABLE BY NEGOTIATION OF YOUR DRAFT(S) AT SIGHT DRAWN ON US FOR FULL INVOICE VALUE BEARING THE CLAUSE "DRAWN UNDER BANK OF CHINA, SINGAPORE CREDIT NO. YN8812 DATED SEP. 20. 2019" ACCOMPANIED BY THE DOCUMENTS HEREIN.

DOCUMENTS:

(1) SIGNED COMMERCIAL INVOICE IN QUADRUPLICATE.

(2) FULL SET CLEAN ON BOARD OCEAN BILLS OF LADING IN TRIPLICATE MADE OUT TO THE ORDER OF BANK OF CHINA AND ENDORSED IN BLANK, NOTIFY APPLICANT AND MARKED FREIGHT PREPAID.

(3) PACKING LIST IN 3 COPIES.

(4) MARINE INSURANCE POLICY/CERTIFICATE, ENDORSED IN BLANK, FOR FULL CIF VALUE PLUS 10% STIPULATING CLAIMS PAYABLE IN SINGAPORE COVERING ALL RISKS AND WAR RISK AS PER C. I. C. OF PICC.

(5) CERTIFICATE OF ORIGIN FORM A CERTIFYING GOODS OF ORIGIN OF CHINA.

(6) BENEFICIARY'S CERTIFICATE CERTIFYING THAT NON-NEGOTIABLE COPY SHIPPING DOCUMENTS HAVE BEEN SENT DIRECTLY TO THE BUYER WITHIN 3 DAYS AFTER SHIPMENT.

EVIDENCING SHIPMENT OF:

CHINESE SILK SKIRT

NO. HY212   1,000CTNS $43.00/CTN CIF SINGAPORE

AS PER S/C NO. 2019AE016 DATED APR. 25, 2019

SHIPMENT: FROM CHINA TO SINGAPORE LATEST NOV. 30, 2019.

PARTIAL SHIPMENT: PROHIBITED

TRANSHIPMENT: ALLOWED

SPECIAL CONDITIONS:

(1) ALL BANK CHARGES ARE FOR ACCOUNT OF APPLICATE.

(2) COMBINED TRANSPORT B/L ACCEPTABLE.

INSTRUCTIONS TO NEGOTIATING BANK:

(1) ALL DOCUMENTS ARE TO BE FORWARDED TO US IN TWO SETS BY CONSECUTIVE REGISTERED AIRMAIL.

(2) SIGNED ORIGINAL BILLS OF LADING MUST BE FORWARDED TO US IN THE FIRST MAIL AND THE THIRD SIGNED ORIGINAL COPY TO BE FORWARDED IN THE SECOND MAIL.

THIS DOCUMENTARY CREDIT IS SUBJECT TO UCP600.

YOURS FAITHFULLY,
BANK OF CHINA, SINGAPORE
(AUTHORISED SIGNATURE)

Other Information:

Invoice No. : DY-N0023

Invoice Date: Nov. 10, 2011

Date of Shipment: Nov. 20, 2011

Ship No. : BBSID V. 2546

B/L No. : WFTY843270

Gross Weight: NO. HY212   1000CTNS   16kg/CTN

Net Weight: NO. HY212   1000CTNS   14kg/CTN

Package: 100 pieces per CTN

Measurement of Package: 70cm * 30cm * 50cm

SHIPPING MARK: NO MARK

REFERENCE NO. : TPWE02465

Issuer:		PACKING LIST			
To:		Invoice No. :		Date:	
Marks and Numbers	Number and kind of packages Description of goods	Quantity	G. W.	N. W.	Meas.
Total: SAY TOTAL PACKAGES IN WORDS:					(Signature)

Chapter 15
Certificate of Origin

Learning Objectives

• To master the general concepts and functions of Certificate of Origin.

• To learn how to make out a certificate of origin according to the relevant stipulations of L/C and other information.

15.1 Introduction

15.1.1 Definition

A certificate of origin(C/O, CO) is an independent document evidencing the origin of goods or manufacturer. It contains the description of goods, quantity, weight, value of goods shipped (only for applicant, it will not be indicated in the original official certificate) and the producing area.

15.1.2 Main Types of C/O

Two kinds of certificates of origin are generally adopted in our country.

One is non-preferential, which is issued by CIQ (China Exit and Entry Inspection and Quarantine Bureau) or CCPIT (The China Council for the Promotion of International Trade). These are also known as "ordinary certificates of origin" and they indicate that the shipped goods don't qualify for tariff-free or reduced tariff treatments under any trade agreements.

The other is preferential. It refers to Generalized System of Preference Certificate of Origin Form A (GSP Form A) which is issued by CIQ. GSP refers to the document evidencing the origin of goods or manufacturer issued by the beneficiary countries for goods exported to preference-giving countries.

15.1.3 Main Principles of GSP

1. Non-discriminatory Principle

All the developing countries should enjoy the preferential treatment without discrimination or exception.

2. Universal Principle

Developed countries should give generalized preferential import tariffs to all the manufactured and semi-manufactured goods of the developing countries.

Chapter 15 Certificate of Origin

3. On-reciprocal Principle

Developed countries should give special tariff concession to the developing countries unilaterally without demanding the same treatment from the developing countries.

15.1.4 Functions

(1) To determine the differential duty rate.

(2) To make sure where the goods come from.

(3) Important document for the exchange settlement.

15.2 Samples

Specimen 1   Certificate of Origin

1. Exporter: (name and address)	Certificate No. : CERTIFICATE OF ORIGIN OF THE PEOPLE'S REPUBLIC OF CHINA
2. Consignee: (name and address)	
3. Means of Transport and Route (as far as known): Departure Date: Vessel/Flight/Train/Vehicle No. : Port of Loading: Port of Discharge:	For Official Use Only
	4. Remarks:

5. Item No. (Max 20)	6. Marks, No. & Kind of Packages; Description of Goods	7. H. S. Code (Six Digit Code)	8. Quantity	9. No. & Date of Invoice	10. Invoice Value

(continued)

11. Declaration by the Exporter: The undersigned hereby declares that the above details and statements are correct, that all the goods were produced in _____ (Country) and that they comply with the origin requirements for the goods exported to _____ (Importing Country) .... Place & Date, Signature of Authorized Signatory.	12. Certification: It is hereby certified that the declaration by the exporter is correct. .... Place & Date, Signature and Stamp of Authorized Body.

Specimen 2 GSP Form A

ORIGINAL	
1. Exporter (full name and address)	Certificate No.: **GENERALIZED SYSTEM OF PREFERENCES CERTIFICATE OF ORIGIN** (Combined declaration and certificate) **FORM A** Issued by THE PEOPLE'S REPUBLIC OF CHINA
2. Consignee (full name and address, country)	
3. Means of Transport and Route (as far as known):	4. For Certifying Authority Use Only

5. Item No.	6. Marks & No. of Packages	7. No. & Kind of Packages; Description of Goods	8. Origin Criterion	9. Gross Weight Or Other Quantity	10. No. & Date of Invoice

Chapter 15 Certificate of Origin

(continued)

11. Certification It is hereby certified, on the basis of control carried out, that the declaration by the exporter is correct. Place & Date, Signature and Stamp of Certifying Authority.	12. Declaration by the Exporter The undersigned hereby declares that the above details and statements are correct; that all the goods were produced in _____ (country). and that they comply with the origin requirements specified for those goods in the Generalized System of Preferences for goods exported to _____ (Importing country). Place and Date, Signature and Stamp of Certifying Authority.

15.3 Composing Details

15.3.1 Certificate of Origin (C/O)

It should indicate "original" on the original certificate and is always printed.

1. Certificate No.

Serial number of a certificate of origin is assigned by the authorized body.

2. Exporter

State the full legal name and address (including country) of the exporter. If the goods is transshipped, the word "via" is added to the exporter. For example,

A Corp.

8 Huaihai Road, Beijing, China

Via Hong Kong Co., Ltd.

33 Guangdong Road, Hong Kong

3. Producer

State the full legal name and address (including country) of the producer. If goods from more than one producer are included in the certificate, list the additional producers, including their full legal name and address (including country). If the exporter or the producer wishes to maintain this information as confidential, it is acceptable to state "Available to the authorized body upon request". If the producer and the exporter are the same, please state "SAME". If the producer is unknown, it is acceptable to state "UNKNOWN".

4. Consignee

State the full legal name and address (including country) of the consignee.

5. Means of Transport and Route

Complete the means of transport and route and specify the departure date, transport vehicle No., port of loading and port of discharge. If transshipment is allowed, the place of transshipment should be marked. The following is an example: FROM DALIAN TO ROTTERDAM VIA HONG KONG BY VESSEL.

6. For Certifying Authority Use Only

It is usually kept in blank. The content is made out by the issuing organization according to the concrete condition.

7. Remarks

Any additional information such as Customer's Order Number, Letter of Credit Number, etc., may be included. In the case where the goods are invoiced by a non-Party operator, the full legal name of the non-Party operator and the producer of the goods shall be indicated in this box.

8. Item Number

State the item number, and the number of items should not exceed 20.

9. Marks, Number and Kind of Packages/Description of Goods

Marks, number and kind of packages shall be specified and in accordance with that in the invoice and B/L.

Provide a full description of each goods. The phrase "As per invoice NO. XXX" or "As per B/L NO. XXX" are not allowed. N/M is filled in while there is no mark.

The description should be sufficiently detailed to enable the goods to be identified by the Customs Officers to examine them and relate it to the invoice description and to the HS description of the goods. If goods are not packed, state "In bulk". When the description of the goods is finished, add " *** " (three stars).

10. H. S. Code

For each goods described in Box 7, Specimen 1, identify the H. S. (The Harmonization System Code) tariff classification to six digits.

11. Weight, Quantity or Other Measures

Gross weight in kilos should be shown here. Other units of measurement, e. g., volume or number of items which would indicate exact quantities may be used when customary.

12. Number and Date of Invoice

Number and date of invoice should be shown here. In the case where the Goods are invoiced by a non-Party operator and the number and date of the commercial invoice are unknown, the number and date of original commercial invoice, issued in the exporting Party, shall be indicated in this box.

13. Invoice Value

Invoice value should be shown here. In the case where the goods are invoiced by a non-Party operator and the invoice value is unknown, the invoice value of the original commercial invoice shall be indicated in this box.

14. Declaration by the Exporter

This box shall be completed, signed and dated by the exporter. The issuing place and date are usually printed here. The date is no later than the date of B/L and no earlier than the date of invoice.

15. Certification

This box shall be completed, hand-signed, dated and stamped by the authorized body. The date should not be earlier than that in the invoice and applying date. The issuer should sign manually with seal.

15.3.2 Generalized System of Preference Certificate of Origin Form A (GSP Form A)

1. Goods Consigned From

The detailed address of the exporter must be made out here.

2. Goods Consigned To

The detailed name and address of the consignee in the preferential giving country, the name of the country is needed here.

3. Means of Transport and Route

Port of departure, destination and means of transport, port of transshipment must be pointed out if any.

4. For Official Use

It is usually kept in blank.

If the goods have been exported already, "ISSUED RETROSPECTIVELY" is printed in red. If the certificate is lost or stolen, "THIS CERTIFICATE IS IN REPLACEMENT OF CERTIFICATE OF ORIGIN NO... DATED... WHICH IS CANCELLED" in red is marked.

5. Item Number

If the same lot has different varieties, "1" "2" "3"... are marked according to the varieties. If there is only one lot, "1" is marked.

6. Marks and Numbers of Packages

They are the same as that in the C/O.

7. Number and Kind of Package, Description of Goods

They are the same as that in the C/O.

8. Origin Criterion

This part is the core content of the certification. The exporter must indicate here the origin criteria on the basis of which he claims that the goods qualify for preferential tariff treatment, in the manner shown in the following table:

原产地标准		本栏填写
完全原产品,不含任何非原产成分,出口到所有给惠国。		P
含有非原产成分	非原产成分的价值未超过产品出厂价的40%,出口到加拿大	F
	非原产成分的价值未超过产品离岸价的40%,出口到欧盟国家、挪威、日本、瑞士	W,其后加上出口产品的 H.S. 品目号
	非原产成分的价值未超过产品离岸价的50%,出口到俄罗斯、白俄罗斯、哈萨克斯坦、乌克兰、捷克、斯洛伐克	Y,其后加上非原产成分价值占该产品离岸价格的百分比
	出口到澳大利亚、新西兰	此栏可留空

9. Gross Weight or Other Quantity

It is the same as that in the C/O.

10. Number and Date of Invoice

Chapter 15 Certificate of Origin

It is the same as that in the C/O.

11. Certification

This box shall be completed, manually-signed and dated by the exporter. The issuing place and date are usually printed here. The date is no later than the date of B/L and no earlier than the date of invoice.

12. Declaration by the Exporter

Except that mentioned in column NO. 14 in certificate of origin, name of the original country and importing country should be marked in corresponding place in this column.

EXERCISES

◇Practice

Ⅰ. Make out a GSP Form A according to the given information.

L/C Information:
BANK OF CHINA, VANCOUVER BRANCH
DATE: SEP. 20, 2019
FORM OF DOCUMENTARY CREDIT: INRREVOCABLE
CREDIT NO. : YN8812
ADVISING BANK: BANK OF CHINA, NANJING BRANCH
APPLICANT: A COMPANY, 1021 DUNSMUIR STREET, VANCOUVER, B. C. , CANADA
BENEFICIARY: B COMPANY, NO. 78 CHANGJIANG ROAD, NANJING, CHINA
AMOUNT: $98,500.00 (SAY US DOLLARS NINETY EIGHT THOUSAND FIVE HUNDRED ONLY)
EXPIRY DATE: DEC. 15, 2019 IN THE COUNTRY OF BENEFICIARY.
DEAR SIR(S),
WE HEREBY ISSUE AN IRREVOCABLE DOCUMENT CREDIT IN YOUR FAVOUR WHICH IS AVAILABLE BY NEGOTIATION OF YOUR DRAFT(S) AT SIGHT DRAWN ON US FOR FULL INVOICE VALUE BEARING THE CLAUSE "DRAWN UNDER BANK OF CHINA, VANCOUVER BRANCH CREDIT NO. YN8812 DATED SEP. 20, 2019" ACCOMPANIED BY THE DOCUMENTS HEREIN.

DOCUMENTS:

1. SIGNED COMMERCIAL INVOICE IN QUADRUPLICATE.

2. FULL SET CLEAN ON BOARD OCEAN BILLS OF LADING IN TRIPLICATE MADE OUT TO THE ORDER OF BANK OF CHINA AND ENDORSED IN BLANK, NOTIFY APPLICANT AND MARKED FREIGHT PREPAID.

3. PACKING LIST IN 3 COPIES.

4. MARINE INSURANCE POLICY/CERTIFICATE, ENDORSED IN BLANK, FOR FULL CIF VALUE PLUS 10% STIPULATING CLAIMS PAYABLE IN CANADA COVERING ALL RISKS AND WAR RISK AS PER C.I.C. OF PICC.

5. CERTIFICATE OF ORIGIN FORM A CERTIFYING GOODS OF ORIGIN OF CHINA.

6. BENEFICIARY'S CERTIFICATE CERTIFYING THAT NON-NEGOTIABLE COPY SHIPPING DOCUMENTS HAVE BEEN SENT DIRECTLY TO THE BUYER WITHIN 3 DAYS AFTER SHIPMENT.

EVIDENCING SHIPMENT OF:

CHINESE SILK SKIRT

NO. HY212   1000CTNS   USD43.00/CTN CIFVANCOUVER

AS PER S/C NO. 2011AE016 DATED APR. 25, 2019

SHIPMENT: FROMSHANGHAI, CHINA TO VANCOUVER, CANADA LATEST NOV. 30, 2019.

PARTIAL SHIPMENT: PROHIBITED

TRANSSHIPMENT: ALLOWED

SPECIAL CONDITIONS:

ALL BANK CHARGES ARE FOR ACCOUNT OF APPLICATE.

COMBINED TRANSPORT B/L ACCEPTABLE.

INSTRUCTIONS TO NEGOTIATING BANK:

1. ALL DOCUMENTS ARE TO BE FORWARDED TO US IN TWO SETS BY CONSECUTIVE REGISTERED AIRMAIL.

2. SIGNED ORIGINAL BILLS OF LADING MUST BE FORWARDED TO US IN THE FIRST MAIL AND THE THIRD SIGNED ORIGINAL COPY TO BE FORWARDED IN THE SECOND MAIL.

Chapter 15 Certificate of Origin

THIS DOCUMENTARY CREDIT IS SUBJECT TO UCP600.

YOURS FAITHFULLY,

BANK OF CHINA, VANCOUVER BRANCH

(AUTHORISED SIGNATURE)

Other Information:

Invoice NO. : DY-N0023

Invoice Date: Nov. 10, 2019

Date of Shipment: Nov. 20, 2019

Ship NO. : BBSID V. 2546

B/L NO. : WFTY843270

Gross Weight: NO. HY212   1,000CTNS   16kg/CTN

Net Weight: NO. HY212   1,000CTNS   14kg/CTN

Measurement of Package: 70cm * 30cm * 50cm

SHIPPING MARK: NO MARK

REFERENCE NO. : TIYE02465

Date of GSP C/O: Nov. 15, 2019

	ORIGINAL	
1. Goods consigned from:	Certificate No. : GENERALIZED SYSTEM OF PREFERENCE CERTIFICATE OF ORIGIN (Combined declaration and certificate) FORM A Issued by THE PEOPLE'S REPUBLIC OF CHINA	
2. Goods consigned to:		
3. Means of transport and route:	4. For official use only	
5. Item No.	6. Marks & No. of packages	7. No. & kind of packages; Description of goods	8. Origin Criterion	9. Gross Weight or other quantity	10. No. & Date of Invoice

(continued)

11. Certification It is hereby certified, on the basis of control carried out, that the declaration by the exporter is correct. _____ .... Place and date, signature and stamp of certifying authority.	12. Declaration by the Exporter The undersigned hereby declares that the above details and statements are correct; that all the goods were produced in _____ (country) and that they comply with the origin requirements specified for those goods in the Generalized System of Preferences for goods exported to _____ (Importing country). .... Place and date, signature and stamp of authorized signatory.

Chapter 16
Other Bills and Documents

Learning Objectives
- To get acquainted with other bills and documents frequently used in transactions.
- To learn the online execution of such bills or documents.

Bills or documents in international trade are by no means confined to the ones in the preceding chapters, which are only some examples concerning certain procedures in the whole course of a transaction. As the scope of business activities in trade is wide and the matters dealt with often differ from each other, there are bills or documents which do not fall under the main categories mentioned before in this book. However, they concern business dealings all the same and the attention paid to them is certain to be worthwhile.

16.1 Inspection Certificate

16.1.1 Introduction

The purpose of inspection, in international trade, is to ensure that the goods are in accordance with the relative laws and decrees of the country. An inspection certificate is a document certifying the result of commodity inspection(quality, quantity, packing and quarantine, etc.) issued by an inspection institution. Inspection certificate is not a basic document in international settlement, but if it does not conform to the terms and conditions of the L/C or the stipulations of the contract, the relevant bank has the right to dishonor the draft or and the buyer may lodge a claim.

Internationally, import and export commodity inspections are executed by a third party generally known as surveyor. Some of the surveyors are governmental institutions while others are run by individuals or trade associations. In our country, the China Exit and Entry Inspection and Quarantine Bureau (CIQ) and China Certification & Inspection (Group) Co. Ltd (CCIC) are the main governmental institutions. The inspection certificates they issue are:

1. Inspection Certificate of Quality.

2. Inspection Certificate of Quantity/Weight.

3. Certificate of Value.

Chapter 16 Other Bills and Documents

4. Certificate of Origin.

5. Certificate of Health.

6. Disinfection Inspection Certificate, etc.

16.1.2 Samples

Sample 1   Application for Export Inspection

中华人民共和国出入境检验检疫

出境货物报检单

报检单位(加盖公章)_____   编号:_____   报检单位登记号:_____

联系人:_____   电话:_____   报检日期:_____

发货人	(中文)	池州 *** 有限责任公司					
	(外文)						
收货人	(中文)						
	(外文)						
货物名称 (中/外文)	H.S编码	产地	数/重量	货物总值	包装各类及数量		
轴承 BEARING	8482100000	池州	15000PCS /990KGS (净重)	157,500 USD	出口纸箱 150(纸箱)		
运输工具 名称号码	海运集装箱		贸易方式	一般贸易	货物存 放地点	XX公司仓库	
合同号	99SC1860056		信用证号	T/T	用途		
发货日期	2010.11.30		输往国家 (地区)	USA	许可证/ 审批号	××××××	
启运地	SHANGHAI		到达口岸	NEW YORK	生产单位 注册号	3******18	
集装箱规格、数量及号码				40'×1			
合同、信用证订立的检验 检疫条款或特殊要求			标记及号码		随附单据(划"√"或补填)		
GB/T307.3-96 SN/T0234-93 需要电子转单 (电子监管)			GBC NEW YORK LOT NO. NB1230 PL7#1-24 MADE IN CHINA		☑合同 信用证 ☑发票 换证凭单 ☑装箱单 ☑厂检单	☑包装性能结果单 许可/审批文件 ☐ ☐ ☐ ☐	
需要证单名称(划"√"或补填)					检验检疫费		

(continued)

		总金额 （人民币）	本局填写
品质证书_正_副 重量证书_正_副 数量证书_正_副 兽医卫生证书_正_副 健康证书_正_副 卫生证书_正_副 动物卫生证书_正_副	□植物检疫证书 _正_副 □熏蒸/消毒证书 _正_副 □出境货物通关单①或 ☑出境货物换证凭单② □ □ □	计费人	本局填写
		收费人	本局填写
报检人郑重证明： 1.本人被授权报检。 2.上列填写内容正确属实，货物无伪造或冒用他人的厂名、标志、认证标志。并承担货物质量责任。 签名：_____		领　取　证　单	
		日期	_____
		签名	_____

注：(1)有"___"的内容由报检单位填写或盖章；

(2)有"□"的内容根据实际情况打"√"；

(3)货物总值，应根据需要不同的单证内容，选择"欧元"或"美元"等外币金额；

(4)所需单证：①宁波口岸出运应选取通关单；②其他口岸出运应选取换证凭单。

Sample 2　Inspection Certificate of Quality

中华人民共和国出入境检验检疫

ENTRY-EXIT INSPECTION AND QUARANTINE

OF THE PEOPLE'S REPUBLIC OF CHINA

品质检验证书

INSPECTION CERTIFICATE of QUALITY

编号 No.：

发货人

Consignor _____

收货人

Consignee _____

标记及号码 Mark & No.	品名 Description of Goods

Chapter 16 Other Bills and Documents

报检数量/重量
Quantity/Weight Declared _____

包装种类及数量
Number and Type of Packages _____

运输工具
Means of Conveyance _____

RESULTS OF INSPECTION:

印章

签证地点 Place of Issue   SHENZHEN, CHINA

签证日期 Date of Issue _____

Official Stamp

授权签字人 Authorized Officer _____   签 名 Signature _____

Sample 3 Customs Clearance of Exit Commodities

中华人民共和国出入境检验检疫 出境货物通关单			
			编号:
1. 发货人 ZHEJIANG GARMENTS IMP./EXP. CORP.			5. 标记及号码 A. V. NEW YORK MADE IN CHINA
2. 收货人 NEW YORK TRADING COMPANY			
3. 合同/信用证号 06－234/609/23262		4. 输往国家或地区 THE USA	
6. 运输工具名称及号码 MARIE V. 275		7. 发货日期 AUGUST 30, 2018	8. 集装箱规格及数量 1 * 20'
9. 货物名称及规格	10. H. S. 编码	11. 申报总值	12. 数/重量、包装数量及种类
LADIES' SILK BLOUSES	621200	$52,000.00	1,000 DOZ 500 CTNS

179

(continued)

13. 证明	
上述货物业经检验检疫，请海关予以放行。	
本通关单有效期至　　2018 年 10 月 25 日	
签字：	日期：2018 年 8 月 25 日
14. 备注	

16.1.3 Composing Details

Inspection certificates vary in terms of what nature the document certifies and which country issues. The following contents are generally included:

1. Name of the Certificate; Name and Place of the Issuing Party

Name of the certificate shall be in strict conformity with the contract and/or the credit stipulations. The exporter has the right to decide the issuing party unless otherwise specified in the relevant L/C.

2. Name and Address of the Consignor

It is usually the name and address of the exporter, which should conform to the contract and/or the credit stipulations.

3. Name and Address of the Consignee

It is usually the name and address of the importer, which should conform to the contract and/or the credit stipulations.

4. Item Names

Items like name of commodity, quantity, weight, packages, and marks shall be in accordance with the commercial invoice and the bill of lading.

5. Results

Results, which are the most important part in the certificate, describe the status of the goods inspected.

6. Date

Date of issuance shall not be late than the date of the B/L.

Chapter 16 Other Bills and Documents

7. Signature and Seal

Seal, in most cases, is as effective as signature. However, some countries stresses the uttermost importance of a signature.

When composing, please pay special attention to the following details: (1) name and address of the exporter; (2) name of the inspection certificate; (3) the invoice number; (4) date of inspection no later than that of the bill of lading; (5) description of goods; (6) marks (N/M if there are no marks); (7) quantity; (8) gross/net weight; (9) inspection results in detail; (10) signature.

16.2 Export License

16.2.1 Introduction

Import and export license system belongs to the non-tariff barrier in international trade. The government stipulates that the importer or exporter has to get the license before the special goods are imported or exported in order to maintain his own country's benefit. Licenses are no longer required for most export products now, but some import products need it. Exporters apply for an export license through the Ministry of Commerce of the People's Republic of China (MOFCOM) or its branches. The customs officer will not let the goods pass if there is no license. It is a system to control the foreign trade and a warrant for customs to release the goods.

16.2.2 Samples

Sample 1　Application for Export Goods

中华人民共和国出口许可证申请表

1. 出口商： 领证人姓名：	代码： 电话：	3. 出口许可证号：
2. 发货人：	代码：	4. 出口许可证有效截止日期： 　　　　年　　月　　日
5. 贸易方式：		8. 进口国(地区)：
6. 合同号：		9. 付款方式：

(continued)

7.报关口岸:			10.运输方式:		
11.商品名称:			商品编码:		
12.规格、等级	13.单位	14.数量	15.单价(币别)	16.总值(币别)	17.总值折美元
18.总计					
19.备 注 申请单位盖章 申领日期:			20.签证机构审批(初审): 经办人: 终审:		

填表说明:(1)本表应用正楷逐项填写清楚,不得涂改、遗漏,否则无效;

(2)本表内容需打印多份许可证的,请在备注栏内注明;

(3)本表填写一式二份。

Sample 2 Export License

中华人民共和国出口许可证

EXPORT LICENCE OF THE PEOPLE'S REPUBLIC OF CHINA

No. 0000000

1.出口商: Exporter	3.出口许可证号: Export licence No.
2.发货人: Consignor	4.出口许可证有效截止日期: Export licence expiry date
5.贸易方式: Terms of trade	8.出口最终目的国(地区): Country/Region of purchase
6.合同号: Contract No.	9.付款方式: Payment
7.报关口岸: Place of clearance	10.运输方式: Mode of transport
11.商品名称: Description of goods	商品编码: Code of goods

(continued)

12. 规格、等级 Specification	13. 单位 Unit	14. 数量 Quantity	15. 单价 Unit price	16. 总值 Amount	17. 总值折美元 Amount in USD
18. 总计 Total					
19. 备　注： Supplementary details 输欧或输美许可证号： 类别号：			20. 发证机关盖章： Issuing authority's stamp 21. 发证日期： Licence date		

16.2.3 Composing Details

(1) Exporter: the seller(s) in the contract.

(2) Consignor: the party who performs the consignment and the clearance.

(3) Export licence number: year ＋ code of the issuing authority ＋ sequence number from the computer system.

(4) Expiry date: automatically generated.

(5) Terms of trade: nature of the export transaction, such as general trade, processing, donation, etc.

(6) Contract number: 17 letters, same number with the one applying for export permit.

(7) Place of clearance: port of export.

(8) Country/region of purchase: the sole destination stipulated in the contract. Name of region such as the EU is not acceptable.

(9) Payment: one from such terms of payment as L/C, collection, remittance.

(10) Mode of transport: by sea, by rail, by road or by air.

(11) Description of goods and code of goods: name of the goods automatically generated when entering the code from the latest Catalogue of Goods Under Export Licence Management.

(12) Specification: no more than 4 grades under the same commodity code. If there are more than four, another export licence should be applied.

(13) Unit: unit when measured.

(14) Quantity: if the measurement is "lot", quantity is marked "1".

(15) Unit price: if the measurement is "1", unit price here should read the total amount.

16.3　Customs Declaration

16.3.1　Introduction

The exporter has to apply for declaration of the commodity to the customs before the shipment. The customs officer will release the customs declaration if the goods are up to the requirements. The person who asks for declaration is required to be qualified, that is to say, he should have the certificate of customs declaration. The examination is held by the General Administration of Customs of PRC.

The customs declaration is in different colors, for example: the white one is made out for general trade and the pink one is used for processing trade. The contents of these documents are similar.

16.3.2　Sample

中华人民共和国海关出口货物报关单

预录入编号：　　　　　　　　　　　　　　　海关编号：

出口口岸		备案号		出口日期		申报日期	
经营单位		运输方式		运输工具名称		提运单号	
发货单位		贸易方式		征免性质		结汇方式	
许可证号		运抵国（地区）		指运港		境内货源地	
批准文号		成交方式		运费		保费		杂费	
合同协议号		件数		包装种类		毛重（千克）		净重（千克）	
集装箱号		随附单据				生产厂家	
标记唛码及备注							
项号	商品编码	商品名称、规格型号	数量及单位	最终目的国（地区）	单价	总价	币制	征免

(continued)

税费征收情况		
录入员 录入单位	兹证明以上申报无讹并承 担法律责任	海关审单批注放行日期(签章)
		审单　　　　　审价
		征税　　　　　统计
报关员		查验　　　　　放行
单位地址	申报单位(签章)	
邮编　　　电话	填制日期	

16.3.3 Composing Details

Composing a customs declaration can be very complicated and the corresponding rules abound. Therefore, just a few details are listed below. For more information, please refer to *Specifications on Completion of the PRC Customs Declaration Form for Imports and Exports*.

(1) Our customs declaration must be applied in Chinese according to the law.

(2) Pre-entry code is different from the customs code.

(3) Date: a date should read in the following order: **** (year) ** (month) ** (date)

(4) Packages: the actual number of packages; the number of containers, or the number of plates for special packing; "1" instead of "0" for nude packing.

(5) Gross weight (kg): the weight of goods and their packages; "1" for the gross weight less than one kilogram.

(6) Net weight (kg): the weight of goods; "1" for the weight less than one kilogram.

(7) Documents attached: the bills or documents sent to the customs together with

the customs declaration. Documents attached, in the declaration does not include contract, invoice, packing list, export/import permit.

(8) Commodity and its specifications: type in for 2 lines, one for name of the goods in Chinese, the other for specifications. All the information should comply with what stated in the commercial invoice.

EXERCISES

◇ **Practice**

Ⅰ. **Make out an application for export inspection according to the following conditions.**

CHIZHOU FOREIGN TRADE CO. LTD (CUSTOMS' CODE: 1234567890, ADD: EAST JIANSHE ROAD, CHIZHOU, ANHUI 247000 PRC, TEL: 2218000) IS READY TO EXPORT MEN'S SHIRTS (H. S. 000000) TO JAPAN FROM SHANGHAI ON MAY 18, 2019. THE RELATIVE INFORMATION IS GIVEN BELOW:

GW: 2MTS, NW: 1. 6 MTS, 160 CARTONS

CHAPTER PRICE: USD1,000/MT CFR KOBE

VESSEL NAME: JIUHUA VOY. 1

B/L NO. : C070808

PAYMENT: L/C

FREIGHT: USD1,150

CONTRACT NO. : 08196

CONTAINER NO. : CZ123

ORIGIN: CHIZHOU

(No need to fill the blanks where the relative information has not been given.)

出境货物报检单

报检单位(加盖公章)_____   编号:_____   报检单位登记号:_____

联系人:_____   电话:_____   报检日期:_____

发货人	(中文)
	(外文)

(continued)

收货人	(中文)					
	(外文)					
货物名称(中/外文)		H.S编码	产地	数/重量	货物总值	包装各类及数量
运输工具名称号码				贸易方式		货物存放地点
合同号				信用证号		用途
发货日期		输往国家(地区)			许可证/审批号	
启运地		到达口岸			生产单位注册号	
集装箱规格、数量及号码						
合同、信用证订立的检验检疫条款或特殊要求		标 记 及 号 码		随附单据(划"√"或补填)		
				☑合同 信用证 ☑发票 换证凭单 ☑装箱单 ☑厂检单	☑包装性能结果单 许可/审批文件 ☐ ☐ ☐ ☐	
需要证单名称(划"√"或补填)				检验检疫费		
品质证书_正_副 重量证书_正_副 数量证书_正_副 兽医卫生证书_正_副 健康证书_正_副 卫生证书_正_副 动物卫生证书_正_副		☐植物检疫证书_正_副 熏蒸/消毒证书_正_副 ☐出境货物通关单①或 ☑出境货物换证凭单② ☐ ☐ ☐		总金额(人民币)	本局填写	
				计费人	本局填写	
				收费人	本局填写	
报检人郑重证明: 1.本人被授权报检。 2.上列填写内容正确属实,货物无伪造或冒用他人的厂名、标志、认证标志。并承担货物质量责任。 签名:				领 取 证 单		
				日期		
				签名		

Ⅱ. Make out an Application for Export Goods according to the following commercial invoice.

安徽机械进出口公司

ANHUI MACHINERY IMPORT & EXPORT CORP.

103, CHANGJIANG ROAD, HEFEI CHINA

INVOICE

TO: HML INDUSTRIAL CO., LTD. 5-1,1-KA, DANGSAN-DONG, YOUNGDEUNGPO-KU, SEOUL, KOREA			INVOICE NO.: AMIE00I66	
			DATE: OCT. 24, 2019	
			S/C NO.: 00SAMI-C065HF	
			L/C NO.: H07U4908ES608	
FROM: TO:				
Marks & Number	Description	Quantity	Unit Price	Amount
N/M	BEARINGS COUNTRY OF ORIGIN CHINA	3,000 KGS	CIF BUSAN PORT, KOREA $30.00/KG	$90,000.00
			TOTAL: $90,000.00	
SAY US DOLLARS NINETY THOUSAND ONLY. TOTAL PACKED IN 200 IRON DRUMS. TOTAL G.W. 3,350 KGS. PAYBLE BY DRAFT AT SIGHT				

中华人民共和国出口许可证申请表

1. 出口商： 代码： 领证人姓名： 电话：	3. 出口许可证号：

（continued）

2. 发货人： 代码：	4. 出口许可证有效截止日期： 年　月　日
5. 贸易方式：	8. 进口国（地区）：
6. 合同号：	9. 付款方式：
7. 报关口岸：	10. 运输方式：

11. 商品名称：　　　　　　　　　　　　　　商品编码：

12. 规格、等级	13. 单位	14. 数量	15. 单价(币别)	16. 总值(币别)	17. 总值折美元
18. 总计					

19. 备　注 申请单位盖章 申领日期：	20. 签证机构审批（初审）： 经办人： 终审：

　　填表说明：(1)本表应用正楷逐项填写清楚，不得涂改、遗漏，否则无效；
　　　　　　(2)本表内容需打印多份许可证的,请在备注栏内注明；
　　　　　　(3)本表填写一式二份。

Part Ⅲ
Practical Training

Part II
Practical Training

Chapter 17
Simulative Training

Learning Objectives

- To understand the whole process of foreign trade.
- To practice the writing of correspondence and the making of documents involved in different stages of foreign trade.

17.1　Simulative Training Ⅰ

17.1.1　Background Information

1. Exporter: Dongguan Little Star Foreign Trade Co., Ltd.

Founded in September 2000, Dongguan Little Star Foreign Trade Co., Ltd. is a privately owned company with import and export rights. It specializes in the production and marketing of a wide range of high-quality clothes for children.

2. Importer: Canadian Hansen Trading Co., Ltd.

Canadian Hansen Trading Co., Ltd. is a newly founded Canadian company. It wants to import some pure cotton children's T-shirts from China to satisfy the needs of local market.

Please choose the role of either the exporter or the importer, and work with a partner to complete the following tasks in sequence. Exchange roles with your partner and practice again.

17.1.2　Tasks for the Exporter

TASK 1: Write a letter of establishment of business relations and try to market your products to the Importer.

TASK 3: Write a letter of firm offer to the Importer based on their enquiry letter.

TASK 5: Write a letter of counter-counter-offer.

TASK 7: Writer a letter of urging the establishment of L/C.

17.1.3　Tasks for the Importer

TASK 2: Writer a letter in reply with a specific enquiry to the Exporter.

TASK 4: Write a counter-offer.

TASK 6: Writer a letter of acceptance, enclosing a Purchase Contract with relevant information.

TASK 8: Writer a letter of urging shipment after the establishment of L/C.

Chapter 17 Simulative Training

17.2 Simulative Training II

17.2.1 Background Information

Dongguan Little Star Foreign Trade Co., Ltd. signed a contract with Canadian Hansen Trading Co., Ltd. on the export of pure cotton children's T-shirts on April 5, 2020 (Contract No. LS040501). On April 20, 2020, Dongguan Little Star Foreign Trade Co., Ltd. received an irrevocable letter of credit issued by Bank of Montreal, Toronto. Please make a complete set of export documents according to the following background materials (Sales Contract, Letter of Credit and other information).

1. Sales Contract

SALES CONTRACT

Contract No.: LS040501

Date: April 5, 2020

Signed at: Guangzhou, China

The Seller: Dongguan Little Star Foreign Trade Co., Ltd.
Address: #105, Guantai Road, Dongguan, Guangdong, China
The Buyer: Canadian Hansen Trading Co., Ltd.
Address: #22, Pigott Road, Vancouver, Canada

This contract is made by and between the Seller and Buyer, whereby the seller agrees to sell and the buyer agrees to buy the under-mentioned commodity according to the terms and conditions stipulated below:

Commodity and Specifications	Quantity	Unit Price	Amount
Pure Cotton Children's T-shirts		CIF TORONTO	
ART NO. 001	2,000	$30/PC	$60,000.00
ART NO. 002	5,000	$15/PC	$75,000.00
ART NO. 003	5,000	$18/PC	$90,000.00
Total	12,000		$225,000.00
Total Amount: SAY USD TWO HUNDRED AND TWENTY FIVE THOUSAND ONLY			

Packing: In polybag of one piece each, then 100 pieces to a carton
Time of Shipment: Before June 30, 2020
Place of Loading and Destination: From Dongguan Port, China to Toronto, Canada

Shipping marks: CHT
  LS040501
    Toronto
     1-120

INSURANCE: To be effected by the sellers for 110% of invoice value covering All Risks and War Risk as per ocean marine cargo clauses of PICC dated Jan. 01,1981.

TERMS OF PAYMENT: The Buyers shall open through a bank acceptable to the sellers an irrevocable letter of credit to reach the Sellers on or before April 30,2020, valid for negotiation in China until 15 days after the month of shipment.

INSPECTION: This contract is made in two original copies and become valid after signature, one copy to be held by each party.

The Seller: Dongguan Little Star Foreign Trade Co., Ltd.
The Buyer: Canadian Hansen Trading Co., Ltd.

2. Letter of Credit

Type of Documentary Credit	40A	IRREVOCABLE
Letter of Credit Number	20	20200411
Date of Issue	31C	200420
Date and Place of Expiry	31D	200730 IN CHINA
Issuing Bank	51D	BANK OF MONTREAL, TORONTO
Applicant	50	CANADIAN HANSEN TRADING CO., LTD. #22, PIGOTT ROAD, VANCOUVER, CANADA
Beneficiary	59	DONGGUAN LITTLE STAR FOREIGN TRADE CO., LTD. #105, GUANTAI ROAD, DONGGUAN, GUANGDONG, CHINA
Currency Code, Amount	32B	CURRENCY USD AMOUNT 225,000.00
Available with... by...	41D	ANY BANK BY NEGOTIATION
Drafts at	42C	AT SIGHT
Drawee	42D	BANK OF MONTREAL, TORONTO
Partial Shipments	43P	NOT ALLOWED
Transshipment	43T	NOT ALLOWED

(continued)

Loading on Board	44A	DONGGUAN, CHINA
For Transportation To	44B	TORONTO, CANADA
Latest Date of Shipment	44C	200630
Description of Goods or Services	45B	PURE COTTON CHILDREN'S T-SHIRTS ART NO. 001 2,000PCS $30/PC ART NO. 002 5,000PCS $15/PC ART NO. 003 5,000PCS $18/PC CIF TORONTO

Documents Required: 46
1. SIGNED COMMERCIAL INVOICE IN TRIPLICATE
2. PACKING LIST IN TRIPLICATE SHOWING NUMBER OF CARTONS, GROSS WEIGHT, NET WEIGHT AND MEASUREMENT.
3. FULL SET OF CLEAN ON BOARD OCEAN BILLS OF LADING ISSUED TO ORDER AND BLANK ENDORSED MARKED "FREIGHT PREPAID" NOTIFYING APPLICANT.
4. INSURANCE POLICY OR CERTIFICATE IN TWO ORIGINALS FOR 110 PCT OF INVOICE VALUE WITH CLAIMS PAYABLE AT DESTINATION IN CURRENCY OF DRAFT COVERING ALL RISKS AND WAR RISK AS PER OCEAN MARINE CARGO CLAUSES OF PICC DATED 1981/01/01.
5. GSP FORM A.

ADDITIONAL INSTRUCTIONS	47A	
Charges	71B	ALL BANKING CHARGES OUTSIDE THE OPENING BANK ARE FOR BENEFICIARY'S ACCOUNT.
Period for Presentation	48	DOCUMENTS MUST BE PRESENTED WITHIN 15 DAYS AFTER THE DATE OF ISSUANCE OF THE TRANSPORT DOCUMENTS BUT WITHIN THE VALIDITY OF THE CREDIT.
Confirmation Instructions	49	WITHOUT

3. Other Information

    Invoice No.: LS 0430; Date of invoice: April 30, 2020; Gross weight of each carton:

12KGS; Net weight of each carton: 11KGS; Measurement of each carton: 0.22CBM; Time of shipment: June 12, 2020; Vessel name: PRINCE; Container No.: TEXU323; Seal No.: 356271; B/L No.: PT24310.

17.2.2 Tasks

1. Commercial Invoice

COMMERCIAL INVOICE				
TO:		Invoice No.: Date: Contract No.: L/C No.:			
Transport Detail FROM		TO			
Marks & No.	Description of Goods	Quantity	Unit Price	Amount
		Total:		
Total (In words):				

2. Packing List

Issuer:		PACKING LIST			
To:		Invoice No.:		Date:	
Marks & No.	No. & kind of packages, Description of goods	Quantity	G.W.	N.W.	Meas.
Total: SAY TOTAL PACKAGES IN WORDS:					
					(Signature)

3. Bill of Lading

Shipper		B/L NO.
Consignee		中国对外贸易运输总公司 CHINA NATIONAL FOREIGN TRADE TRANSPORT CORPORATION
Notify Party		
Pre-carriage by	Port of Loading	直运或转船提单 BILL OF LADING DIRECT OR WITH TRANSSHIPMENT
Vessel	Port of Transshipment	
Port of Discharge	Final Destination	

Marks & No.	No. & Kind of Packages; Description of Goods	Gross Weight (KGS.)	Measurement (M^3)

REGARDING TRANSSHIPMENT INFORMATION PLEASE CONTACT		Freight and Charge	
Ex. rate	Prepaid at	Freight Payable at	Place of Issue Date of Issue
	Total Prepaid	Number of Original Bs/L	Signed for or on Behalf of the Master

4. Bill of Exchange

BILL OF EXCHANGE

Drawn under: _____ L/C No. _____ Dated: _____

No. _____ Exchange for _____ Place and Date: _____

At _____ sight of this FIRST of Exchange (Second of Exchange being unpaid)

pay to the order of _____

the sum of _____

(continued)

| To: _____ |
| Signature: _____ |

5. Insurance Policy

The People's Insurance (Property) Company of China, Ltd.	
Invoice No.:	Policy No.:
MARINE CARGO TRANSPORTATION INSURANCE POLICY	
Insured:	
This policy of Insurance witnesses that the People's Insurance (Property) Company of China, Ltd. (hereinafter called "The Company"), at the request of the Insured and in consideration of the agreed premium paid by the Insured, undertakes to insure the under-mentioned goods in transportation subject to conditions of the Policy as per the Clauses printed overleaf and other special clauses attached hereon.	

Marks of Goods	Packing Unit	Descriptions of Goods	Amount Insured

Total Amount Insured:			
Premium:	Slg. on or abt.:		Per conveyance S.S.:
Conditions (Coverage):			
From:	VIA:		To:
In the event of loss or damage which may result in acclaim under this Policy, immediate notice must be given to the Company's Agent as mentioned hereunder. Claims, if any, one of the Original Policy which has been issued in 2 original(s) together with the relevant documents shall be surrendered to the Company. If one of the Original Policy has been accomplished, the others to be void.			
Claim payable at:			Date:
			(Signature)

6. Certificate of Origin GSP FORM A

ORIGINAL	
1. Goods consigned from:	Certificate No. : GENERALIZED SYSTEM OF PREFERENCES CERTIFICATE OF ORIGIN (Combined declaration and certificate) FORM A Issued by THE PEOPLE'S REPUBLIC OF CHINA
2. Goods consigned to:	
3. Means of transport and route:	4. For official use

5. Item No.	6. Marks & No. of packages	7. No. & kind of packages; Description of goods	8. Origin Criterion	9. Gross weight or other quantity	10. No. & date of invoice

| 11. Certification

It is hereby certified, on the basis of control carried out, that the declaration by the exporter is correct.

....
Place and date, signature and stamp of certifying authority. | 12. Declaration by the exporter

The undersigned hereby declares that the above details and statements are correct; that all the goods were produced in

_____
(country)

and that they comply with the origin requirements specified for those goods in the Generalized System of Preferences for goods exported to

_____
(Importing country).
....
Place and date, signature and stamp of certifying authority. |

17.3 Simulative Training III

17.3.1 Background Information

1. Exporter: Chizhou Sincere Ceramics Co., Ltd.

Founded in September 2009, Chizhou Sincere Ceramics Co., Ltd. is a privately owned company with import and export rights. It specializes in the production and marketing of a wide range of high-quality domestic ceramics, including porcelain tableware, tea sets, coffee sets, wine sets, etc.

2. Importer: Nippon Ceramic Industrial Limited

Nippon Ceramic Industrial Limited is a newly founded Japanese company. It wants to import some daily ceramics from China to satisfy the needs of local market.

Please choose the role of either the exporter or the importer, and work with a partner to complete the following tasks in sequence. Exchange roles with your partner and practice again. Inquire about port, bank and other relevant information online if necessary.

17.3.2 Tasks for the Importer

TASK 1: Writer a letter of specific enquiry to the Exporter.

TASK 3: Write a counter-offer.

TASK 5: Apply for the opening of an irrevocable documentary letter of credit.

Letter of Credit

Type of Documentary Credit	40A	
Letter of Credit Number	20	
Date of Issue	31C	
Date and Place of Expiry	31D	
Issuing Bank	51D	
Applicant	50	
Beneficiary	59	
Currency Code, Amount	32B	
Available with... by...	41D	

Chapter 17 Simulative Training

(continued)

Drafts at	42C	
Drawee	42D	
Partial Shipments	43P	
Transshipment	43T	
Loading on Board	44A	
For Transportation To	44B	
Latest Date of Shipment	44C	
Description of Goods or Services	45B	
Documents Required: 46 1. SIGNED COMMERCIAL INVOICE 2. FULL SET OF CLEAN ON BOARD OCEAN BILLS OF LADING 3. PACKING LIST 4. CERTIFICATE OF ORIGIN 5. INSURANCE POLICY		
ADDITIONAL INSTRUCTIONS 47A		
Charges	71B	ALL BANKING CHARGES OUTSIDE THE OPENING BANK ARE FOR BENEFICIARY'S ACCOUNT.
Period for Presentation	48	DOCUMENTS MUST BE PRESENTED WITHIN 15 DAYS AFTER THE DATE OF ISSUANCE OF THE TRANSPORT DOCUMENTS BUT WITHIN THE VALIDITY OF THE CREDIT.
Confirmation Instructions	49	WITHOUT

TASK 7: Reply to the Exporter after L/C amendment (This step can be omitted if there is no discrepancy.)

Send the Shipping Instructions to the Exporter.

17.3.2 Tasks for the Exporter

TASK 2: Write a letter of firm offer to the Importer based on their enquiry letter.

TASK 4: Writer a letter of acceptance, enclosing the following Sales Contract with relevant information.

SALES CONTRACT

Contract NO.:

Date:

Signed at:

The Seller:　　　　　　　　　　The Buyer:

Address:　　　　　　　　　　　Address:

This contract is made by and between the Seller and Buyer, whereby the seller agrees to sell and the buyer agrees to buy the under-mentioned commodity according to the terms and conditions stipulated below:

Commodity and Specifications	Quantity	Unit Price	Amount
Total			

Total Amount:

Packing:

Time of Shipment:

Place of Loading and Destination:

Shipping marks:

INSURANCE:

TERMS OF PAYMENT:

INSPECTION:

This contract is made in two original copies and become valid after signature, one copy to be held by each party.

The Seller:　　　　　　　　　　The Buyer:

TASK 6: Check the L/C according to the Sales Contract.

Send a letter to ask for L/C amendment if there is any discrepancy(This step can

Chapter 17 Simulative Training

be omitted if there is no discrepancy.).

TASK 8: Start preparing the products and relevant documents, including Commercial Invoice, Packing List and Certificate of Origin.

COMMERCIAL INVOICE				
TO:				Invoice No.: Date: Contract No.: L/C No.:
Transport Detail FROM TO				
Marks and Numbers	Description of Goods	Quantity	Unit Price	Amount
	Total:			
Total (In words):				

Packing List

Issuer:		PACKING LIST			
To:		Invoice No.:		Date:	
Marks and numbers	Number and kind of package Description of goods	Quantity	G. W.	N. W.	Meas.
Total: SAY TOTAL PACKAGES IN WORDS:					
					(Signature)

Certificate of Origin GSP FORM A

ORIGINAL	
1. Goods consigned from:	Certificate No.: GENERALIZED SYSTEM OF PREFERENCES CERTIFICATE OF ORIGIN (Combined declaration and certificate) FORM A Issued by THE PEOPLE'S REPUBLIC OF CHINA
2. Goods consigned to:	
3. Means of transport and route:	4. For official use

5. Item No.	6. Marks & No. of packages	7. No. & kind of packages; Description of goods	8. Origin Criterion	9. Gross weight or other quantity	10. No. & date of invoice

| 11. Certification

It is hereby certified, on the basis of control carried out, that the declaration by the exporter is correct.

—————————————
Place and date, signature and stamp of certifying authority. | 12. Declaration by the exporter

The undersigned hereby declares that the above details and statements are correct; that all the goods were produced in

—————————
(country)
and that they comply with the origin requirements specified for those goods in the Generalized System of Preferences for goods exported to

—————————
(Importing country).

—————————————
Place and date, signature and stamp of certifying authority. |

TASK 9: Go through the formalities of Customs Declaration (Customs Declaration

Form, omitted), obtain Bill of Lading and Insurance Policy。

Bill of Lading

Shipper		B/L NO. 中国对外贸易运输总公司 CHINA NATIONAL FOREIGN TRADE TRANSPORT CORPORATION 直运或转船提单 BILL OF LADING DIRECT OR WITH TRANSSHIPMENT	
Consignee			
Notify Party			
Pre-carriage by	Port of Loading		
Vessel	Port of Transshipment		
Port of Discharge	Final Destination		
Marks and No.	No. & Kind of Packages; Description of Goods	Gross Weight (KGS.)	Measurement (M^3)
REGARDING TRANSSHIPMENT INFORMATION PLEASE CONTACT		Freight and Charge	
Ex. rate	Prepaid at	Freight Payable at	Place of Issue Date of Issue
	Total Prepaid	Number of Original Bs/L	Signed for or on Behalf of the Master

Insurance Policy

The People's Insurance (Property) Company of China, Ltd.	
Invoice No.:	Policy No.:
MARINE CARGO TRANSPORTATION INSURANCE POLICY	
Insured:	
This policy of Insurance witnesses that the People's Insurance (Property) Company of China, Ltd. (hereinafter called "The Company"), at the request of the Insured and in consideration of the agreed premium paid by the Insured, undertakes to insure the under-mentioned goods in transportation subject to conditions of the Policy as per the Clauses printed overleaf and other special clauses attached hereon.	

(continued)

Marks of Goods	Packing Unit	Descriptions of Goods	Amount Insured

Total Amount Insured:		
Premium:	Slg. on or abt.:	Per-conveyance S. S.:
Conditions (Coverage):		
From:	VIA:	To:
In the event of loss or damage which may result in acclaim under this Policy, immediate notice must be given to the Company's Agent as mentioned hereunder. Claims, if any, one of the Original Policy which has been issued in 2 original(s) together with the relevant documents shall be surrendered to the Company. If one of the Original Policy has been accomplished, the others to be void.		
Claim payable at:	Date:	
		(Signature)

TASK 10: Send a Shipping Advice to the Importer.

TASK 11: Draw a draft. And present all the documents (Draft, Commercial Invoice, Bill of Lading, Insurance Policy, Packing List, Certificate of Origin) to the Negotiating Bank.

BILL OF EXCHANGE

Drawn under: _____ L/C No. _____ Dated: _____

No. _____ Exchange for _____ Place and Date: _____

At _____ sight of this FIRST of Exchange (Second of Exchange being unpaid)

pay to the order of _____

the sum of _____

To: _____

Signature: _____.

Appendices

Appendix I

《跟单信用证统一惯例(UCP600)》

Article 1　Application of UCP

第一条　统一惯例的适用范围

The Uniform Customs and Practice for Documentary Credits, 2007 Revision, ICC Publication No. 600 ("UCP") are rules that apply to any documentary credit ("credit") (including, to the extent to which they may be applicable, any standby letter of credit) when the text of the credit expressly indicates that it is subject to these rules. They are binding on all parties thereto unless expressly modified or excluded by the credit.

《跟单信用证统一惯例(2007年修订本)》,国际商会第600号出版物,适用于所有在正文中标明按本惯例办理的跟单信用证(包括本惯例适用范围内的备用信用证)。除非信用证中另有规定,本惯例对一切有关当事人均具有约束力。

Article 2　Definitions

第二条　定义

For the purpose of these rules:

就本惯例而言:

Advising bank means the bank that advises the credit at the request of the issuing bank.

通知行意指应开证行要求通知信用证的银行。

Applicant means the party on whose request the credit is issued.

申请人意指发出开立信用证申请的一方。

Banking day means a day on which a bank is regularly open at the place at which an act subject to these rules is to be performed.

银行日意指银行在其营业地正常营业,按照本惯例行事的行为得以在银行履行的日子。

Beneficiary means the party in whose favour a credit is issued.

受益人意指信用证中受益的一方。

Complying presentation means a presentation that is in accordance with the terms and conditions of the credit, the applicable provisions of these rules and international standard banking practice.

相符交单意指与信用证中的条款及条件、本惯例中所适用的规定及国际标准银行实务相一致的提示。

Confirmation means a definite undertaking of the confirming bank, in addition to that of the issuing bank, to honour or negotiate a complying presentation.

保兑意指保兑行在开证行之外对于相符交单做出兑付或议付的确定承诺。

Confirming bank means the bank that adds its confirmation to a credit upon the issuing bank's authorization or request.

保兑行意指应开证行的授权或请求对信用证加具保兑的银行。

Credit means any arrangement, however named or described, that is irrevocable and thereby constitutes a definite undertaking of the issuing bank to honour a complying presentation.

信用证意指一项约定,无论其如何命名或描述,该约定不可撤销并因此构成开证行对于相符交单予以兑付的确定承诺。

Honour means:

a. to pay at sight if the credit is available by sight payment.

b. to incur a deferred payment undertaking and pay at maturity if the credit is available by deferred payment.

c. to accept a bill of exchange ("draft") drawn by the beneficiary and pay at maturity if the credit is available by acceptance.

兑付意指:

a. 对于即期付款信用证即期付款。

b. 对于延期付款信用证发出延期付款承诺并到期付款。

c. 对于承兑信用证承兑由受益人出具的汇票并到期付款。

Issuing bank means the bank that issues a credit at the request of an applicant or on its own behalf.

开证行意指应申请人要求或代表其自身开立信用证的银行。

Negotiation means the purchase by the nominated bank of drafts (drawn on a bank other than the nominated bank) and/or documents under a complying presentation, by advancing or agreeing to advance funds to the beneficiary on or before the banking day on which reimbursement is due to(to be paid the nominated bank).

议付意指指定银行在其应获得偿付的银行日或在此之前,通过向受益人预付或者同意向受益人预付款项的方式购买相符提示项下的汇票(汇票付款人为被指定银行以外的银行)及/或单据。

Nominated bank means the bank with which the credit is available or any bank in the case of a credit available with any bank.

指定银行意指有权使用信用证的银行,对于可供任何银行使用的信用证而言,任何银行均为指定银行。

Presentation means either the delivery of documents under a credit to the issuing bank or nominated bank or the documents so delivered.

交单意指信用证项下单据被提交至开证行或指定银行,抑或按此方式提交的单据。

Presenter means a beneficiary, bank or other party that makes a presentation.

交单人意指做出提示的受益人、银行或其他一方。

Article 3   Interpretations
第三条   释义

For the purpose of these rules:

就本惯例而言:

Where applicable, words in the singular include the plural and in the plural include the singular.

在适用的条款中,词汇的单复数同义。

A credit is irrevocable even if there is no indication to that effect.

信用证是不可撤销的,即使信用证中对此未作指示也是如此。

A document may be signed by handwriting, facsimile signature, perforated signature, stamp, symbol or any other mechanical or electronic method of authentication.

单据可以通过手签、签样印制、穿孔签字、盖章、符号表示的方式签署,也可以通过其他任何机械或电子证实的方法签署。

A requirement for a document to be legalized, visard, certified or similar will be satisfied by any signature, mark, stamp or label on the document which appears to satisfy that requirement.

当信用证含有要求使单据合法、签证、证实或对单据有类似要求的条件时,这些条件可由在单据上签字、标注、盖章或标签来满足,只要单据表面已满足上述条件即可。

Branches of a bank in different countries are considered to be separate banks.

一家银行在不同国家设立的分支机构均视为另一家银行。

Terms such as "first class" "well known" "qualified" "independent" "official" "competent" or "local" used to describe the issuer of a document allow any issuer except the beneficiary to issue that document.

诸如"第一流""著名""合格""独立""正式""有资格""当地"等用语用于描述单据出单人的身份时,单据的出单人可以是除受益人以外的任何人。

Unless required to be used in a document, words such as "prompt" "immediately" or "as soon as possible" will be disregarded.

除非确需在单据中使用,银行对诸如"迅速""立即""尽快"之类词语将不予置理。

The expression "on or about" or similar will be interpreted as a stipulation that an event is to occur during a period of five calendar days before until five calendar days after the specified date, both start and end dates included.

"于或约于"或类似措辞将被理解为一项约定,按此约定,某项事件将在所述日期前后各五天内发生,起讫日均包括在内。

The words "to" "until" "till" "from" and "between" when used to determine a period of shipment include the date or dates mentioned, and the words "before" and "after" exclude the date mentioned.

词语"×月×日止"(to)、"至×月×日"(until)、"直至×月×日"(till)、"从×月×日"(from) 及"在×月×日至×月×日之间"(between) 用于确定装运期限时,包括所述日期。词语"×月×日之前"(before) 及"×月×日之后"(after) 不包括所述日期。

The words "from" and "after" when used to determine a maturity date exclude the date mentioned.

词语"从×月×日"(from)以及"×月×日之后"(after) 用于确定到期日时不包括所述日期。

The terms "first half" and "second half" of a month shall be construed respectively as the 1st to the 15th and the 16th to the last day of the month, all dates inclusive.

术语"上半月"和"下半月"应分别理解为自每月"1 日至 15 日"和"16 日至月末最后一天",包括起讫日期。

The terms "beginning" "middle" and "end" of a month shall be construed respectively as the 1st to the 10th, the 11th to the 20th and the 21st to the last day of the month, all dates inclusive.

术语"月初""月中"和"月末"应分别理解为每月 1 日至 10 日、11 日至 20 日和 21 日至月末最后一天,包括起讫日期。

Article 4　Credits v. Contracts
第四条　信用证与合同

a. A credit by its nature is a separate transaction from the sale or other contract on which it may be based. Banks are in no way concerned with or bound by such contract, even if any reference whatsoever to it is included in the credit. Consequently, the undertaking of a bank to honour, to negotiate or to fulfil any other obligation under the credit is not subject to claims or defences by the applicant resulting from its relationships with the issuing bank or the beneficiary.

A beneficiary can in no case avail itself of the contractual relationships existing between banks or between the applicant and the issuing bank.

a. 就性质而言,信用证与可能作为其依据的销售合同或其他合同,是相互独立的交易。即使信用证中提及该合同,银行亦与该合同完全无关,且不受其约束。因此,一家银行作出兑付、议付或履行信用证项下其他义务的承诺,并不受申请人与开证行之间或与受益人之间在已有关系下产生的索偿或抗辩的制约。

受益人在任何情况下,不得利用银行之间或申请人与开证行之间的契约关系。

b. An issuing bank should discourage any attempt by the applicant to include, as an integral part of the credit, copies of the underlying contract, proforma invoice and the like.

b. 开证行应劝阻申请人将基础合同、形式发票或其他类似文件的副本作为信用证整体组成部分的做法。

Article 5　Documents v. Goods, Services or Performance
第五条　单据与货物/服务/履约行为

Banks deal with documents and not with goods, services or performance to which the documents may relate.

银行处理的是单据,而不是单据所涉及的货物、服务或履约行为。

Article 6 Availability, Expiry Date and Place for Presentation
第六条 有效性、截止日及交单地点

a. A credit must state the bank with which it is available or whether it is available with any bank. A credit available with a nominated bank is also available with the issuing bank.

a. 信用证必须规定可在其处兑用的银行,或者信用证是否可在任何银行兑用。对于指定银行有效的信用证同样也可以在开证行兑用。

b. A credit must state whether it is available by sight payment, deferred payment, acceptance or negotiation.

b. 信用证必须规定它是否适用于即期付款、延期付款、承兑抑或议付。

c. A credit must not be issued available by a draft drawn on the applicant.

c. 不得开立包含以申请人为汇票付款人条款的信用证。

d. i. A credit must state an expiry date for presentation. An expiry date stated for honour or negotiation will be deemed to be an expiry date for presentation.

d. i. 信用证必须规定交单截止日。规定的用于兑付或者议付的截止日将被认为是交单截止日。

ii. The place of the bank with which the credit is available is the place for presentation. The place for presentation under a credit available with any bank is that of any bank. A place for presentation other than that of the issuing bank is in addition to the place of the issuing bank.

ii. 可以在其处兑用信用证的银行所在的地点即为交单地点。可在任何银行兑用的信用证其交单地点是任何银行所在地。除规定交单地点外,开证行所在地也是交单地点。

e. Except as provided in sub-article 29(a), a presentation by or on behalf of the beneficiary must be made on or before the expiry date.

e. 除非如第二十九条(a)款中规定,否则受益人或代表受益人的交单必须在截止日当日或在此之前提交。

Article 7 Issuing Bank Undertaking
第七条 开证行的承诺

a. Provided that the stipulated documents are presented to the nominated bank or to the issuing bank and that they constitute a complying presentation, the issuing bank must honour if the credit is available by:

倘若规定的单据被提交至指定银行或开证行并构成相符交单,开证行必须按下述信用证所适用的情形予以兑付:

i. sight payment, deferred payment or acceptance with the issuing bank;

i. 由开证行即期付款、延期付款或者承兑;

ii. sight payment with a nominated bank and that nominated bank does not pay;

ii. 由指定银行即期付款而该指定银行未予付款;

iii. deferred payment with a nominated bank and that nominated bank does not incur its deferred payment undertaking or, having incurred its deferred payment undertaking, does not pay at maturity;

iii. 由指定银行延期付款而该指定银行未承担其延期付款承诺,或者虽已承担延期付款承诺但到期未予付款;

iv. Acceptance with a nominated bank and that nominated bank does not accept a draft drawn on it or, having accepted a draft drawn on it, does not pay at maturity;

iv. 由指定银行承兑而该指定银行未予承兑以其为付款人的汇票,或者虽已承兑以其为付款人的汇票但到期未予付款;

v. negotiation with a nominated bank and that nominated bank does not negotiate.

v. 由指定银行议付而该指定银行未予议付。

b. An issuing bank is irrevocably bound to honour as of the time it issues the credit.

b. 自信用证开立之时起,开证行即不可撤销地受到兑付责任的约束。

c. An issuing bank undertakes to reimburse a nominated bank that has honoured or negotiated a complying presentation and forwarded the documents to the issuing bank. Reimbursement for the amount of a complying presentation under a credit available by acceptance or deferred payment is due at maturity, whether or not the nominated bank prepaid or purchased before maturity. An issuing bank's undertaking to reimburse a nominated bank is independent of the issuing bank's undertaking to the beneficiary.

c. 开证行保证向对于相符交单已经予以兑付或者议付并将单据寄往开证行的指定银行进行偿付。无论指定银行是否于到期日前已经对相符交单予以预付或者购买,对于承兑或延期付款信用证项下相符交单的金额的偿付于到期日进行。开证行偿付指定银行的承诺独立于开证行对于受益人的承诺。

Article 8　Confirming Bank Undertaking
第八条　保兑行的承诺

a. Provided that the stipulated documents are presented to the confirming bank or to any other nominated bank and that they constitute a complying presentation, the confirming bank must:

a. 倘若规定的单据被提交至保兑行或者任何其他指定银行并构成相符交单,保兑行必须:

i. honour, if the credit is available by:

i. 兑付,如果信用证适用于:

a) sight payment, deferred payment or acceptance with the confirming bank;

a) 由保兑行即期付款、延期付款或者承兑;

b) sight payment with another nominated bank and that nominated bank does not pay;

b) 由另一家指定银行即期付款而该指定银行未予付款;

c) deferred payment with another nominated bank and that nominated bank does not incur its deferred payment undertaking or, having incurred its deferred payment undertaking, does not pay at maturity;

c) 由另一家指定银行延期付款而该指定银行未承担其延期付款承诺,或者虽已承担延期付款承诺但到期未予付款;

d) acceptance with another nominated bank and that nominated bank does not accept a draft drawn on it or, having accepted a draft drawn on it, does not pay at maturity;

d) 由另一家指定银行承兑而该指定银行未予承兑以其为付款人的汇票,或者虽已承兑以其为付款人的汇票但到期未予付款;

e) negotiation with another nominated bank and that nominated bank does not negotiate.

e) 由另一家指定银行议付而该指定银行未予议付。

ii. Negotiate, without recourse, if the credit is available by negotiation with the confirming bank.

ii. 若信用证由保兑行议付,无追索权地议付。

b. A confirming bank is irrevocably bound to honour or negotiate as of the time it adds its confirmation to the credit.

b. 自为信用证加具保兑之时起，保兑行即不可撤销地受到兑付或者议付责任的约束。

c. A confirming bank undertakes to reimburse another nominated bank that has honoured or negotiated a complying presentation and forwarded the documents to the confirming bank. Reimbursement for the amount of a complying presentation under a credit available by acceptance or deferred payment is due at maturity, whether or not another nominated bank prepaid or purchased before maturity. A confirming bank's undertaking to reimburse another nominated bank is independent of the confirming bank's undertaking to the beneficiary.

c. 保兑行保证向对于相符交单已经予以兑付或者议付并将单据寄往开证行的另一家指定银行进行偿付。无论另一家指定银行是否于截止日前已经对相符交单予以预付或者购买，对于承兑或延期付款信用证项下相符交单的金额的偿付于到期日进行。保兑行偿付另一家指定银行的承诺独立于保兑行对于受益人的承诺。

d. If a bank is authorized or requested by the issuing bank to confirm a credit but is not prepared to do so, it must inform the issuing bank without delay and may advise the credit without confirmation.

d. 如开证行授权或要求另一家银行对信用证加具保兑，而该银行不准备照办时，它必须不延误地告知开证行并仍可通知此份未经加具保兑的信用证。

Article 9   Advising of Credits and Amendments
第九条   信用证及其修改通知

a. A credit and any amendment may be advised to a beneficiary through an advising bank. An advising bank that is not a confirming bank advises the credit and any amendment without any undertaking to honour or negotiate.

a. 信用证及其修改可以通过通知行通知受益人。除非已对信用证加具保兑，通知行通知信用证不构成兑付或议付的承诺。

b. By advising the credit or amendment, the advising bank signifies that it has satisfied itself as to the apparent authenticity of the credit or amendment and that the advice accurately reflects the terms and conditions of the credit or amendment received.

b. 通过通知信用证或修改，通知行即表明其认为信用证或修改的表面真实性得到满足，且通知准确地反映了所收到的信用证或修改的条款及条件。

c. An advising bank may utilize the services of another bank ("second advising bank") to advise the credit and any amendment to the beneficiary. By advising the credit or amendment, the second advising bank signifies that it has satisfied itself as to the apparent authenticity of the advice it has received and that the advice accurately reflects the terms and conditions of the credit or amendment received.

c. 通知行可以利用另一家银行的服务("第二通知行")向受益人通知信用证及其修改。通过通知信用证或修改,第二通知行即表明其认为所收到的通知的表面真实性得到满足,且通知准确地反映了所收到的信用证或修改的条款及条件。

d. A bank utilizing the services of an advising bank or second advising bank to advise a credit must use the same bank to advise any amendment thereto.

d. 如一家银行利用另一家通知行或第二通知行的服务将信用证通知给受益人,它也必须利用同一家银行的服务通知修改书。

e. If a bank is requested to advise a credit or amendment but elects not to do so, it must so inform, without delay, the bank from which the credit, amendment or advice has been received.

e. 如果一家银行被要求通知信用证或修改但决定不予通知,它必须不延误通知向其发送信用证、修改或通知的银行。

f. If a bank is requested to advise a credit or amendment but cannot satisfy itself as to the apparent authenticity of the credit, the amendment or the advice, it must so inform, without delay, the bank from which the instructions appear to have been received. If the advising bank or second advising bank elects nonetheless to advise the credit or amendment, it must inform the beneficiary or second advising bank that it has not been able to satisfy itself as to the apparent authenticity of the credit, the amendment or the advice.

f. 如果一家被要求通知信用证或修改,但不能确定信用证、修改或通知的表面真实性,就必须不延误地告知向其发出该指示的银行。如果通知行或第二通知行仍决定通知信用证或修改,则必须告知受益人或第二通知行其未能核实信用证、修改或通知的表面真实性。

Article 10   Amendments
第十条   修改

a. Except as otherwise provided by Article 38, a credit can neither be amended nor cancelled without the agreement of the issuing bank, the confirming bank, if any, and the beneficiary.

a. 除本惯例第三十八条另有规定外,凡未经开证行、保兑行(如有)以及受益人同意,信用证既不能修改也不能撤销。

b. An issuing bank is irrevocably bound by an amendment as of the time it issues the amendment. A confirming bank may extend its confirmation to an amendment and will be irrevocably bound as of the time it advises the amendment. A confirming bank may, however, choose to advise an amendment without extending its confirmation and, if so, it must inform the issuing bank without delay and inform the beneficiary in its advice.

b. 自发出信用证修改书之时起,开证行就不可撤销地受其发出修改的约束。保兑行可将其保兑承诺扩展至修改内容,且自其通知该修改之时起,即不可撤销地受到该修改的约束。然而,保兑行可选择仅将修改通知受益人而不对其加具保兑,但必须不延误地将此情况通知开证行和受益人。

c. The terms and conditions of the original credit (or a credit incorporating previously accepted amendments) will remain in force for the beneficiary until the beneficiary communicates its acceptance of the amendment to the bank that advised such amendment. The beneficiary should give notification of acceptance or rejection of an amendment. If the beneficiary fails to give such notification, a presentation that complies with the credit and to any not yet accepted amendment will be deemed to be notification of acceptance by the beneficiary of such amendment. As of that moment the credit will be amended.

c. 在受益人向通知修改的银行表示接受该修改内容之前,原信用证(或包含先前已被接受修改的信用证)的条款和条件对受益人仍然有效。受益人应发出接受或拒绝接受修改的通知。如受益人未提供上述通知,当其提交至被指定银行或开证行的单据与信用证以及尚未表示接受的修改的要求一致时,则该事实即视为受益人已作出接受修改的通知,并从此时起,该信用证已被修改。

d. A bank that advises an amendment should inform the bank from which it received the amendment of any notification of acceptance or rejection.

d. 通知修改的银行应当通知向其发出修改书的银行任何有关接受或拒绝接受修改的通知。

e. Partial acceptance of an amendment is not allowed and will be deemed to be notification of rejection of the amendment.

e. 不允许部分接受修改,部分接受修改将被视为拒绝接受修改的通知。

f. A provision in an amendment to the effect that the amendment shall enter into force unless rejected by the beneficiary within a certain time shall be disregarded.

f. 修改书中作出的除非受益人在某一时间内拒绝接受修改,否则修改将开始生效的条款将被不予置理。

Article 11　Teletransmitted and Pre-Advised Credits and Amendments

第十一条　电讯传递与预先通知的信用证和修改

a. An authenticated teletransmission of a credit or amendment will be deemed to be the operative credit or amendment, and any subsequent mail confirmation shall be disregarded.

If a teletransmission states "full details to follow" (or words of similar effect), or states that the mail confirmation is to be the operative credit or amendment, then the teletransmission will not be deemed to be the operative credit or amendment. The issuing bank must then issue the operative credit or amendment without delay in terms not inconsistent with the teletransmission.

a. 经证实的信用证或修改的电讯文件将被视为有效的信用证或修改,任何后续的邮寄确认书将被不予置理。

若该电讯文件声明"详情后告"(或类似词语)或声明随后寄出的邮寄确认书为有效信用证或修改,则该电讯文件将被视为无效的信用证或修改。开证行必须随即不延误地开立有效信用证或修改,且条款不得与电讯文件相矛盾。

b. A preliminary advice of the issuance of a credit or amendment ("pre-advice") shall only be sent if the issuing bank is prepared to issue the operative credit or amendment. An issuing bank that sends a pre-advice is irrevocably committed to issue the operative credit or amendment, without delay, in terms not inconsistent with the pre-advice.

b. 只有准备开立有效信用证或修改的开证行,才可以发出开立信用证或修改的预先通知书。发出预先通知的开证行应不可撤销地承诺将不延误地开立有效信用证或作出修改,且条款不得与预先通知书相矛盾。

Article 12 Nomination
第十二条 指定

a. Unless a nominated bank is the confirming bank, an authorization to honour or negotiate does not impose any obligation on that nominated bank to honour or negotiate, except when expressly agreed to by that nominated bank and so communicated to the beneficiary.

a. 除非指定银行是保兑行,对被指定银行进行兑付或议付的授权并不构成其必须兑付或议付的义务,被指定银行明确同意并照此通知受益人的情形除外。

b. By nominating a bank to accept a draft or incur a deferred payment undertaking, an issuing bank authorizes that nominated bank to prepay or purchase a draft accepted or a deferred payment undertaking incurred by that nominated bank.

b. 通过指定一家银行承兑汇票或承担延期付款承诺,开证行即授权该指定银行预付或购买经其承兑的汇票或由其承担延期付款的承诺。

c. Receipt or examination and forwarding of documents by a nominated bank that is not a confirming bank does not make that nominated bank liable to honour or negotiate, nor does it constitute honour or negotiation.

c. 非保兑行身份的指定银行接受、审核并寄送单据的行为既不使得该指定银行具有兑付或议付的义务,也不构成兑付或议付。

Article 13 Bank-to-Bank Reimbursement Arrangements
第十三条 银行间偿付约定

a. If a credit states that reimbursement is to be obtained by a nominated bank ("claiming bank") claiming on another party ("reimbursing bank"), the credit must state if the reimbursement is subject to the ICC rules for bank-to-bank reimbursements in effect on the date of issuance of the credit.

a. 如果信用证规定指定银行("索偿行")须通过向另一方银行("偿付行")索偿,则信用证中必须声明是否按照信用证开立时有效的国际商会《银行间偿付规则》办理。

b. If a credit does not state that reimbursement is subject to the ICC rules for bank-to-bank reimbursements, the following apply:

b. 如果信用证中未声明是否按照国际商会《银行间偿付规则》办理,则适用于下列条款:

i. An issuing bank must provide a reimbursing bank with a reimbursement authorization that conforms with the availability stated in the credit. The reimbursement authorization should not be subject to an expiry date.

i. 开证行必须向偿付行提供偿付授权书,该授权书须与信用证中声明的有效性一致。偿付授权书不应规定有效日期。

ii. A claiming bank shall not be required to supply a reimbursing bank with a certificate of compliance with the terms and conditions of the credit.

ii. 不应要求索偿行向偿付行提供证实单据与信用证条款及条件相符的证明。

iii. An issuing bank will be responsible for any loss of interest, together with any expenses incurred, if reimbursement is not provided on first demand by a reimbursing bank in accordance with the terms and conditions of the credit.

iii. 如果偿付行未能按照信用证的条款及条件在首次索偿时即行偿付,则开证行应对索偿行的利息损失以及产生的费用负责。

iv. A reimbursing bank's charges are for the account of the issuing bank. However, if the charges are for the account of the beneficiary, it is the responsibility of an issuing bank to so indicate in the credit and in the reimbursement authorization. If a reimbursing bank's charges are for the account of the beneficiary, they shall be deducted from the amount due to a claiming bank when reimbursement is made. If no reimbursement is made, the reimbursing bank's charges remain the obligation of the issuing bank.

iv. 偿付行的费用应由开证行承担。然而,如果费用系由受益人承担,则开证行有责任在信用证和偿付授权书中予以注明。如偿付行的费用系由受益人承担,则该费用应在偿付时从支付索偿行的金额中扣除。如果未发生偿付,开证行仍有义务承担偿付行的费用。

c. An issuing bank is not relieved of any of its obligations to provide reimbursement if reimbursement is not made by a reimbursing bank on first demand.

c. 如果偿付行未能于首次索偿时即行偿付,则开证行不能解除其自身的偿付责任。

Article 14 Standard for Examination of Documents
第十四条 单据审核标准

a. A nominated bank acting on its nomination, a confirming bank, if any, and the issuing bank must examine a presentation to determine, on the basis of the documents alone, whether or not the documents appear on their face to constitute a complying presentation.

a. 按照指定行事的指定银行、保兑行（如有）以及开证行必须对提示的单据进行审核，并仅以单据为基础，以决定单据在表面上看来是否构成相符提示。

b. A nominated bank acting on its nomination, a confirming bank, if any, and the issuing bank shall each have a maximum of five banking days following the day of presentation to determine if a presentation is complying. This period is not curtailed or otherwise affected by the occurrence on or after the date of presentation of any expiry date or last day for presentation.

b. 按照指定行事的指定银行、保兑行（如有）以及开证行，自其收到提示单据的翌日起算，应各自拥有最多不超过五个银行工作日的时间以决定提示是否相符。该期限不因单据提示日适逢信用证有效期或最迟提示期或在其之后而被缩减或受到其他影响。

c. A presentation including one or more original transport documents subject to Articles 19, 20, 21, 22, 23, 24 or 25 must be made by or on behalf of the beneficiary not later than 21 calendar days after the date of shipment as described in these rules, but in any event not later than the expiry date of the credit.

c. 提示若包含一份或多份按照本惯例第十九条、二十条、二十一条、二十二条、二十三条、二十四条或二十五条出具的正本运输单据，则必须由受益人或其代表按照相关条款在不迟于装运日后的二十一个公历日内提交，但无论如何不得迟于信用证的到期日。

d. Data in a document, when read in context with the credit, the document itself and international standard banking practice, need not be identical to, but must not conflict with, data in that document, any other stipulated document or the credit.

d. 单据中内容的描述不必与信用证、信用证对该项单据的描述以及国际标准银行实务完全一致，但不得与该项单据中的内容、其他规定的单据或信用证相冲突。

e. In documents other than the commercial invoice, the description of the goods, services or performance, if stated, may be in general terms not conflicting with their description in the credit.

e. 除商业发票外，其他单据中的货物、服务或行为描述若须规定，可使用统称，但不得与信用证规定的描述相矛盾。

f. If a credit requires presentation of a document other than a transport document, insurance document or commercial invoice, without stipulating by whom the document is to be issued or its data content, banks will accept the document as presented if its content appears to fulfil the function of the required document and otherwise complies with sub-article 14 (d).

f. 如果信用证要求提示运输单据、保险单据和商业发票以外的单据,但未规定该单据由何人出具或单据的内容。如信用证对此未做规定,只要所提交单据的内容看来满足其功能需要且其他方面与十四条(d)款相符,银行将对提示的单据予以接受。

g. A document presented but not required by the credit will be disregarded and may be returned to the presenter.

g. 提交信用证中未要求提交的单据,银行将不予置理。如果收到此类单据,可以退还交单人。

h. If a credit contains a condition without stipulating the document to indicate compliance with the condition, banks will deem such condition as not stated and will disregard it.

h. 如果信用证中包含某项条件,但未规定需提交与之相符的单据,银行将认为未列明此条件,并对此不予置理。

i. A document may be dated prior to the issuance date of the credit, but must not be dated later than its date of presentation.

i. 单据的出单日期可以早于信用证开立日期,但不得晚于交单日期。

j. When the addresses of the beneficiary and the applicant appear in any stipulated document, they need not be the same as those stated in the credit or in any other stipulated document, but must be within the same country as the respective addresses mentioned in the credit. Contact details (telefax, telephone, email and the like) stated as part of the beneficiary's and the applicant's address will be disregarded. However, when the address and contact details of the applicant appear as part of the consignee or notify party details on a transport document subject to Articles 19, 20, 21, 22, 23, 24 or 25, they must be as stated in the credit.

j. 当受益人和申请人的地址显示在任何规定的单据上时,不必与信用证或其他规定单据中显示的地址相同,但必须与信用证中述及的各自地址处于同一国家内。用于联系的资料(电传、电话、电子邮箱及类似方式)如作为受益人和申请人地址的组成部分将被不予置理。然而,当申请人的地址及联系信息作为按照十九条、二十条、二十一条、二十二条、二十三条、二十四条或二十五条出具的运输单据中收货人或通知方详址的组成部分时,则必须按照信用证规定予以显示。

k. The shipper or consignor of the goods indicated on any document need not be the beneficiary of the credit.

k. 显示在任何单据中的货物的托运人或发货人不必是信用证的受益人。

l. A transport document may be issued by any party other than a carrier, owner, master or charterer provided that the transport document meets the requirements of Articles 19, 20, 21, 22, 23 or 24 of these rules.

l. 假如运输单据能够满足本惯例第十九条、二十条、二十一条、二十二条、二十三条或二十四条的要求，则运输单据可以由承运人、船东、船长或租船人以外的任何一方出具。

Article 15　Complying Presentation
第十五条　相符交单

a. When an issuing bank determines that a presentation is complying, it must honour.

a. 当开证行确定交单相符时，必须予以兑付。

b. When a confirming bank determines that a presentation is complying, it must honour or negotiate and forward the documents to the issuing bank.

b. 当保兑行确定交单相符时，必须予以兑付或议付并将单据寄往开证行。

c. When a nominated bank determines that a presentation is complying and honours or negotiates, it must forward the documents to the confirming bank or issuing bank.

c. 当指定银行确定交单相符并予以兑付或议付时，必须将单据寄往保兑行或开证行。

Article 16　Discrepant Documents, Waiver and Notice
第十六条　不符单据及不符点的放弃与通知

a. When a nominated bank acting on its nomination, a confirming bank, if any, or the issuing bank determines that a presentation does not comply, it may refuse to honour or negotiate.

a. 当按照指定行事的指定银行、保兑行（如有）或开证行确定交单不符时，可以拒绝兑付或议付。

b. When an issuing bank determines that a presentation does not comply, it may in its sole judgement approach the applicant for a waiver of the discrepancies. This does not, however, extend the period mentioned in sub-article 14 (b).

b. 当开证行确定交单不符时，可以依据其独立的判断联系申请人放弃有关不符点。

然而,这并不因此延长第十四条(b)款中述及的期限。

c. When a nominated bank acting on its nomination, a confirming bank, if any, or the issuing bank decides to refuse to honour or negotiate, it must give a single notice to that effect to the presenter.

The notice must state:

c. 当按照指定行事的指定银行、保兑行(如有)或开证行决定拒绝兑付或议付时,必须给予交单人一份单独的拒付通知。

通知必须声明:

i. That the bank is refusing to honour or negotiate; and

i. 银行拒绝兑付或议付;及

ii. Each discrepancy in respect of which the bank refuses to honour or negotiate; and

ii. 银行凭以拒绝兑付或议付的各个不符点;及

iii. a) That the bank is holding the documents pending further instructions from the presenter; or

iii. a) 银行留存单据等候交单人进一步指示;或

b) That the issuing bank is holding the documents until it receives a waiver from the applicant and agrees to accept it, or receives further instructions from the presenter prior to agreeing to accept a waiver; or

b) 开证行留存单据直至收到申请人通知弃权并同意接受该弃权,或在同意接受弃权前从交单人处收到进一步指示;或

c) That the bank is returning the documents; or

c) 银行退回单据;或

d) That the bank is acting in accordance with instructions previously received from the presenter.

d) 银行按照先前从交单人处收到的指示行事。

d. The notice required in sub-article 16 (c) must be given by telecommunication or, if that is not possible, by other expeditious means no later than the close of the fifth banking day following the day of presentation.

d. 第十六条(c)款中要求的通知必须以电讯方式发出,或者,如果不可能以电讯方式通知时,则以其他快捷方式通知,但不得迟于提示单据日期翌日起第五个银行工作日

终了。

e. A nominated bank acting on its nomination, a confirming bank, if any, or the issuing bank may, after providing notice required by sub-article 16 (c) (iii) a) or b), return the documents to the presenter at any time.

e. 按照指定行事的指定银行、保兑行(如有)或开证行可以在提供第十六条(c)款(iii)a)款或b)款要求提供的通知后,于任何时间将单据退还交单人。

f. If an issuing bank or a confirming bank fails to act in accordance with the provisions of this article, it shall be precluded from claiming that the documents do not constitute a complying presentation.

f. 如果开证行或保兑行未能按照本条款的规定行事,将无权宣称交单不相符。

g. When an issuing bank refuses to honour or a confirming bank refuses to honour or negotiate and has given notice to that effect in accordance with this article, it shall then be entitled to claim a refund, with interest, of any reimbursement made.

g. 当开证行拒绝兑付或保兑行拒绝兑付或议付,并已经按照本条款发出通知时,该银行将有权就已经履行的偿付索取退款及其利息。

Article 17 Original Documents and Copies
第十七条 单据正本和副本

a. At least one original of each document stipulated in the credit must be presented.

a. 信用证中规定的各种单据必须至少提供一份正本。

b. A bank shall treat as an original any document bearing an apparently original signature, mark, stamp, or label of the issuer of the document, unless the document itself indicates that it is not an original.

b. 除非单据本身表明其不是正本,银行将视任何单据表面上具有单据出具人正本签字、标志、图章或标签的单据为正本单据。

c. Unless a document indicates otherwise, a bank will also accept a document as original if it:

c. 除非单据另有说明,银行将接受单据作为正本单据如果该单据:

i. Appears to be written, typed, perforated or stamped by the document issuer's hand; or

i. 单据看似由出单人手写、打字、穿孔签字或盖章;或

ii. Appears to be on the document issuer's original stationery; or

ii. 单据看似使用出单人的正本信笺出具;或

iii. States that it is original, unless the statement appears not to apply to the document presented.

iii. 声明单据为正本,除非该项声明看似与所提交的单据不符。

d. If a credit requires presentation of copies of documents, presentation of either originals or copies is permitted.

d. 如果信用证要求提交单据副本,则提交正本或副本均可。

e. If a credit requires presentation of multiple documents by using terms such as "in duplicate" "in two fold" or "in two copies", this will be satisfied by the presentation of at least one original and the remaining number in copies, except when the document itself indicates otherwise.

e. 如果信用证使用诸如"一式两份""两张""两份"等术语要求提交多份单据,则可以提交至少一份正本,其余份数以副本来满足。但单据本身另有说明除外。

Article 18　Commercial Invoice
第十八条　商业发票

a. A commercial invoice：

a. 商业发票：

i. Must appear to have been issued by the beneficiary (except as provided in article 38);

i. 必须看似系由受益人出具(第三十八条另有规定者除外);

ii. Must be made out in the name of the applicant (except as provided in sub-article 38 (g));

ii. 必须做成以申请人为抬头(第三十八条(g)款另有规定者除外);

iii. Must be made out in the same currency as the credit; and

iii. 必须与信用证币种相同;以及

iv. Need not be signed.

iv. 无须签字。

b. A nominated bank acting on its nomination, a confirming bank, if any, or the issuing bank may accept a commercial invoice issued for an amount in excess of the amount permitted by the credit, and its decision will be binding upon all parties, provided the bank in question has not honoured or negotiated for an amount in excess of that permitted by the credit.

b. 按照指定行事的指定银行、保兑行（如有）或开证行可以接受金额超过信用证所允许金额的商业发票，倘若有关银行已兑付或已议付的金额没有超过信用证所允许的金额，则该银行的决定对各有关方均具有约束力。

c. The description of the goods, services or performance in a commercial invoice must correspond with that appearing in the credit.

c. 商业发票中货物、服务或行为的描述必须与信用证中显示的内容相符。

Article 19　Transport Document Covering at Least Two Different Modes of Transport

第十九条　至少包括两种不同运输方式的运输单据

a. A transport document covering at least two different modes of transport (multimodal or combined transport document), however named, must appear to:

a. 至少包括两种不同运输方式的运输单据（即多式运输单据或联合运输单据），不论其称谓如何，必须在表明上看来：

i. Indicate the name of the carrier and be signed by:

i. 显示承运人名称并由下列人员签署：

• The carrier or a named agent for or on behalf of the carrier, or

• 承运人或承运人的具名代理或代表，或

• The master or a named agent for or on behalf of the master.

• 船长或船长的具名代理或代表。

Any signature by the carrier, master or agent must be identified as that of the carrier, master or agent.

承运人、船长或代理的任何签字必须分别表明承运人、船长或代理的身份。

Any signature by an agent must indicate whether the agent has signed for or on behalf of the carrier or for or on behalf of the master.

代理的签字必须显示其是否作为承运人或船长的代理或代表签署提单。

ii. Indicate that the goods have been dispatched, taken in charge or shipped on board at the place stated in the credit, by:

ii. 通过下述方式表明货物已在信用证规定的地点发运、接受监管或装运

• Pre-printed wording, or

• 预先印就的措词,或

• A stamp or notation indicating the date on which the goods have been dispatched, taken in charge or shipped on board.

• 注明货物已发运、接受监管或装载日期的图章或批注。

The date of issuance of the transport document will be deemed to be the date of dispatch, taking in charge or shipped on board, and the date of shipment. However, if the transport document indicates, by stamp or notation, a date of dispatch, taking in charge or shipped on board, this date will be deemed to be the date of shipment.

运输单据的出具日期将被视为发运、接受监管或装载以及装运日期。然而,如果运输单据以盖章或批注方式标明发运、接受监管或装载日期,则此日期将被视为装运日期。

iii. Indicate the place of dispatch, taking in charge or shipment and the place of final destination stated in the credit, even if:

iii. 显示信用证中规定的发运、接受监管或装载地点以及最终目的地,即使:

a) The transport document states, in addition, a different place of dispatch, taking in charge or shipment or place of final destination, or

a) 运输单据另外显示了不同的发运、接受监管或装载地点或最终目的地,或

b) The transport document contains the indication "intended" or similar qualification in relation to the vessel, port of loading or port of discharge.

b) 运输单据包含"预期"或类似限定有关船只、装货港或卸货港的限定语。

iv. Be the sole original transport document or, if issued in more than one original, be the full set as indicated on the transport document.

iv. 系仅有的一份正本运输单据,或者,如果出具了多份正本运输单据,应是运输单据中显示的全套正本份数。

v. Contain terms and conditions of carriage or make reference to another source containing the terms and conditions of carriage (short form or blank back transport document). Contents of terms and conditions of carriage will not be examined.

v. 包含承运条件须参阅包含承运条件条款及条件的某一出处(简式或背面空白的运输单据)者,银行对此类承运条件的条款及条件内容不予审核。

vi. Contain no indication that it is subject to a charter party.

vi. 未注明运输单据受租船合约约束。

b. For the purpose of this article, transhipment means unloading from one means of conveyance and reloading to another means of conveyance (whether or not in different modes of transport) during the carriage from the place of dispatch, taking in charge or shipment to the place of final destination stated in the credit.

b. 就本条款而言,转运意指货物在信用证中规定的发运、接受监管或装载地点到最终目的地的运输过程中,从一个运输工具卸下并重新装载到另一个运输工具上(无论是否为不同运输方式)的运输。

c. i. A transport document may indicate that the goods will or may be transhipped provided that the entire carriage is covered by one and the same transport document.

c. i. 只要同一运输单据包括运输全程,则运输单据可以注明货物将被转运或可被转运。

ii. A transport document indicating that transhipment will or may take place is acceptable, even if the credit prohibits transhipment.

ii. 即使信用证禁止转运,银行也将接受注明转运将发生或可能发生的运输单据。

Article 20 Bill of Lading
第二十条 提单

a. A bill of lading, however named, must appear to:

a. 无论其称谓如何,提单必须表面上看来:

i. Indicate the name of the carrier and be signed by:

i. 显示承运人名称并由下列人员签署:

- The carrier or a named agent for or on behalf of the carrier, or
- 承运人或承运人的具名代理或代表,或
- The master or a named agent for or on behalf of the master.
- 船长或船长的具名代理或代表。

Any signature by the carrier, master or agent must be identified as that of the carrier, master or agent.

承运人、船长或代理的任何签字必须分别表明其承运人、船长或代理的身份。

Any signature by an agent must indicate whether the agent has signed for or on behalf of the carrier or for or on behalf of the master.

代理的签字必须显示其是否作为承运人或船长的代理或代表签署提单。

ii. Indicate that the goods have been shipped on board a named vessel at the port of loading stated in the credit by:

ii. 通过下述方式表明货物已在信用证规定的装运港装载上具名船只：

• Pre-printed wording, or

• 预先印就的措词，或

• An on board notation indicating the date on which the goods have been shipped on board.

• 注明货物已装船日期的装船批注。

The date of issuance of the bill of lading will be deemed to be the date of shipment unless the bill of lading contains an on board notation indicating the date of shipment, in which case the date stated in the on board notation will be deemed to be the date of shipment.

提单的出具日期将被视为装运日期，除非提单包含注明装运日期的装船批注，在此情况下，装船批注中显示的日期将被视为装运日期。

If the bill of lading contains the indication "intended vessel" or similar qualification in relation to the name of the vessel, an on board notation indicating the date of shipment and the name of the actual vessel is required.

如果提单包含"预期船"字样或类似有关限定船只的词语时，装上具名船只必须由注明装运日期以及实际装运船只名称的装船批注来证实。

iii. Indicate shipment from the port of loading to the port of discharge stated in the credit.

iii. 注明货物从信用证规定的装货港运至卸货港。

If the bill of lading does not indicate the port of loading stated in the credit as the port of loading, or if it contains the indication "intended" or similar qualification in relation to the port of loading, an on board notation indicating the port of loading as stated in the credit, the date of shipment and the name of the vessel is required. This provision applies even when loading on board or shipment on a named vessel is indicated by pre-printed wording on the bill of lading.

如果提单未注明以信用证规定的装货港作为装货港，或包含"预期"或类似有关限定装货港的标注者，则需要提供注明信用证中规定的装货港、装运日期以及船名的装船批注。即使提单上已注明印就的"已装船"或"已装具名船只"措词，本规定仍然适用。

iv. Be the sole original bill of lading or, if issued in more than one original, be the full set as indicated on the bill of lading.

ⅳ. 系仅有的一份正本提单,或者,如果出具了多份正本,应是提单中显示的全套正本份数。

ⅴ. Contain terms and conditions of carriage or make reference to another source containing the terms and conditions of carriage (short form or blank back bill of lading). Contents of terms and conditions of carriage will not be examined.

ⅴ. 包含承运条件须参阅包含承运条件条款及条件的某一出处(简式或背面空白的提单)者,银行对此类承运条件的条款及条件内容不予审核。

ⅵ. Contain no indication that it is subject to a charter party.

ⅵ. 未注明运输单据受租船合同约束。

b. For the purpose of this article, transhipment means unloading from one vessel and reloading to another vessel during the carriage from the port of loading to the port of discharge stated in the credit.

b. 就本条款而言,转运意指在信用证规定的装货港到卸货港之间的海运过程中,将货物由一艘船卸下再装上另一艘船的运输。

c. ⅰ. A bill of lading may indicate that the goods will or may be transhipped provided that the entire carriage is covered by one and the same bill of lading.

c. ⅰ. 只要同一提单包括运输全程,则提单可以注明货物将被转运或可被转运。

ⅱ. A bill of lading indicating that transhipment will or may take place is acceptable, even if the credit prohibits transhipment, if the goods have been shipped in a container, trailer or LASH barge as evidenced by the bill of lading.

ⅱ. 银行可以接受注明将要发生或可能发生转运的提单。即使信用证禁止转运,只要提单上证实有关货物已由集装箱、拖车或子母船运输,银行仍可接受注明将要发生或可能发生转运的提单。

d. Clauses in a bill of lading stating that the carrier reserves the right to tranship will be disregarded.

d. 对于提单中包含的声明承运人保留转运权利的条款,银行将不予置理。

Article 21　Non-Negotiable Sea Waybill
第二十一条　非转让海运单

a. A non-negotiable sea waybill, however named, must appear to:

a. 无论其称谓如何,非转让海运单必须表面上看来:

i. Indicate the name of the carrier and be signed by:

i. 显示承运人名称并由下列人员签署：

• The carrier or a named agent for or on behalf of the carrier, or

• 承运人或承运人的具名代理或代表，或

• The master or a named agent for or on behalf of the master.

• 船长或船长的具名代理或代表。

Any signature by the carrier, master or agent must be identified as that of the carrier, master or agent.

承运人、船长或代理的任何签字必须分别表明其承运人、船长或代理的身份。

Any signature by an agent must indicate whether the agent has signed for or on behalf of the carrier or for or on behalf of the master.

代理的签字必须显示其是否作为承运人或船长的代理或代表签署提单。

ii. Indicate that the goods have been shipped on board a named vessel at the port of loading stated in the credit by:

ii. 通过下述方式表明货物已在信用证规定的装运港装载上具名船只：

• Pre-printed wording, or

• 预先印就的措词，或

• An on board notation indicating the date on which the goods have been shipped on board.

• 注明货物已装船日期的装船批注。

The date of issuance of the non-negotiable sea waybill will be deemed to be the date of shipment unless the non-negotiable sea waybill contains an on board notation indicating the date of shipment, in which case the date stated in the on board notation will be deemed to be the date of shipment.

非转让海运单的出具日期将被视为装运日期，除非非转让海运单包含注明装运日期的装船批注，在此情况下，装船批注中显示的日期将被视为装运日期。

If the non-negotiable sea waybill contains the indication "intended vessel" or similar qualification in relation to the name of the vessel, an on board notation indicating the date of shipment and the name of the actual vessel is required.

如果非转让海运单包含"预期船"字样或类似有关限定船只的词语时，装上具名船只必须由注明装运日期以及实际装运船只名称的装船批注来证实。

iii. Indicate shipment from the port of loading to the port of discharge stated in the credit.

iii. 注明货物从信用证规定的装货港运至卸货港。

If the non-negotiable sea waybill does not indicate the port of loading stated in the credit as the port of loading, or if it contains the indication "intended" or similar qualification in relation to the port of loading, an on board notation indicating the port of loading as stated in the credit, the date of shipment and the name of the vessel is required. This provision applies even when loading on board or shipment on a named vessel is indicated by pre-printed wording on the non-negotiable sea waybill.

如果非转让海运单未注明以信用证规定的装货港作为装货港，或包含"预期"或类似有关限定装货港的标注者，则需要提供注明信用证中规定的装货港、装运日期以及船名的装船批注。即使非转让海运单上已注明印就的"已装船"或"已装具名船只"措词，本规定仍然适用。

iv. Be the sole original non-negotiable sea waybill or, if issued in more than one original, be the full set as indicated on the non-negotiable sea waybill.

iv. 系仅有的一份正本非转让海运单，或者，如果出具了多份正本，应是非转让海运单中显示的全套正本份数。

v. Contain terms and conditions of carriage or make reference to another source containing the terms and conditions of carriage (short form or blank back non-negotiable sea waybill). Contents of terms and conditions of carriage will not be examined.

v. 包含承运条件须参阅包含承运条件条款及条件的某一出处（简式或背面空白的提单）者，银行对此类承运条件的条款及条件内容不予审核。

vi. Contain no indication that it is subject to a charter party.

vi. 未注明运输单据受租船合同约束。

b. For the purpose of this article, transhipment means unloading from one vessel and reloading to another vessel during the carriage from the port of loading to the port of discharge stated in the credit.

b. 就本条款而言，转运意指在信用证规定的装货港到卸货港之间的海运过程中，将货物由一艘船卸下再装上另一艘船的运输。

c. i. A non-negotiable sea waybill may indicate that the goods will or may be transhipped provided that the entire carriage is covered by one and the same non-negotiable sea waybill.

c. i. 只要同一非转让海运单包括运输全程,则非转让海运单可以注明货物将被转运或可被转运。

ii. A non-negotiable sea waybill indicating that transhipment will or may take place is acceptable, even if the credit prohibits transhipment, if the goods have been shipped in a container, trailer or LASH barge as evidenced by the non-negotiable sea waybill.

ii. 银行可以接受注明将要发生或可能发生转运的非转让海运单。即使信用证禁止转运,只要非转让海运单上证实有关货物已由集装箱、拖车或子母船运输,银行仍可接受注明将要发生或可能发生转运的非转让海运单。

d. Clauses in a non-negotiable sea waybill stating that the carrier reserves the right to tranship will be disregarded.

d. 对于非转让海运单中包含的声明承运人保留转运权利的条款,银行将不予置理。

Article 22 Charter Party Bill of Lading
第二十二条 租船合同提单

a. A bill of lading, however named, containing an indication that it is subject to a charter party (charter party bill of lading), must appear to:

a. 无论其称谓如何,倘若提单包含有提单受租船合同约束的指示(即租船合约提单),则必须在表面上看来:

i. Be signed by:

i. 由下列当事方签署:

- The master or a named agent for or on behalf of the master, or
- 船长或船长的具名代理或代表,或
- The owner or a named agent for or on behalf of the owner, or
- 船东或船东的具名代理或代表,或
- The charterer or a named agent for or on behalf of the charterer.
- 租船主或租船主的具名代理或代表。

Any signature by the master, owner, charterer or agent must be identified as that of the master, owner, charterer or agent.

船长、船东、租船主或代理的任何签字必须分别表明其船长、船东、租船主或代理的身份。

Any signature by an agent must indicate whether the agent has signed for or on behalf of the master, owner or charterer.

代理的签字必须显示其是否作为船长、船东或租船主的代理或代表签署提单。

An agent signing for or on behalf of the owner or charterer must indicate the name of the owner or charterer.

代理人代理或代表船东或租船主签署提单时必须注明船东或租船主的名称。

ii. Indicate that the goods have been shipped on board a named vessel at the port of loading stated in the credit by:

ii. 通过下述方式表明货物已在信用证规定的装运港装载上具名船只：

- Pre-printed wording, or
- 预先印就的措词，或
- An on board notation indicating the date on which the goods have been shipped on board.
- 注明货物已装船日期的装船批注。

The date of issuance of the charter party bill of lading will be deemed to be the date of shipment unless the charter party bill of lading contains an on board notation indicating the date of shipment, in which case the date stated in the on board notation will be deemed to be the date of shipment.

租船合同提单的出具日期将被视为装运日期，除非租船合约提单包含注明装运日期的装船批注，在此情况下，装船批注中显示的日期将被视为装运日期。

iii. Indicate shipment from the port of loading to the port of discharge stated in the credit. The port of discharge may also be shown as a range of ports or a geographical area, as stated in the credit.

iii. 注明货物由信用证规定的装货港运至卸货港。卸货港可以按信用证中的规定显示为一组港口或某个地理区域。

iv. Be the sole original charter party bill of lading or, if issued in more than one original, be the full set as indicated on the charter party bill of lading.

iv. 系仅有的一份正本租船合同提单，或者，如果出具了多份正本，应是租船合同提单中显示的全套正本份数。

b. A bank will not examine charter party contracts, even if they are required to be presented by the terms of the credit.

b. 即使信用证中的条款要求提交租船合同，银行也将对该租船合同不予审核。

Article 23　Air Transport Document

第二十三条　空运单据

a. An air transport document, however named, must appear to:

a. 无论其称谓如何，空运单据必须在表面上看来：

i. Indicate the name of the carrier and be signed by:

i. 注明承运人名称并由下列当事方签署：

- The carrier, or
- 承运人，或
- A named agent for or on behalf of the carrier.
- 承运人的具名代理或代表。

Any signature by the carrier or agent must be identified as that of the carrier or agent.

承运人或代理的任何签字必须分别表明其承运人或代理的身份。

Any signature by an agent must indicate that the agent has signed for or on behalf of the carrier.

代理的签字必须显示其是否作为承运人的代理或代表签署空运单据。

ii. Indicate that the goods have been accepted for carriage.

ii. 注明货物已收妥待运。

iii. Indicate the date of issuance. This date will be deemed to be the date of shipment unless the air transport document contains a specific notation of the actual date of shipment, in which case the date stated in the notation will be deemed to be the date of shipment.

iii. 注明出具日期。这一日期将被视为装运日期，除非空运单据包含注有实际装运日期的专项批注，在此种情况下，批注中显示的日期将被视为装运日期。

Any other information appearing on the air transport document relative to the flight number and date will not be considered in determining the date of shipment.

空运单据显示的其他任何与航班号和起飞日期有关的信息不能被视为装运日期。

iv. Indicate the airport of departure and the airport of destination stated in the credit.

iv. 表明信用证规定的起飞机场和目的地机场。

v. Be the original for consignor or shipper, even if the credit stipulates a full set of originals.

v. 为开给发货人或拖运人的正本,即使信用证规定提交全套正本。

vi. Contain terms and conditions of carriage or make reference to another source containing the terms and conditions of carriage. Contents of terms and conditions of carriage will not be examined.

vi. 载有承运条款和条件,或提示条款和条件参见别处。银行将不审核承运条款和条件的内容。

b. For the purpose of this article, transhipment means unloading from one aircraft and reloading to another aircraft during the carriage from the airport of departure to the airport of destination stated in the credit.

b. 就本条而言,转运是指在信用证规定的起飞机场到目的地机场的运输过程中,将货物从一飞机卸下再装上另一飞机的行为。

c. i. An air transport document may indicate that the goods will or may be transhipped, provided that the entire carriage is covered by one and the same air transport document.

c. i. 空运单据可以注明货物将要或可能转运,只要全程运输由同一空运单据涵盖。

ii. An air transport document indicating that transhipment will or may take place is acceptable, even if the credit prohibits transhipment.

ii. 即使信用证禁止转运,注明将要或可能发生转运的空运单据仍可接受。

Article 24　Road, Rail or Inland Waterway Transport Documents
第二十四条　公路、铁路或内陆水运单据

a. A road, rail or inland waterway transport document, however named, must appear to:

a. 公路、铁路或内陆水运单据,无论名称如何,必须看似:

i. Indicate the name of the carrier and:

i. 表明承运人名称,并且

- Be signed by the carrier or a named agent for or on behalf of the carrier, or

- 由承运人或其具名代理人签署,或者

- Indicate receipt of the goods by signature, stamp or notation by the carrier or a named agent for or on behalf of the carrier.

- 由承运人或其具名代理人以签字、印戳或批注表明货物收讫。

Any signature, stamp or notation of receipt of the goods by the carrier or agent must be identified as that of the carrier or agent.

承运人或其具名代理人的售货签字、印戳或批注必须标明其承运人或代理人的身份。

Any signature, stamp or notation of receipt of the goods by the agent must indicate that the agent has signed or acted for or on behalf of the carrier.

代理人的收获签字、印戳或批注必须标明代理人系代表承运人签字或行事。

If a rail transport document does not identify the carrier, any signature or stamp of the railway company will be accepted as evidence of the document being signed by the carrier.

如果铁路运输单据没有指明承运人,可以接受铁路运输公司的任何签字或印戳作为承运人签署单据的证据。

ii. Indicate the date of shipment or the date the goods have been received for shipment, dispatch or carriage at the place stated in the credit. Unless the transport document contains a dated reception, stamp, an indication of the date of receipt or a date of shipment, the date of issuance of the transport document will be deemed to be the date of shipment.

ii. 表明货物在信用证规定地点的发运日期,或者收讫代运或代发送的日期。运输单据的出具日期将被视为发运日期,除非运输单据上盖有带日期的收货印戳,或注明了收货日期或发运日期。

iii. Indicate the place of shipment and the place of destination stated in the credit.

iii. 表明信用证规定的发运地及目的地。

b. i. A road transport document must appear to be the original for consignor or shipper or bear no marking indicating for whom the document has been prepared.

b. i. 公路运输单据必须看似为开给发货人或托运人的正本,或没有认可标记表明单据开给何人。

ii. A rail transport document marked "duplicate" will be accepted as an original.

ii. 注明"第二联"的铁路运输单据将被作为正本接受。

iii. A rail or inland waterway transport document will be accepted as an original whether marked as an original or not.

iii. 无论是否注明正本字样,铁路或内陆水运单据都被作为正本接受。

c. In the absence of an indication on the transport document as to the number of originals issued, the number presented will be deemed to constitute a full set.

c. 如运输单据上未注明出具的正本数量,提交的分数即视为全套正本。

d. For the purpose of this article, transhipment means unloading from one means of conveyance and reloading to another means of conveyance, within the same mode of transport, during the carriage from the place of shipment, dispatch or carriage to the place of destination stated in the credit.

d. 就本条而言,转运是指在信用证规定的发运、发送或运送的地点到目的地之间的运输过程中,在同一运输方式中从一运输工具卸下再装上另一运输工具的行为。

e. i. A road, rail or inland waterway transport document may indicate that the goods will or may be transhipped provided that the entire carriage is covered by one and the same transport document.

e. i. 只要全程运输由同一运输单据涵盖,公路、铁路或内陆水运单据可以注明货物将要或可能被转运。

ii. A road, rail or inland waterway transport document indicating that transhipment will or may take place is acceptable, even if the credit prohibits transhipment.

ii. 即使信用证禁止转运,注明将要或可能发生转运的公路、铁路或内陆水运单据仍可接受。

Article 25　Courier Receipt, Post Receipt or Certificate of Posting
第二十五条　快递收据、邮政收据或投邮证明

a. A courier receipt, however named, evidencing receipt of goods for transport, must appear to:

a. 证明货物收讫待运的快递收据,无论名称如何,必须看似:

i. Indicate the name of the courier service and be stamped or signed by the named courier service at the place from which the credit states the goods are to be shipped; and

i. 表明快递机构的名称,并在信用证规定的货物发运地点由该具名快递机构盖章或签字;并且

ii. Indicate a date of pick-up or of receipt or wording to this effect. This date will be deemed to be the date of shipment.

ii. 表明取件或收件的日期或类似词语。该日期将被视为发运日期。

b. A requirement that courier charges are to be paid or prepaid may be satisfied by a transport document issued by a courier service evidencing that courier charges are for the account of a party other than the consignee.

b. 如果要求显示快递费用付讫或预付，快递机构出具的表明快递费由收货人以外的一方支付的运输单据可以满足该项要求。

c. A post receipt or certificate of posting, however named, evidencing receipt of goods for transport, must appear to be stamped or signed and dated at the place from which the credit states the goods are to be shipped. This date will be deemed to be the date of shipment.

c. 证明货物收讫待运的邮政收据或投邮证明，无论名称如何，必须看似在信用证规定的货物发运地点盖章或签署并注明日期。该日期将被视为发运日期。

Article 26 "On Deck" "Shipper's Load and Count" "Said by Shipper to Contain" and Charges Additional to Freight

第二十六条 "货装舱面""托运人装载和计数""内容据托运人报称"及运费之外的费用

a. A transport document must not indicate that the goods are or will be loaded on deck. A clause on a transport document stating that the goods may be loaded on deck is acceptable.

a. 运输单据不得表明货物装于或者将装于舱面。声明货物可能被装于舱面的运输单据条款可以接受。

b. A transport document bearing a clause such as "shipper's load and count" and "said by shipper to contain" is acceptable.

b. 载有诸如"托运人装载和计数"或"内容据托运人报称"条款的运输单据可以接受。

c. A transport document may bear a reference, by stamp or otherwise, to charges additional to the freight.

c. 运输单据上可以以印戳或其他方式提及运费之外的费用。

Article 27 Clean Transport Document

第二十七条 清洁运输单据

A bank will only accept a clean transport document. A clean transport document is one bearing no clause or notation expressly declaring a defective condition of the goods or their packaging. The word "clean" need not appear on a transport document, even if a credit has a requirement for that transport document to be "clean on board".

银行只接受清洁运输单据。清洁运输单据指未载有明确宣称货物或包装有缺陷的条款或批注的运输单据。"清洁"一词并不需要在运输单据上出现,即使信用证要求运输单据为"清洁已装船"的。

Article 28 Insurance Document and Coverage
第二十八条 保险单据及保险范围

a. An insurance document, such as an insurance policy, an insurance certificate or a declaration under an open cover, must appear to be issued and signed by an insurance company, an underwriter or their agents or their proxies.

a. 保险单据,例如保险单或预约保险项下的保险证明书或者声明书,必须看似由保险公司或承保人或其代理人或代表出具并签署。

Any signature by an agent or proxy must indicate whether the agent or proxy has signed for or on behalf of the insurance company or underwriter.

代理人或代表的签字必须标明其系代表保险公司或承保人签字。

b. When the insurance document indicates that it has been issued in more than one original, all originals must be presented.

b. 如果保险单据表明其以多份正本出具,所有正本均须提交。

c. Cover notes will not be accepted.

c. 暂保单将不被接受。

d. An insurance policy is acceptable in lieu of an insurance certificate or a declaration under an open cover.

d. 可以接受保险单代替预约保险项下的保险证明书或声明书。

e. The date of the insurance document must be no later than the date of shipment, unless it appears from the insurance document that the cover is effective from a date not later than the date of shipment.

e. 保险单据日期不得晚于发运日期,除非保险单据表明保险责任不迟于发运日生效。

f. i. The insurance document must indicate the amount of insurance coverage and be in the same currency as the credit.

f. i. 保险单据必须表明投保金额并以与信用证相同的货币表示。

ii. A requirement in the credit for insurance coverage to be for a percentage of the value of the goods, of the invoice value or similar is deemed to be the minimum amount of coverage required.

ii. 信用证对于投保金额为货物价值、发票金额或类似金额的某一比例的要求,将被视为对最低保额的要求。

iii. If there is no indication in the credit of the insurance coverage required, the amount of insurance coverage must be at least 110% of the CIF or CIP value of the goods.

iii. 如果信用证对投保金额未作规定,投保金额须至少为货物的 CIF 或 CIP 价格的 110%。

iv. When the CIF or CIP value cannot be determined from the documents, the amount of insurance coverage must be calculated on the basis of the amount for which honour or negotiation is requested or the gross value of the goods as shown on the invoice, whichever is greater.

iv. 如果从单据中不能确定 CIF 或者 CIP 价格,投保金额必须基于要求承付或议付的金额,或者基于发票上显示的货物总值来计算,两者之中取金额较高者。

v. The insurance document must indicate that risks are covered at least between the place of taking in charge or shipment and the place of discharge or final destination as stated in the credit.

v. 保险单据须标明承包的风险区间至少涵盖从信用证规定的货物监管地或发运地开始到卸货地或最终目的地为止。

g. A credit should state the type of insurance required and, if any, the additional risks to be covered. An insurance document will be accepted without regard to any risks that are not covered if the credit uses imprecise terms such as "usual risks" or "customary risks".

g. 信用证应规定所需投保的险别及附加险(如有的话)。如果信用证使用诸如"通常风险"或"惯常风险"等含义不确切的用语,则无论是否有漏保之风险,保险单据将被照样接受。

h. When a credit requires insurance against "all risks" and an insurance document is presented containing any "all risks" notation or clause, whether or not bearing the heading "all risks", the insurance document will be accepted without regard to any risks stated to be excluded.

h. 当信用证规定投保"一切险"时,如保险单据载有任何"一切险"批注或条款,无论是否有"一切险"标题,均将被接受,即使其声明任何风险除外。

i. An insurance document may contain reference to any exclusion clause.

i. 保险单据可以援引任何除外责任条款。

j. An insurance document may indicate that the cover is subject to a franchise or excess (deductible).

j. 保险单据可以注明受免赔率或免赔额(减除额)约束。

Article 29 Extension of Expiry Date or Last Day for Presentation
第二十九条 截止日或最迟交单日的顺延

a. If the expiry date of a credit or the last day for presentation falls on a day when the bank to which presentation is to be made is closed for reasons other than those referred to in Article 36, the expiry date or the last day for presentation, as the case may be, will be extended to the first following banking day.

a. 如果信用证的截止日或最迟交单日适逢接受交单的银行非因第三十六条所述原因而歇业,则截止日或最迟交单日,视何者适用,将顺延至其重新开业的第一个银行工作日。

b. If presentation is made on the first following banking day, a nominated bank must provide the issuing bank or confirming bank with a statement on its covering schedule that the presentation was made within the time limits extended in accordance with sub-article 29 (a).

b. 如果在顺延后的第一个银行工作日交单,指定银行必须在其致开证行或保兑行的面涵中声明交单是在根据第二十九条(a)款顺延的期限内提交的。

c. The latest date for shipment will not be extended as a result of sub-article 29 (a).

c. 最迟发运日不因第二十九条(a)款规定的原因而顺延。

Article 30 Tolerance in Credit Amount, Quantity and Unit Prices
第三十条 信用证金额、数量与单价的增减幅度

a. The words "about" or "approximately" used in connection with the amount of the credit or the quantity or the unit price stated in the credit are to be construed as allowing a tolerance not to exceed 10% more or 10% less than the amount, the quantity or the unit price to which they refer.

a. "约"或"大约"用语信用证金额或信用证规定的数量或单价时,应解释为允许有关金额或数量或单价有不超过10%的增减幅度。

b. A tolerance not to exceed 5% more or 5% less than the quantity of the goods is allowed, provided the credit does not state the quantity in terms of a stipulated number of packing units or individual items and the total amount of the drawings does not exceed the amount of the credit.

b. 在信用证未以包装单位件数或货物自身件数的方式规定货物数量时,货物数量允许有5%的增减幅度,只要总支取金额不超过信用证金额。

c. Even when partial shipments are not allowed, a tolerance not to exceed 5% less than the amount of the credit is allowed, provided that the quantity of the goods, if stated in the credit, is shipped in full and a unit price, if stated in the credit, is not reduced or that sub-article 30 (b) is not applicable. This tolerance does not apply when the credit stipulates a specific tolerance or uses the expressions referred to in sub-article 30 (a).

c. 如果信用证规定了货物数量,而该数量已全部发运,及如果信用证规定了单价,而该单价又未降低,或当第三十条(b)款不适用时,则即使不允许部分装运,也允许支取的金额有5%的减幅。若信用证规定有特定的增减幅度或使用第三十条(a)款提到的用语限定数量,则该减幅不适用。

Article 31　Partial Drawings or Shipments
第三十一条　分批支款或分批装运

a. Partial drawings or shipments are allowed.

a. 允许分批支款或分批装运。

b. A presentation consisting of more than one set of transport documents evidencing shipment commencing on the same means of conveyance and for the same journey, provided they indicate the same destination, will not be regarded as covering a partial shipment, even if they indicate different dates of shipment or different ports of loading, places of taking in charge or dispatch. If the presentation consists of more than one set of transport documents, the latest date of shipment as evidenced on any of the sets of transport documents will be regarded as the date of shipment.

b. 表明使用同一运输工具并经由同次航程运输的数套运输单据在同一次提交时,

只要显示相同目的地,将不视为部分发运,即使运输单据上标明的发运日期不通或装卸港、接管地或发送地点不同。如果交单由数套运输单据构成,其中最晚的一个发运日将被视为发运日。

A presentation consisting of one or more sets of transport documents evidencing shipment on more than one means of conveyance within the same mode of transport will be regarded as covering a partial shipment, even if the means of conveyance leave on the same day for the same destination.

含有一套或数套运输单据的交单,如果表明在同一种运输方式下经由数件运输工具运输,即使运输工具在同一天出发运往同一目的地,仍将被视为部分发运。

c. A presentation consisting of more than one courier receipt, post receipt or certificate of posting will not be regarded as a partial shipment if the courier receipts, post receipts or certificates of posting appear to have been stamped or signed by the same courier or postal service at the same place and date and for the same destination.

c. 含有一份以上快递收据、邮政收据或投邮证明的交单,如果单据看似由同一块地或邮政机构在同一地点和日期加盖印戳或签字并且表明同一目的地,将不视为部分发运。

Article 32 Instalment Drawings or Shipments
第三十二条 分期支款或分期装运

If a drawing or shipment by instalments within given periods is stipulated in the credit and any instalment is not drawn or shipped within the period allowed for that instalment, the credit ceases to be available for that and any subsequent instalment.

如信用证规定在指定的时间段内分期支款或分期发运,任何一期未按信用证规定期限支取或发运时,信用证对该期及以后各期均告失效。

Article 33 Hours of Presentation
第三十三条 交单时间

A bank has no obligation to accept a presentation outside of its banking hours.
银行在其营业时间外无接受交单的义务。

Article 34 Disclaimer on Effectiveness of Documents
第三十四条 关于单据有效性的免责

A bank assumes no liability or responsibility for the form, sufficiency, accuracy, genuineness, falsification or legal effect of any document, or for the general or particular conditions stipulated in a document or superimposed thereon; nor does it assume any liability or responsibility for the description, quantity, weight, quality, condition, packing, delivery, value or existence of the goods, services or other performance represented by any document, or for the good faith or acts or omissions, solvency, performance or standing of the consignor, the carrier, the forwarder, the consignee or the insurer of the goods or any other person.

银行对任何单据的形式、充分性、准确性、内容真实性、虚假性或法律效力,或对单据中规定或添加的一般或特殊条件,概不负责;银行对任何单据所代表的货物、服务或其他履约行为的描述、数量、重量、品质、状况、包装、交付、价值或其存在与否,或对发货人、承运人、货运代理人、收货人、货物的保险人或其他任何人的诚信与否,作为或不作为、清偿能力、履约或资信状况,也概不负责。

Article 35 Disclaimer on Transmission and Translation

第三十五条 关于信息传递和翻译的免责

A bank assumes no liability or responsibility for the consequences arising out of delay, loss in transit, mutilation or other errors arising in the transmission of any messages or delivery of letters or documents, when such messages, letters or documents are transmitted or sent according to the requirements stated in the credit, or when the bank may have taken the initiative in the choice of the delivery service in the absence of such instructions in the credit.

当报文、信件或单据按照信用证的要求传输或发送时,或当信用证未作指示,银行自行选择传送服务时,银行对报文传输或信件或单据的递送过程中发生的延误、中途遗失、残缺或其他错误产生的后果,概不负责。

If a nominated bank determines that a presentation is complying and forwards the documents to the issuing bank or confirming bank, whether or not the nominated bank has honoured or negotiated, an issuing bank or confirming bank must honour or negotiate, or reimburse that nominated bank, even when the documents have been lost in transit between the nominated bank and the issuing bank or confirming bank, or between the confirming bank and the issuing bank.

如果指定银行确定交单相符并将单据发往开证行或保兑行,无论指定的银行是否已经承付或议付,开证行或保兑行必须承付或议付,或偿付指定银行,即使单据在指定银行送往开证行或保兑行的途中,或保兑行送往开证行的途中丢失。

A bank assumes no liability or responsibility for errors in translation or interpretation of technical terms and may transmit credit terms without translating them.

银行对技术术语的翻译或解释上的错误,不负责任,并可不加翻译地传送信用证条款。

Article 36　Force Majeure
第三十六条　不可抗力

A bank assumes no liability or responsibility for the consequences arising out of the interruption of its business by Acts of God, riots, civil commotions, insurrections, wars, acts of terrorism, or by any strikes or lockouts or any other causes beyond its control.

银行对由于天灾、暴动、骚乱、叛乱、战争、恐怖主义行为或任何罢工、停工或其无法控制的任何其他原因导致的营业中断的后果,概不负责。

A bank will not, upon resumption of its business, honour or negotiate under a credit that expired during such interruption of its business.

银行恢复营业时,对于在营业中断期间已逾期的信用证,不再进行承付或议付。

Article 37　Disclaimer for Acts of an Instructed Party
第三十七条　关于被指示方行为的免责

a. A bank utilizing the services of another bank for the purpose of giving effect to the instructions of the applicant does so for the account and at the risk of the applicant.

a. 为了执行申请人的指示,银行利用其他银行的服务,其费用和风险由申请人承担。

b. An issuing bank or advising bank assumes no liability or responsibility should the instructions it transmits to another bank not be carried out, even if it has taken the initiative in the choice of that other bank.

b. 即使银行自行选择了其他银行,如果发出指示未被执行,开证行或通知行对此亦不负责。

c. A bank instructing another bank to perform services is liable for any commissions, fees, costs or expenses ("charges") incurred by that bank in connection with its instructions.

c. 指示另一银行提供服务的银行有责任负担被指执行放因执行指示而发生的任何佣金、手续费、成本或开支("费用")。

If a credit states that charges are for the account of the beneficiary and charges cannot be collected or deducted from proceeds, the issuing bank remains liable for payment of charges.

如果信用证规定费用由受益人负担,而该费用未能收取或从信用证款项中扣除,开证行依然承担支付此费用的责任。

A credit or amendment should not stipulate that the advising to a beneficiary is conditional upon the receipt by the advising bank or second advising bank of its charges.

信用证或其修改不应规定向受益人的通知以通知行或第二通知行收到其费用为条件。

d. The applicant shall be bound by and liable to indemnify a bank against all obligations and responsibilities imposed by foreign laws and usages.

d. 外国法律和惯例加诸于银行的一切义务和责任,申请人应受其约束,并就此对银行负补偿之责。

Article 38 Transferable Credits
第三十八条 可转让信用证

a. A bank is under no obligation to transfer a credit except to the extent and in the manner expressly consented to by that bank.

a. 银行无办理转让信用证的义务,除非该银行明确同意其转让范围和转让方式。

b. For the purpose of this article:

b. 就本条款而言:

Transferable credit means a credit that specifically states it is "transferable". A transferable credit may be made available in whole or in part to another beneficiary ("second beneficiary") at the request of the beneficiary ("first beneficiary").

转让信用证意指明确表明其"可以转让"的信用证。根据受益人("第一受益人")的请求,转让信用证可以被全部或部分地转让给其他受益人("第二受益人")。

Transferring bank means a nominated bank that transfers the credit or, in a credit available with any bank, a bank that is specifically authorized by the issuing bank to transfer and that transfers the credit. An issuing bank may be a transferring bank.

转让银行意指办理信用证转让的被指定银行,或者,在适用于任何银行的信用证中,转让银行是由开证行特别授权并办理转让信用证的银行。开证行也可担任转让银行。

Transferred credit means a credit that has been made available by the transferring bank to a second beneficiary.

转让信用证意指经转让银行办理转让后可供第二受益人使用的信用证。

c. Unless otherwise agreed at the time of transfer, all charges (such as commissions, fees, costs or expenses) incurred in respect of a transfer must be paid by the first beneficiary.

c. 除非转让时另有约定,所有因办理转让而产生的费用(诸如佣金、手续费、成本或开支)必须由第一受益人支付。

d. A credit may be transferred in part to more than one second beneficiary provided partial drawings or shipments are allowed.

d. 倘若信用证允许分批支款或分批装运,信用证可以被部分地转让给一个以上的第二受益人。

A transferred credit cannot be transferred at the request of a second beneficiary to any subsequent beneficiary. The first beneficiary is not considered to be a subsequent beneficiary.

第二受益人不得要求将信用证转让给任何次序位居其后的其他受益人。第一受益人不属于此类其他受益人之列。

e. Any request for transfer must indicate if and under what conditions amendments may be advised to the second beneficiary. The transferred credit must clearly indicate those conditions.

e. 任何有关转让的申请必须指明是否以及在何种条件下可以将修改通知第二受益人。转让信用证必须明确指明这些条件。

f. If a credit is transferred to more than one second beneficiary, rejection of an amendment by one or more second beneficiary does not invalidate the acceptance by any other second beneficiary, with respect to which the transferred credit will be amended accordingly. For any second beneficiary that rejected the amendment, the transferred credit will remain unamended.

f. 如果信用证被转让给一个以上的第二受益人,其中一个或多个第二受益人拒绝接受某个信用证修改并不影响其他第二受益人接受修改。对于接受修改的第二受益人而言,信用证已做相应的修改;对于拒绝接受修改的第二受益人而言,该转让信用证仍未被修改。

g. The transferred credit must accurately reflect the terms and conditions of the credit, including confirmation, if any, with the exception of:

g. 转让信用证必须准确转载原证的条款及条件,包括保兑(如有),但下列项目除外:

- The amount of the credit,
- 信用证金额,
- Any unit price stated therein,
- 信用证规定的任何单价,
- The expiry date,
- 到期日,
- The period for presentation, or
- 交单期限,或
- The latest shipment date or given period for shipment.
- 最迟装运日期或规定的装运期间。

Any or all of which may be reduced or curtailed.

以上任何一项或全部均可减少或缩短。

The percentage for which insurance cover must be affected may be increased to provide the amount of cover stipulated in the credit or these articles.

必须投保的保险金额的投保比例可以增加,以满足原信用证或本惯例规定的投保金额。

The name of the first beneficiary may be substituted for that of the applicant in the credit.

可以用第一受益人的名称替换原信用证中申请人的名称。

If the name of the applicant is specifically required by the credit to appear in any document other than the invoice, such requirement must be reflected in the transferred credit.

如果原信用证特别要求开证申请人名称应在除发票以外的任何单据中出现时,则转让信用证必须反映出该项要求。

h. The first beneficiary has the right to substitute its own invoice and draft, if any, for those of a second beneficiary for an amount not in excess of that stipulated in the credit, and upon such substitution the first beneficiary can draw under the credit for the difference, if any, between its invoice and the invoice of a second beneficiary.

h. 第一受益人有权以自己的发票和汇票(如有),替换第二受益人的发票和汇票(如有),其金额不得超过原信用证的金额。在如此办理单据替换时,第一受益人可在原信用证项下支取自己发票与第二受益人发票之间产生的差额(如有)。

i. If the first beneficiary is to present its own invoice and draft, if any, but fails to do so on first demand, or if the invoices presented by the first beneficiary create discrepancies that did not exist in the presentation made by the second beneficiary and the first beneficiary fails to correct them on first demand, the transferring bank has the right to present the documents as received from the second beneficiary to the issuing bank, without further responsibility to the first beneficiary.

i. 如果第一受益人应当提交其自己的发票和汇票(如有),但却未能在收到第一次要求时照办;或第一受益人提交的发票导致了第二受益人提示的单据中本不存在的不符点,而其未能在收到第一次要求时予以修正,则转让银行有权将其从第二受益人处收到的单据向开证行提示,并不再对第一受益人负责。

j. The first beneficiary may, in its request for transfer, indicate that honour or negotiation is to be effected to a second beneficiary at the place to which the credit has been transferred, up to and including the expiry date of the credit. This is without prejudice to the right of the first beneficiary in accordance with sub-article 38 (h).

j. 第一受益人可以在其提出转让申请时,表明可在信用证被转让的地点,在原信用证的到期日之前(包括到期日)向第二受益人予以兑付或议付。本条款并不损害第一受益人在第三十八条(h)款下的权利。

k. Presentation of documents by or on behalf of a second beneficiary must be made to the transferring bank.

k. 由第二受益人或代表第二受益人提交的单据必须向转让银行提示。

Article 39　Assignment of Proceeds
第三十九条　款项让渡

The fact that a credit is not stated to be transferable shall not affect the right of the beneficiary to assign any proceeds to which it may be or may become entitled under the credit, in accordance with the provisions of applicable law. This article relates only to the assignment of proceeds and not to the assignment of the right to perform under the credit.

信用证未表明可转让,并不影响受益人根据所适用的法律规定,将其在该信用证项下有权获得的款项让渡与他人的权利。本条款所涉及的仅是款项的让渡,而不是信用证项下执行权力的让渡。

Appendix Ⅱ

《检验证书》内容规范

检验证书因其本身所需证明的内容不同以及各国标准不一而有所区别。然而各种检验证书一般都有以下内容:

(1)出证机关、地点及证书的名称。如果信用证并未规定出具的机关,则由出口商决定。如果信用证规定了"有权机构"(COMPETENT AUTHORITY)出证,因为有权机构是指有公证资格或经政府授权的机构,则应根据具体情况由有关的商检机构出具。检验证明书的出证地点应中货物装船口岸,除非信用证另有规定。检验证明书的名称则应与合同或信用证规定相符。

(2)发货人名称及地址。一般为出口商名址。该栏内容应符合合同或信用证的规定,并与其他单据保持一致。

(3)收货人名称与地址,一般为进口商,收货人应与合同或信用证及其他单据保持一致。

(4)品名、报验数量、重量、包装种类及数量、到达口岸、运输工具、唛头等项目应与商业发票及提单上所描述的内容完全一致。货物名称可以用统称。

(5)检验结果,此栏是检验证明书中最重要的一项,在此栏中记载报验货物经检验的现状。货物现状是衡量货物是否符合合同或信用证规定的的凭证,亦是交接货物或索赔、理赔的具有法律效力的证明文件。

(6)签证日期,检验证明书的出具日期应不迟于提单日期,但也不得过早于提单日期,最好在提单日之前一两天或至少与提单日期相同。

(7)签字盖章,一般而言,盖章与签字一样有效。但是有的国家则要求出具的检验证有书一定要经手签,在这种情况下,只有盖章而无签字的检验证明书则被视作无效。

检验证明书有以下要目:A、出口厂家的名称和地址;B、商检证书的名称;C、发票号码;D、不迟于提单日期的检验日;E、商品名称;F、唛头,如无唛头,填 N/M;G、数量;H、填写毛,净重;I、已按检验结果填写详细内容;J、经办人签字及加盖公章。

Appendix Ⅲ

《中华人民共和国出口许可证》证面内容规范

第一项：出口商

指出口合同签订单位，应与出口批准文件一致。出口商代码为《进出口经营者资格证书》、《对外贸易经营者备案登记表》或《外商投资企业批准证书》中的13位企业代码。

第二项：发货人

指具体执行合同发货报关的单位。配额以及配额招标商品的发货人应与出口商保持一致。

第三项：出口许可证号

结构为：××-××-×××××××
　　　　（1）-（2）-（3）

（1）为年份。

（2）为发证机构代码。

（3）为顺序号，由发证系统自动生成。

第四项：出口许可证有效截止日期

按《货物出口许可证管理办法》确定的有效期，由发证系统自动生成。

第五项：贸易方式

指该项出口货物的贸易性质。包括：一般贸易、进料加工、来料加工、出料加工、外资企业出口、捐赠、赠送等。只能填报一种。

第六项：合同号

指申请出口许可证时提交出口合同的编号，长度为17个英文字符。只能填报一个合同号。

第七项：报关口岸

指出口口岸，只允许填报一个关区。

出口许可证实行"一证一关"制。对指定口岸的出口商品，按国家有关规定执行。

第八项：进口国（地区）

指合同目的地。只能填报一个国家（地区）。不能使用地区名，如欧盟等。如对中国保税区出口，进口国（地区）应打印"中国"。

第九项:付款方式

包括:信用证、托收、汇付等。只能填报一种。

第十项:运输方式

指货物离境时的运输方式。包括:海上运输、铁路运输、公路运输、航空运输等。只能填报一种。如对远洋出口冷冻商品,运输方式不得打印陆运,包括铁路运输、公路运输。

第十一项:商品名称、商品编码

按商务部公布的年度《出口许可证管理货物目录》中的 10 位商品编码填报,商品名称由发证系统自动生成。只能填报一个商品编码并应与出口批准文件一致。

第十二项:规格、等级

只能填报同一商品编码下的 4 种不同规格等级,超过 4 种规格等级的,另行申请许可证。

第十三项:单位

指计量单位。按商务部公布的年度《出口许可证管理货物目录》中的计量单位执行,发证系统自动生成。如合同使用的计量单位与规定的计量单位不一致,应换算成规定的计量单位。无法换算的,可在备注栏注明。

第十四项:数量

指申请出口商品数量。最大位数为 9 位阿拉伯数字,最小保留小数点后 1 位。如数量过大,可分证办理;如数量过小,可在备注栏内注明。计量单位为"批"的,此栏均为"1"。

第十五项:单价(币别)

指与第十三项"单位"所使用的计量单位相应的单价和货币种类。计量单位为 1 批的,此栏为总金额。

第十六、十七、十八项:总值、总值折美元、总计

由发证系统自动计算。

第十九项:备注

用于注明其他需要说明的情况。如不是一批一证报关的出口许可证,在此栏注明"非一批一证"。

第二十项:发证机关签章

发证机构发放出口许可证前在此栏加盖《中华人民共和国出口许可证专用章》。

第二十一项:发证日期

由发证系统自动生成。

Bibliography

[1] A. N. Yianopoulos. *Ocean Bill of Lading*. Kluwer Law International,1995.

[2] Christopher Hill. *Maritime Law*. 4th ed. London:Lloyds of London Press,1995.

[3] Clive M Schmitthoff. *Export Trade. The Law and Practice of International Trade*. London:Sweet & Maxwell,2000.

[4] Paul Todd. *Cases and Materials on Bills of Lading*. London:BSP Professional Books,1990.

[5] R H Brown. *Dictionary of Marine Insurance Terms and Clauses*. London:Witherby & Co Ltd,1989.

[6] Wim Albert Timmermans. *Carriage of Goods by Sea in the Practice of the USSR Maritime Arbitration Commission*. Leiden:Martinus Nijhoff Publishers,1991.

[7] 陈火怀. 外贸电子商务与实用英语全真教程[M]. 广州:广东经济出版社,2010.

[8] 程同春,程欣. 新编国际商务英语函电[M]. 南京:东南大学出版社,2013.

[9] 葛萍,周维家. 外贸英语函电(第三版)[M]. 上海:复旦大学出版社,2014.

[10] 顾建华. 外贸单证实务[M]. 北京:清华大学出版社,2010.

[11] 广银芳. 外贸单证制作实务[M]. 北京:清华大学出版社,2007.

[12] 郭纯凡. 英文信函格式范例[M]. 广州:广东经济出版社,2003.

[13] 国际商会中国国家委员会 ICC CHINA. UNCTAD/ICC 多式运输单据规则(中英文对照本). 北京:中国民主法制出版社,2004.

[14] 国际商会中国国家委员会 ICC CHINA. 见索即付保函统一规则(URDG 458)(中英文对照本). 北京:中国民主法制出版社 1992.

[15] 国际商会中国国家委员会 ICC CHINA. 跟单信用证统一惯例(URDG 600)(中英文对照本),北京:中国民主法制出版社,2007.

[16] 国际商会中国国家委员会 ICC CHINA. ICC CHINA 银行委员会意见汇编 1998—2003. 北京:中国民主法制出版社,2003.

[17] 国际商会中国国家委员会 ICC CHINA. 关于审核跟单信用证项下单据的国际标准银行实务(ISBP)(中英文对照本). 北京:中国民主法制出版社,2003.

[18]姜妹.外贸英语函电实训教程[M].武汉:武汉大学出版社,2014.

[19]焦微玲.外贸英语函电——从基础到实践[M].北京:电子工业出版社,2013.

[20]兰天.外贸英语函电[M].大连:东北财经大学出版社,2004.

[21]李辉,白丹.外贸英文函电[M].北京:电子工业出版社,2016.

[22]李京.国际贸易单证[M].北京:北京理工大学出版社,2006.

[23]梁晓玲.国际商务英语函电[M].北京:对外经济贸易大学出版社,2005.

[24]梁宇贤.票据法新论(修订新版)[M].北京:中国人民大学出版社,2004.

[25]刘德标.国际结算规则[M].北京:对外经济贸易大学出版社,2004.

[26]刘启萍,周树玲.外贸英文制单[M].北京:对外经济贸易大学出版社,2006.

[27]孟建国.外贸英语函电[M].杭州:浙江大学出版社,2009.

[28]万宁,潘维琴.外经贸英语函电[M].北京:机械工业出版社,2006.

[29]王海欧.外贸单证实务[M].北京:清华大学出版社,2011.

[30]王俐俐.外贸英语函电与单证[M].北京:机械工业出版社,2010.

[31]向平.商务汉语综合教程 第3册[M].北京:对外经济贸易大学出版社,2010.

[32]许德金.1+1实操商务英语教程 函电[M].北京:首都经济贸易大学出版社,2009.

[33]徐薇.国际贸易单证实务与操作[M].北京:人民邮电出版社,2011.

[34]杨金玲,张建华.国际商务单证操作实训[M].北京:首都经济贸易大学出版社,2009.

[35]尹小莹.外贸英语函电——商务英语应用文写作[M].西安:西安交通大学出版社,2004.

[36]余心之,徐美荣.新编外贸单证实务[M].北京:对外经济贸易大学出版社,2005.

[37]曾元胜,陈春媚.外贸函电与单证实训教程[M].北京:对外经济贸易大学出版社,2010.

[38]章安平.外贸单证操作[M].北京:高等教育出版社,2008.

[39]张丽芳.外贸单证[M].北京:机械工业出版社,2007.

[40]张天桥.国际贸易实务[M].北京:北京师范大学出版社,2007.

[41]张欣.银行信用证风险管理的变化和趋势[J].当代经济,2005(10).

[42]赵薇.国际结算—国际贸易融资支付方法[M].南京:东南大学出版社,2012.

[43]周辉斌.银行保函与备用信用证法律实务[M].北京:中信出版社,2003.

[44]庄乐梅.国际贸易结算实务精要[M].北京:中国纺织出版社,2004.

[45]http://en.wikipedia.org/wiki/Commercial_invoice

Bibliography

[46] http://edu.56156.com/article_16832.html

[47] http://bbs.fobshanghai.com/

[48] http://blog.sina.com.cn/s/blog_498830960100039f.html

[49] http:www.doc88.com/p—774453132058.html

[50] http://www.wesiedu.com/waimao/wxy/dao/201112/71270.html

[51] http://www.365export.com/

[52] http://info.china.alibaba.com/detail/1000646063.html

[53] http://www.cnie.cn/

[54] http://www.yuhuan.org/qqjm/index.asp

[55] http://www.cantonfair.org.cn/cn/index.asp

[56] http://www.snet.com.cn/